A Brave and Beautiful Spirit
Dora Marsden (1882 – 1960)

by

Dr. Les Garner

Union of Egoists
2019

A Brave and Beautiful Spirit / Dora Marsden (1882 –
    1960)
1. Great Britain. Feminism, Marsden, Dora (1882 –
    1960)
2. Title

ISBN 978-1-944651-14-5
SA1127

Previously published by Avebury Gower (Aldershot 1990).

Cover design by Kevin I. Slaughter.
"Closed Gate Bridge" (p. 31) by Duncan Harris at flickr.com, attribution 2.0 Generic (CC BY 2.0).
The Freewoman (p. 123), *The New Freewoman* (p. 189), *The Egoist* (p. 245) thanks to The Modernist Journals Project (searchable database). Brown and Tulsa Universities, ongoing. http://www.modjourn.org

Proofreading by Teresa Bergen.
All remaining errors are the responsibility of the publisher.

Published by Union of Egoists
UnionOfEgoists.com

127 House: at every turn in its thought, society will find us – waiting.

Please send corrections and comments to:

    Trevor Blake
    P. O. Box 2321
    Portland OR 97208-2321
    United States

Table of Contents

Acknowledgements

I have been given so much help and support in my pursuit of Dora Marsden by so many people that it would be impossible to acknowledge them all here. I only hope that those who are omitted will accept my apologies alongside my thanks and gratitude. I must, however, acknowledge the crucial contributions of several people whose assistance has been so vital. Principal among these must be Dora Marsden's niece, Mrs. Elaine Bate (*née* Dyson). Elaine allowed me free access to her papers, now sadly in America, and gave me much encouragement and support. She was extremely generous with both her time and hospitality and I am only too pleased to record this here, for without her help (which goes back to the mid-1970s) I doubt whether this biography could have been written.

I must also record the assistance of local historians Alan and Jill Matthews who freely provided me with much information on Dora's birthplace and family. Their enthusiastic willingness to help constantly astounded me, though their eagerness on one damp, grey afternoon in the local graveyard led to the eerie discovery that the Marsden family tombstone was built by a mason with my own surname, Garner. As a testimony to Dora Marsden, I hope this book lasts as long as that Victorian memorial.

Other assistance has come from Kay Davison and Margaret Gloss (on Grace Jardine and Rona Robinson); the late T. E. Marsden (on Dora's family); the editors of the *Huddersfield Examiner*, the *Colne Valley Reporter*, the *Westmoreland Gazette* and the *Cumberland and Westmoreland Herald* (for publishing appeals for information); Steve Caunce (for letting me view the late Gloden Dallas' work on *The Freewoman*; Gloden was one of the first historians to discover and realize the paper's importance); S. E. Parker (for advice on Max Stirner and Egoism); Jane Lidderdale and Mary Nicholson, whose excellent yet undervalued *Dear Miss Weaver* provided so many crucial clues; Ronnie Cox (for showing me around Seldom Seen and reminiscing about his mother's work for Dora); George S. Stirling, Consultant Psychiatrist at Crichton Royal (for help on Dora's stay there).

I would also like to take this opportunity to thank the workers at various libraries and record offices, especially those in Manchester, Huddersfield, Altrincham, Leeds, Cheshire and Essex. I must not omit those at the British Library and the Institute of Historical Research too. Thanks are also due to Jean and Tim for doing the typing so well, Caroline Lane and Sarah Sutton my original and present editors, and Pauline Ripley, Ursula de la Mare and, once again, Ann Hughes for their discussions on women's history. Thanks too to René Sillet (for translations of French articles on Dora) and Digby Ingle (for comments on Dora's psychological make-up), both at Southwark College. The ILEA also deserve my thanks for allowing me a term's unpaid leave to finish the manuscript.

Finally, I would like to express my gratitude to those friends who did not really have to put up with my obsessional ramblings yet did so with great tolerance and humour. Special thanks must therefore be paid to Moira Spence (who also helped to trace Dora's family tree) and Polly Curran. Last but by no means least I must again thank Pauline Bacon, who in spite of her own misgivings and political objections, gave me so much support throughout. She and all those mentioned above are in no way responsible for what follows, but I hope they at least recognize something of value in my attempt to construe a worthwhile biography of a truly re-markable woman.

Note: These acknowledgements were written in 1990 and still stand though I would like to add in 2019 my thanks to Trevor Blake for his encouragement, help and support throughout the whole process of republication of this book.

Foreword to New Edition

When Trevor Blake first approached me in 2017 to enquire whether I would be interested in a reprint of *A Brave and Beautiful Spirit*, it came as a surprise but his timing was spot on. Thoughts of Dora had returned to me as the centenary celebration of some women getting the vote in 1918 approached. I wondered if Dora and others were again to be ignored. Storm Jameson had written to her in 1928 that "I hope you don't have to wait till you are dead to be seen and known." In spite of further work (principally by Blake and Kevin I. Slaughter at UnionOfEgoists.com) since the publication of *Brave and Beautiful*, I fear in many ways, she still is, especially with regard to the Women's Suffrage movement and early Twentieth Century England.

Authors in my situation have three options – to simply reprint the work with no new comments, to add a new introduction or to rewrite. The last option was tempting but would undoubtedly have mirrored the endless rewriting and procrastination of Dora herself from 1914 onwards. It would have sorely tried the patience of my new publisher. Obviously, I have had a great interest for many years in Marsden but I do not want to replicate some of her most trying mannerisms and ways of working. Also, besides the continual rewriting and dithering I would, like her, have to go into isolation, to become seldom seen. To do this I would have to withdraw from political activity – as an active member of a reborn socialist Labour Party in Great Britain, something I was not prepared to do. The first option (though initially tempting) was also ruled out, as it would represent a lost opportunity to add to the discourse on Dora. The option I have chosen has its own pitfalls and, like the biography itself, is far from above criticism, but I hope both are of some value. Lastly, it apparently took some time for Trevor to track me down but I am glad he did. His perspective and interests in Dora are different from mine but we are united in recovering, in Rebecca West's words "one of the most marvellous personalities the nation has ever produced."

Dora Marsden, as a proud, independent individualist, would argue she should not be claimed by anyone but herself. Others, including feminists, anarchists, egoists, imagists and modernists though have done so. Perhaps – following a more detailed analysis of her later work – experts in the history of religion and philosophy (and even those interested in linguistics) will do so too. A cursory search on that destroyer of wonder, cognitive development and social interaction – Google – reveals a range of relevant research and work with perhaps a focus on modernism, literature and the Imagists, alongside (to the credit of The Union of Egoists), Stirner and Egoism. There is also some work on Dora before 1914 including some useful comments in the *Women's History Review* of 2002. The work on suffrage by Delap follows my exploration of Marsden's analysis of the limitations of suffragism but (as with the other articles in the *Review*) does so without acknowledging *A Brave and Beautiful Spirit* published thirteen years previously –

then as now, the only biography in existence.

I make my own perspective clear in the introduction of the book. I still regard the primary importance of Marsden is in achieving a greater understanding of early Twentieth Century feminism and the limitations of suffragism. Such an approach is crucial also to a more nuanced and critical analysis of the Women's Social and Political Union (WSPU). And in spite of her own loud denials, her life and published work post-*Freewoman,* living in isolation in Southport and the Lake District, still provides some evidence of a continuing feminist perspective. Other commentators – modernists, imagists and Egoists – can and will continue to disagree. This I welcome. My reply is "Let a thousand flowers bloom." As they do, I fondly imagine the woman with "a face like a Florentine Angel[1]" looking down, smiling, finally enjoying the attention she deserves.

My own interest in Dora Marsden stemmed originally from the development of feminist perspectives in the left in the 1960s and 1970s. This led to a PhD at Liverpool University on the ideas of the women's suffrage movement, subsequently reworked as *Stepping Stones for Women's Liberty: Feminist Ideas in the Women's Suffrage Movement 1900-1918* (1984). Discovering Dora via the eminent historian Sheila Rowbotham, who referred me to the pioneering work of Gloden Dallas, was a revelation. In leading to a greater understanding of suffragism and feminism it was a godsend – appropriately enough perhaps given Dora later claimed God was

---

[1] *Stepping Stones,* pg 61.

female. Through a study of Marsden in the early Twentieth Century so much could be revealed and learned about many fields and issues. Amongst many others, these included the pivotal and developmental role for women of education and teaching, the radicalism of Manchester, the potential and limits of suffragism and the suffragettes and the WSPU. It also further reflected on the remarkable political militancy that threatened to create the "strange Death of Liberal England," a revolution stopped only perhaps by the slaughter of the beginning of the First World War in 1914. And of course, Marsden and *The Freewoman* had much to reveal about the incredible diverse and revolutionary ideas developing within Edwardian feminism. *The Freewoman* could indeed "have been edited on a mountain top, it breathed so heavily of freedom[1]."

If *The Freewoman* was Dora Marsden's greatest legacy, her illumination of the restrictions and conservatism of Emmeline and Christabel Pankhurst's WSPU comes a close second. I do not wish to repeat arguments made in the first few chapters but do want to emphasise a few points. Firstly, can I make a plea to writers to refer to Emmeline and Christabel's WSPU rather than the WSPU? Sylvia and Adela Pankhurst both took different political perspectives and eventually became Communists. Alongside many others in the WSPU, they disagreed with the autocracy of their mother and sister, evidenced by the numerous splits from the organisation. Over the years a more critical view of the WSPU – and the contribution of suffragists – has developed but it is

---

[1]   Harriet Shaw Weaver. See page 364. Grayson, see page 361.

depressing to note the overwhelming focus on Emmeline and Christabel that pervades in the 2018 celebrations. Indeed, at the time of writing a BBC History review poll revealed that Emmeline Pankhurst was regarded the third most important woman of modern times, above Mary Wollstonecraft, Marie Stopes and Mary Seacole[1].

Of course Christabel and Emmeline Pankhurst's WSPU was important as – in spite of its limitations – the woman's suffrage movement as a whole. As Victor Grayson, the Socialist MP for Colne Valley (which included Dora's home village of Marsden) put it:

> the right of woman to the vote must be discussed on another basis than the value of the franchise. Their claim is to be recognised as human beings.

Grayson, syndicalists and others were developing radical if not revolutionary ideas about political power while Dora and others were sympathetic to these ideas and wary of restricting all into what was a limited demand for a vote for some women. Dora and others did indeed become S.O.S. – Sick of Suffrage, which Theresa Billington-Grieg illustrated in her sharp *The Militant Suffrage Movement – Emancipation in a Hurry*, published in 1911. In this Billington-Grieg wrote that many activists have "began to realise that the 'vote' cannot secure of itself any single women's emancipation... [suffragists] fail to see that large areas where emancipation's needed lie entirely outside the scope of the vote... a slave woman with a vote will essentially be a slave."

---

[1]   *BBC History Review,* August 2018.

Yet the actions of the suffragettes not only destroyed notions of what women could do but also led to a much wider discussion of what they might want. The ingenuity and bravery of the actions of the suffragettes was remarkable and inspiring, none so more perhaps than those of Miss Marsden chronicled below. It is perhaps worth reflecting for a moment that you are only reading this because Dora was just caught from falling to her death by a policeman when being escorted from the top of the Empire building in Southport following her amazing ambush of Churchill in 1909. "You ought to be grateful to me" the police inspector said, "If I hadn't caught your foot you would have gone to your glory."

Looking back, it could be argued that by 1910 feminism was enclosed in a pressure cooker. Energised by suffragism, inspired by ever daring acts of militancy yet constricted by the overemphasis on the vote and the autocracy of Emmeline and Christabel's WSPU restricting feminist discourse, feminism was getting ready to burst. When it did that "nauseous publication," "that disgusting publication... indecent, immoral and filthy," read once and once only before being ripped into small pieces by the leader of the National Union of Women's Suffrage Societies (NUWSS), Millicent Fawcett, exploded on the scene: *The Freewoman* was born[1].

Again, for me *The Freewoman* was Dora Marsden's greatest achievement. The paper did not last long and quickly changed but if nothing else, it showed the in-

---

[1]   *Stepping Stones*, pg 64.

credible and radical width of feminist debate before 1914. As Caroline Boord wrote "the Freewoman wants no ready sphere... the Freewoman wants the whole wide world to chose from[1]." From Boord's position – a position clearly shared by many readers – debates on monogamy, marriage, prostitution, domesticity, sex, contraception, motherhood, childcare and the rest freely followed. As Dora said in a pre-publication press interview in October 1911, *The Freewoman* was to give feminism:

> ... a new significance... the great change which the Feminist Movement seeks to bring about is not merely a matter of political readjustment... carried to success, it would accomplish a vast revolution in the centre field of human affairs, intellectual, sexual, domestic, economic, legal and political.

This change and the view expressed by Boord were sentiments that in many ways carried throughout Dora's life even though the terminology may have changed, especially as she was drawn to individualism and the work of Max Stirner which first appeared in the paper in August 1912.

But let us pause and reflect on Dora Marsden in 1911 – a mature woman about to become thirty in March 1912. She had already had a remarkable and public life. Her world at this time was exciting yet was also a heady brew with a dangerous mix. A high sense of self-worth that had begun and developed as a teacher had been heightened by her public exploits as a suffragette. She had become a nationally known figure with

---

[1] *Stepping Stones,* pg 65.

her photograph on the front page of the *Daily Mirror*. She had been described as "the sweetest, gentlest and bravest of suffragettes" by one Emmeline, (Pethick-Lawrence), of the WSPU while lauded following a much publicised arrest in London by the other Emmeline (Pankhurst) as a woman who "had more courage than any other man of the nation." Yet within a year Marsden left London to live with her mother Hannah, in Southport.

Of course her involvement and writing continued, but her isolation and removal from active political engagement had two seminal effects. Firstly, the writing was to be increasingly important, if not central to her feelings of self-worth and esteem – rejection, or lack of acknowledgement, risked a heavy price as indeed it turned out to be the case in 1930. Secondly, the fact that Dora had taken full advantage of new opportunities for women in education at the turn of the century and through her own efforts had become a successful teacher, it is conceivable that Marsden saw her success resulting from an act of will making, of course, the work of Stirner appealing to her. And as Dora remained in isolation up North, concentrating more and more on her own writings, her control of the paper changed allowing increasing influence by a literary set including Pound and others.

As editor of *The Freewoman*, Dora encouraged a wide variety of radical ideas and was thus exposed and then attracted to, anarchism and individualism. The latter had a personal appeal to Dora who could justifiably argue she had achieved a great deal through her own efforts, through her own will. In this we can see the eventual attraction to Egoism and a move away from feminism. Indeed, as early as the second issue of *The Freewoman* Dora described feminism as a temporary theory, necessary to balance current "masculinism" and "when one is strong enough to equate the other, both will become merged in a common doctrine of Humanism[1]. From this – as Dora further explored anarchism and Stirner – a logical development took place. *The Freewoman* became "A Weekly Humanist Review" in May 1912; *The New Freewoman* "An Individualist Review" in June 1913, and that in turn became *The Egoist* in January 1914. And while all this was taking place Dora was removing herself from direct political activity. The validations of her efforts were now to come from loyal – and often abused – friends and, she hoped, her writing. Not surprisingly, perhaps Dora's health began to suffer in 1911 and by 1912 she was exhausted and complaining of neurasthenia – fatigue caused by stress and overwork, a condition possibly linked to depression. Ominous signs for the future.

Though my focus on Dora Marsden was – and remains – on her contribution to a fuller understanding of the Women's Suffrage movement, feminism and the radical times of 1910-14, others choose to concentrate on her relation to Imagism, literature, modernism and Egoism. I make comments on these in the book but will leave to others with more empathy and expertise in these areas to analyse Dora's contribution in these fields. However, I cannot refrain from suggesting that these de-

---

[1] *The Freewoman*, 30 November 1911.

velopments took away the vitality and political radicalism of *The Freewoman* where Socialism, Syndicalism as well as a range of radical feminist issues were openly debated.

The change from November 1911 onwards (from my perspective) was reflected in the steady decline in readers, and the perpetual struggle with finance. In the resurrection of the paper as *The New Freewoman* in 1913 showed, this was only ultimately resolved with the financial contribution of Harriet Shaw Weaver. From this year on, Dora would not have been able to survive, none of her publications would have seen the light of day without the lifelong financial and emotional support of *Dear Miss Weaver*[1]. The change from the early days of *The Freewoman* was also reflected in the decline of the remarkable and innovative Freewoman Discussion Circles. These attracted sizable audiences and sometimes were addressed by Dora. Significantly, increasing demands for direct political action were made. Sadly these were not activated and the Circles collapsed.

Yet it could be argued that Dora and others were ultimately seeking a small target audience whether the avant-garde of literature and the arts or "advanced women." In this there was an element of elitism and an inevitable disconnection from the ordinary lives, experiences and struggles of ordinary women (and men). After all, as Dora said in the second issue of *The Freewoman*, she was appealing to "freewomen, and not ordinary women. [We appeal] to those who have already shown

---

[1]   Lidderdale and Nicholson (1970).

signs of individuality and strength[1]." She had already dismissed in the first issue criticism of the high price of the paper (3d compared to 1d for the suffragist weeklies) as "we are not proposing to write for women whose highest journalistic needs are realised by a penny[2]." It is surely unlikely that the growing number of literary contributors were seeking a mass audience but rather avant-garde reputations among their small circle.

The lack of relevance to ordinary lives and the emphasis on individualism was linked to the work of Max Stirner who first made an appearance in 1912 in a review of Stirner's *The Ego and His Own*[3], a tome heavily criticised by Marx but described by Dora as "the most powerful book that has ever emerged from a single mind[4]." Again, I leave to others with more sympathy to Stirner to examine his value and Marsden's contribution to the development of his work. I make my own objections in the book; for those interested in Stirner, I strongly advise them to visit the work of the Union of Egoists – publishers of this reprint[5].

---

[1]   30 November 1911.
[2]   *The Freewoman,* 23 November 1911.
[3]   *The Freewoman,* 8 August 1912.
[4]   *The New Freewoman,* 1 Sept 1913.
[5]   See for example *Der Geist,* Vol 1, No 1 Winter 2017.

Many feminist and suffragist supporters of *The Freewoman* surely would have been shocked to read Dora's comments in the first edition of *The New Freewoman*:

> Woman's movement forsooth. Why does not someone start a straight nose movement.... or any other accidental physical contournation[1]?

Yet, as outlined above, this could in part be explained by Marsden's sympathy with Humanism and her growing belief in neither men nor women but individuals. In common parlance Marsden was implying that gender was indeed socially constructed. As she rather colourfully put it:

> 'If we take away female reproductive organs from the concept "Woman" what have we left? Absolutely nothing, save a mountain of sentimental mush.' Dora argued that 'a limited number of individual women[2] emphasise that they are individuals and cannot be lumped together into a class, a sex, or a "movement. " They – this small number regard themselves neither as wives, mothers, spinsters, women or men... the only fitting description is that of Individual Ends-in-Themselves. They are Egoists[3].'

Dora still made specific references to women but within a different context leading Floyd Dell's to describe her as "the Max Stirner of feminism," Dora still made supportive and radical comments on strike action, the Irish struggles led by Larkin and syndicalism but re-

---

[1]   *Stepping Stones,* pg 77; *The New Freewoman,* 1 July 1913.
[2]   e.g. one Dora Marsden.
[3]   *The New Freewoman.*

22

mained no believer in any "cause" no joiner of collective action. As with Stirner, the resolution of opposing wills and power, or indeed how the post was organised and delivered, or how her paper was made or how inequality was and still is based on the economic and social inequality, was never explained.

Yet ultimately, the exploration of St. Max led Dora, *The New Freewoman* and *The Egoist* down a lonely and obtuse path. The moment *The Egoist* was born – whatever its literary merits – made the possibility of continuing the remarkable spirit and tenor of the original journal, *The Freewoman*, less likely. *The Freewoman* was originally a paper, which combined relevant, revolutionary, political, and sexual radicalism with discussion on cultural and literary issues – an opportunity for this identity to be consolidated was lost as the changes from 1912 developed.

The declining influence of Dora – in spite of her support to James Joyce in the publication of *A Portrait of a Young Man* in the *Egoist* and in determinedly supporting Weaver in the publication of *Ulysses* – continued apace in Southport during the War. It went even further as she moved to the aptly-named Seldom Seen in the Lake District where she eked out an existence in the 1920s and early 1930s. By 1919 Dora was isolated, had few friends and relied on Weaver for funds. As I wrote in the biography, a brave and beautiful spirit perhaps but "a lonely and forgotten one, a *Kami* in the wilderness." I also wrote in 1990 that it was difficult to write about her life from 1920 to the end in 1960 – it still is. Dora continued to write – on philosophy, religion, space and time

– but took prevarication and excruciating prose to new levels or depths. At one point in 1924 she was working on four volumes – *The Nature of Philosophical Enquiry* (her first venture), *Mind, The Nature of Life* and *Space and Time*. Some material she asked for was even in French. Her health continued to deteriorate in the difficult environment of Seldom Seen, the isolation acute. But Dora – being Dora – struggled on and eventually published *Definition of the Godhead* in 1928 and *Mysteries of Christianity* in 1930. Yet these hit the world with a resounding silent thud. Only six copies of *Definition* were sold and none at all it would seem of *Mysteries*. Sadly, reviews were often hidden from Dora for fear of the effect they would have on her. The only way for Dora to be saved was through her work but the world was not ready to save her and she had a breakdown after the failure of *Mysteries*, increasingly withdrawn, not eating and depressed[1]. After a somewhat desperate attempt to go back into teaching at the age of fifty-three, she attempted suicide in 1935.

With regard to her later work, I will again leave to others to evaluate the quality, if they can get through what one reviewer of *Definition* described as Marsden's "execrable" prose although "one or two phrases almost make the book worth reading[2]." There were – in for example, her condemnation of 'masculine monotheism' and the reference to God as female – comments that could perhaps have some link to feminism. Her last work – and her most successful selling – perhaps has

---

[1]   Dumfries records.
[2]   *The New Age.*

something to say too on space and time but I will leave philosophers and those interested in religion to determine the value of her work.

After the 'accident' of 1935 Dora lived for another twenty-five years in Dumfries. Throughout her time in Scotland, Dora sporadically made reference to working on her Magnus Opus again. She remained quiet and kept herself to herself but did succeed in publishing of *The Philosophy of Time* in 1955 (entirely funded by Weaver). Though selling few copies this was her most successful book, it needs others to judge the value of this work but her concentration on religion, space, time and philosophy were a long, long way from the heady days of 1911 though she had begun an interest in Philosophy as a student at Manchester. At the age of seventy-six she wrote to Weaver that she was considering "one last cosmo-historical book... it constitutes the promised Book of Truth which is Heaven's Covenant with Creation." On this, the Dumfries records she worked furiously during 1958-9.

In the early Twentieth Century as an active suffragette, feminist and editor of *The Freewoman*, Dora was part of, and was making, history. And as someone once said, people do make history if not always in circumstances of their own choosing. In the political context of the early Twentieth Century it was possible for Dora to make the mark she did. But this was clearly less likely once she went into self-imposed exile. Dora too at *The Freewoman* certainly interpreted the world without fear and in some ways actively engaged in trying to change it. She may have continued to interpret the world (albeit form a different and esoteric point that radically differed from 1911), once in Southport, Seldom Seen and Scotland but did little to change it. This requires political engagement and organisation with others.

This is the only biography on Dora Marsden but it is far, far from being the last word – there is more, much more to come from the pupil teacher, teacher, graduate, suffragette, radical feminist, egoist and philosopher. For me, I remain convinced that Dora's legacy is to feminism. Others have lauded her relation to Egoism and literature, and one day even her work in Seldom Seen and Dumfries may attract praise. In the end it may be as her friend Rebecca West wrote about Dora's work in the 1920s, "... that the wisdom she has obtained is not communicable, but I am sure some far peak of wisdom she must have attained." Whatever the validity of this assertion, my conclusion remains the same as it was in the 1980s – "It is as a feminist that this certainly brave, often beautiful and ultimately tragic spirit should be remembered and seen."

Dr. Les Garner

London 2019

Introduction

Dora Marsden was once described by the feminist writer Rebecca West as:

> one of the most marvellous personalities that the nation has ever produced. She had, to begin with, the most exquisite beauty of person. She was hardly taller than a child, but she was not just a small woman; she was a perfectly proportioned fairy. She was the only person I have ever met who could so accurately have been described as flower-like that one could have put it down on her passport. And on many other planes she was remarkable[1].

If all this is true then a biography of Dora Marsden is long overdue. Dora was born in Yorkshire in 1882 and died seventy-eight years later, in Dumfries, Scotland. She had indeed what can only be described as a remarkable life – teacher at thirteen, a university student at eighteen and headmistress of a teachers' training centre in her twenties, Dora had already become a successful and independent woman before joining the struggle for women's suffrage. Turning her back on a promising career in education to become a full-time activist in Emmeline and Christabel Pankhursts' Women's Social and Political Union (WSPU), she became a prominent and much-loved suffragette, renowned for her ingenuity and bravery. Her first arrest in 1909 propelled her into the national limelight, while her other exploits, particularly her harassment of Winston Churchill, quickly entered

---

[1]   *Time and Tide,* 16 July 1926.

suffragette folklore. Her courage was accentuated by her fragile beauty and her diminutive stature – she was just over four foot six inches.

Yet in spite of almost giving her life to the WSPU, and certainly sacrificing her health, Dora became disenchanted with the Suffrage Movement. She found Christabel and Emmeline Pankhurst too dictatorial, and clashed bitterly with them and Emmeline Pethick-Lawrence in 1910. Dora also felt that the ideology of suffragism was too narrow and that it especially stifled feminist debate on issues affecting women. Thus, with little capital and even less journalistic experience, Dora and her friend Mary Gawthorpe founded that "nauseous publication," *The Freewoman – A Weekly Feminist Review*. Though it only survived a year, and in its original form only six months, *The Freewoman* was a truly outstanding, if not the most outstanding feminist journal of the 1900s. Its frank and unrestricted exploration of morality, sexual oppression and women's issues in general was extremely radical, invoking threats of prosecution by the state and boycotts by distributors. It acted as a barometer of radical ideas and became a forum open to the talents of H. G. Wells, Rebecca West, Stella Browne, Edward Carpenter, Ada Neild Chew and others.

After a short break, *The Freewoman* reappeared as *The New Freewoman* in June 1913 and again as *The Egoist* in January 1914. Dora regarded herself in this period more as a rugged individualist, a follower of Max Stirner, than a feminist, though she continued to make astute observations on the position of women and the WSPU. A more literary element, encouraged by Rebecca

West and others, was introduced as Dora began to concentrate on her own "philosophical individualism." In particular, Ezra Pound and Richard Aldington became involved with the paper and were, with Dora, responsible for its change of title in January 1914. Dora remained as editor of *The Egoist* for a few months until her friend and benefactor, Harriet Shaw Weaver, somewhat reluctantly took over. Though Dora was now concentrating on her own philosophical research, she was still concerned with the paper's affairs. To Dora's belated credit, and to the credit of *The Egoist* as a whole, it was she, for example, who accepted James Joyces's *A Portrait of The Artist as a Young Man* for serialization. As Rebecca West later claimed, *The Egoist* "did a magnificent thing for literature" in publishing Joyce; it was also open to the work of Pound, Aldington, H. D., Margaret Storm Jameson and T. S. Eliot.

After *The Egoist* folded at the end of 1919, Dora and her mother moved to Glencoyne in the Lake District. Here, in increasing personal and social isolation, Dora continued with her research; ultimately publishing two volumes, *The Definition of the Godhead* (1928) and *The Mysteries of Christianity* (1930). These were not well received and after a continual decline in mental as well as physical health she suffered several breakdowns, the most serious in 1935. In that year she left Glencoyne and was admitted to the Royal Crichton Hospital in Dumfries. Dora remained as a patient there for the next twenty-five years, dying on 13 December 1960.

She has until recently been largely ignored, though interest in her, and in particular her contribution to

Twentieth-Century feminism and literature, has begun to grow. This is the first attempt to trace and evaluate her whole life. It aims not only to recover yet another woman who for too long has remained "hidden from history" but also to integrate her life and writing with her political environment and involvement. Its aim is to further our understanding of the movements she was involved with, notably the women's movement before 1914, and the circles she moved in. It aims, too, to introduce the reader to her published work, much of which has direct relevance to modern concerns and issues, particularly on women and power[1].

This last aim could possibly have been pursued through the increasingly popular "scissors-and-paste" approach – a selection of her writings with an introduction to each. Though in many ways easier to organize, this method has its pitfalls and can fail to integrate the author's life with her work; the snapshots do not give a complete picture. It can perhaps also fail to appreciate her contributions to areas other than those that are principally seen as her own. The clearest example of this might be the contribution Dora made to the career of James Joyce. None the less, Dora's concerns often went off at tangents, touching areas that if exhaustively covered here would triple the length of the book and delay its publication even further. Thus, for example, the volume leaves to others a fuller exploration of her relationship with Imagism: if indeed such a relationship ex-

---

[1] Since writing this, again I am convinced Marsden's writings before 1914 are relevant to contemporary discourse on gender as a social construct.

isted[1].

However, biography has its own pitfalls. It seems to me that the biographer has two distinct approaches – the narrative and what can be called the psychoanalytical. Both have their advantages but both share a major flaw, if only by implication. They can both foster the notion that history, after all, is made by great individuals – great men and women. In other words, they can ignore the political context in which these individuals operated and which also made them important and influential. People do make history, to paraphrase Marx, but not in circumstances of their own choosing; the role of the biographer is to understand and evaluate both.

A biography, particularly a first biography, should of course discover what its subject did, but a mere chronicle of events would surely not guarantee to reveal the life as a whole. But to explore and understand the life and psyche of our closest contemporaries, let alone those of people who lived so many years ago, is extremely difficult and inevitably bound to generate subjective commentary. In Marsden's case the problem has been exacerbated by her self-imposed seclusion in her later years, followed by her long hospital confinement. It has been made more difficult too by the death of nearly all her contemporaries. The few who are still alive are unable through illness and old age to recall much of her, while her surviving relatives were only children when they knew her in the 1920s.

---

[1] Imagism was a new type of poetry pioneered by the American poet, Ezra Pound, just before the First World War.

31

Lastly, the destruction – sometimes deliberate, sometimes accidental – of some of her personal correspondence has frustrated the attempt to present a full account of her life. None of these obstacles, though, could justify a retreat into pure narrative. There is more than enough evidence to provide a picture of Dora Marsden's life and, as with other historical approaches, no valid reason to avoid interpretation and evaluation. In any case, narrative itself relies on selection, and on the judgement of the author.

It is at this point that I should perhaps explain my motives in writing this biography. I first came across Dora Marsden during my research for a thesis on the women's suffrage movement which was published as *Stepping Stones to Women's Liberty – Feminist Ideas in the Women's Suffrage Movement 1900 to 1918*. Initially, my interest in her focused on her role as a feminist critic of suffragism but widened as I came to appreciate what a fascinating character she was. Where did she come from? How did she become involved in the suffrage movement? What happened to her after *The Freewoman*? These were the first questions that led to a trail that stretched from Colchester to Chester, from London to the Lake District, from Marsden to Dumfries, and even to Canada and the USA. It seemed singularly inappropriate to "drop" Marsden after *The Freewoman*; to do so would only subscribe to the view that feminism somehow died after 1918, miraculously to re-emerge from nowhere in the 1960s.

Finally, some feminists might question the right of a male historian to write this book, while others would see the gender of the author as irrelevant. Certainly, it is an issue that has divided my feminist friends. My own view is that apart from wishing the study to be judged on its own merits, there is a need to avoid the marginalization of "women's history." A vague term – does it mean history by women, history about women, or history written from a feminist point of view? To avoid marginalization, women's history[1], like all "history from below" (socialist history, black history, and so on) must challenge, transform, enrich, indeed become mainstream history and not be content to fill in a few gaps here and there. To succeed, this goal would of course involve more than just intellectual debate but as such it becomes the concern of us all, particularly those socialist historians like myself who wish to see the eradication of sexual, racial and economic inequality and who, while stressing the central importance of class, would define the equality that socialism would bring in that way.

Whether Dora Marsden would share these sentiments is debatable but without question she was a fascinating woman, a "brave and beautiful spirit," but a tragic one too. This book is dedicated to her and her memory; I hope it gives her the recognition she deserves.

---

[1] For a fascinating discussion on women's history, see "What is Women's History?," *History Today* (June 1985). See also E. Fox-Genovese, "Placing Women's History in History," *New Left Review*, 113 (1982).

Beginnings and Influences, 1882 – 1900

Marsden Village

Dora Marsden was born in the Yorkshire village of Marsden which lies at the head of the Colne Valley, seven miles from Huddersfield. A settlement there can be traced back to medieval times but the village did not flourish until the growth of the textile industry in the Eighteenth and Nineteenth Centuries. Aided by the development of the Pennine roads and later by the Manchester-Leeds canal and railway, Marsden became a thriving centre of the West Riding economy, mainly concentrating on cloth, but with its own foundry, Taylor and Sons, too[1].

Marsden village shared the radical and independent traditions of the Colne valley. For example, the Luddites, workers who wrecked the new machinery which threatened their jobs, were active in the area. One local industrialist, William Horsfall, was even murdered on 28 April 1812. Marsden workers were also involved in the agitation for a shorter working day which culminated in the 1830s campaign for the Ten Hours Bill. There is some evidence too of local support for Chartism, a somewhat divided and fluctuating movement of the 1830s and 1840s which pressed for the enactment of the People's Charter. Among other demands, this called for a wider franchise (but not, in spite of pressure from women Chartists, female suffrage) and greater working-class representation in Parliament.

Though Chartism collapsed through the late 1840s

---

[1] For further details of the local history of Marsden see Whitehead (1942) and Lockwood, (1936). For full details of works cited in notes, see Bibliography.

and early 1850s its aims and the wider goals of labour could not be suppressed. They re-emerged in the 1880s with the growth of socialism and the rest of the aggressive and militant New Unionism. The latter began after the famous Match Girls Strike in the summer of 1888 when women workers at Bryant and May's struck for better pay and conditions. It appealed generally to poorer workers and was in part a reaction against the staid "New Model Unions" which represented a labour aristocracy of skilled workers and craftsmen. The new militancy of the Labour Movement was also reflected in the demand for independent representation in Parliament which ultimately resulted in the birth of the Labour Party.

All these changes were clearly evident in the industrial areas of the North of England. New Unionism had a considerable impact among unskilled workers while the Independent Labour Party (ILP), led by Keir Hardie, had its roots in the textile towns of the West Riding and Lancashire. The first ILP branch was created at Bradford in 1891. The Marxist Social Democrat Federation (SDF) which was formed by C. F. Hyndman in 1884 and enrolled Marx's daughter Eleanor, was influential too. Socialist ideas were made accessible through Robert Blatchford's newspaper *The Clarion* which began in 1891 and enjoyed a wide circulation throughout the North. A "Clarion Movement" of cycling clubs and choirs became popular too.

Colne Valley played a crucial role in many of these developments even though trade unionism was slow to take hold in the area. This was in part due to population distribution in the valley scattered as it was in villages but also because many of the mills were small-scale family concerns run by paternalistic employers. The success of New Unionism however had an impact even if this cannot be measured by startling increases in trade union membership. The eventual success of the bitter strike against cuts in piece-rates at the Manningham Mills, Bradford in 1890 could only have inspired others in the area involved in similar attacks on their wages and conditions. Moreover, though small, Marsden and its neighbour Slaithwaite both had branches of the Amalgamated Society of Railway Servants and the Weavers and Textile Workers Union in the 1890s. The latter was formed initially as a result of the "Two Loom Question," essentially an attempt by employers to get weavers to work more than one loom. Finally, the impact of New Unionism cannot be judged purely by union membership. There were several examples of strikes by workers in the area who did not in fact belong to a union at all[1].

The militancy of the working class in the Colne Valley was also reflected in their vital contribution to the movement for Independent Labour representation in Parliament. Though the voters (which excluded many men as well as all women) never elected a Conservative to represent them, dissatisfaction with the Liberals grew. This culminated in the creation of the Colne Valley Labour Union (CVLU) at Slaithwaite in 1891. Members initially came from Slaithwaite, Marsden and Linthwaite but workers from other villages in the valley soon be-

---

[1] For the political history of the Colne Valley, see Clark (1981).

came involved too. The CVLU was active in the formation of the Independent Labour Party and put forward its own candidate, Tom Mann, in the General Election of 1895[1].

Mann did not win the election but the CVLU had been successful in promoting Labour and Socialist issues throughout the valley. One novel and principal way in which this was achieved was through the Union's creation of Labour Clubs. The first was formed in Slaithwaite in 1891, then Marsden in 1892, and many others followed. They organized meetings and arranged guest speakers to lecture on various political and industrial topics. Social events, usually tea and dancing interspersed with an address, were popular too. A marvellous mix of political and social activity was created which was ideally suited to the small and remote communities of the Valley.

The Clubs were not only a vital arm of the CVLU but were crucial to the progress of Socialism in the area. On a formal level this was achieved through debate provoked by guest speakers but it clearly occurred through informal discussion too. This would frequently be inspired by Robert Blatchford's *Clarion*, which was widely read throughout the valley. Blatchford's analysis was more ethical than economic, but he wrote with great clarity and wit, making Socialism both accessible and attractive to his readers. The discussion of his work, including his *Merrie England* which was serialized in the

---

[1]   Thomas Mann was a major figure in Labour and Socialist circles and an extremely popular speaker. Originally the SDF, he became prominent in the ILP and was later a major supporter of Syndicalism.

paper in 1892 and 1893, encouraged visions of a new life under Socialism and contributed to the growth of a counter-culture centred in the clubs. This was furthered by Clarion Choirs and cycling clubs, though these only developed in this area in the 1900s[1].

Blatchford was no feminist but *The Clarion*, along with the Labour Clubs, did much to promote issues that concerned working women. Many outstanding suffragists and feminists wrote for the paper, including Margaret McMillan and Enid Stacey[2], both frequent visitors to the area. Women speakers such as Isabella Ford of the ILP and National Union of Women's Suffrage Societies, and Annie Marland of the Women's Trade Union League, addressed Club meetings on topics such as women and trade unions, education and other social issues. These women built on and developed the local tradition of women's independence. This had come about through their involvement in paid work outside the home. As in the Lancashire towns of Oldham and elsewhere, women workers in the textile industry in the Colne Valley had become an integral part of the labour force. Though by no means guaranteed equal pay or equal opportunity, this work gave women the chance to organize collectively. If nothing else, their wages would at least tend to shift the balance of power at home and foster a stronger and more positive image of women

---

[1]   Clark (1981), pp. 124 – 5, 184. Clark records that at least one member of *The Clarion*'s staff spoke in the area.

[2]   Margaret McMillan was in the ILP and became a nationally known Labour figure. Stacey was also in the ILP, a popular speaker and writer who struggled for feminism, and the suffrage, within the Labour Movement.

than in areas where such work was not available to them. The independent spirit of the Colne was not restricted to men.

The greatest triumph of the Colne Valley's independent and Socialist traditions came in 1907 with the success of Victor Grayson in a by-election in June. This was a sensational victory not only because of Grayson's revolutionary Socialism, but also because the Labour Party refused to endorse him. The CVLU stuck by their candidate who astounded his Liberal and Tory opponents not only by winning the seat, but by claiming after the result was announced that "this epoch-making victory has been won for pure revolutionary Socialism." His success, he admitted, was due to the "idealism of the people of the Colne Valley[1]," and though the details of Grayson's extraordinary career need not concern us here, the significance of his victory in 1907 lay in its reflection of the independence, radicalism and nonconformity of villages like Marsden. It is singularly appropriate therefore that Dora should bear the name of her birthplace, for these qualities remained with her throughout her life.

❦

Dora was born on 5 March 1882, the fourth child and third daughter of Fred and Hannah Marsden. Fred, aged thirty, and Hannah, twenty-nine, already had John six, Marion five and Eleanor two. Their fifth and last child, Ewart, was born soon after. Many years later, in some autobiographical notes[2], Dora claimed that 5

---

[1]   Clark (1981), p. 157. See also Clark (1985).
[2]   These were written many years later in the 1950s when Dora was a

March was the pre-Christian New Year and thus she was bound to become a woman of destiny. Given the difficulties of her early life this seemed unlikely even though she was not born into poverty. Her family, whose local connections went back to the Seventeenth Century, were reasonably well off, if not bourgeois. This was reflected in her birthplace, The Hey, a large, stone house standing in its own grounds, atypical mill-owner's or businessman's home. Dora called it a "gentleman's residence" in her autobiographical notes. It is far from clear how Dora's grandfather, John, came to own the house. He had been a skilled worker, a draughtsman at the foundry, and was involved too in the Mechanics Institute[1]. He might too have been involved in gamekeeping on the local moors[2]. John died in 1870 before Dora was born but his wife Sarah knew her (she died in 1887).

The Marsdens then were clearly not poor but by the time of Dora's birth the impression is of a family under strain if not in absolute decline. The Hey had been divided into two units sometime after 1881, with Fred's sister living in one half with her three daughters, Margarite, Mary and Clarice (and later a son, Ewart), and Fred, his mother, wife and children in the other. This may of course have been done for family convenience but Fred, described in the 1881 census as a "woollen

---

resident of Crichton Royal Hospital in Dumfries. I have not seen them myself but Mrs. E. Bate, Dora's niece, kindly took some notes from them for my benefit.

[1] The Mechanics Institute, with its own magnificent building in the centre of the village, was part of the local workers' education movement.

[2] T. E. Marsden to Garner 22 April 1985.

waste dealer," was already in financial difficulties[1]. It is likely too that Fred Marsden, like others in the textile industry, was suffering from a recession in the 1880s and 1890s and consequently he was experiencing a fall in income. This was not helped by his reputation as a gambler and a man increasingly to be found in the local Junction Inn. By the time of Dora's birth he was certainly restless and possibly even bored with life in Marsden, and it seems clear that he was gambling and frittering the family money away[2].

Whatever the reasons, the result of Fred Marsden's troubles was drastic – around 1890 he left his family and the village for the USA. It was not unusual for men to seek their fortune in the colonies or the United States where, through the textile trade, the village already had strong connections[3], yet it was a momentous decision for a man with five children to make. It is not known whether he intended his wife to follow him but in any event Hannah refused to go. His eldest son, John, who shared his father's weakness for drink, did finally follow him to Philadelphia. Here Fred Marsden set up a textile mill, and died in mysterious circumstances – possibly murder or suicide – on 21 November 1913.

Fred Marsden never saw his wife, Dora or Eleanor again. Contact of a sort must have been maintained for the family had inscribed on the gravestone of his parents the words: "Also of Fred their son who died on Novem-

---

[1]   T. E. Marsden to Garner 22 April 1985. T. E. Marsden claimed Fred was one of the first factory owners to recover wool from rags and call it shoddy.
[2]   T. E. Marsden to Garner 22 April 1985. Also records at Dumfries and conversations with Elaine Bate.
[3]   Pearson (1982).

ber 21 1913 in Philadelphia U.S.A. Age 62. At Rest."
Contact may well have continued through Marion Marsden who settled with her husband in Glastonbury, Connecticut. She was later one of Dora's American subscribers to *The Freewoman*[1].

Whatever Fred Marsden's motives were, the effect on Hannah and the children was severe. The relationship between Hannah and Fred during Dora's formative years had already been strained. And, whatever the emotional turmoil it created at the time (or stored up for the future), the financial repercussions meant that Hannah had to leave The Hey, taking Dora, (then aged between eight and ten) Ewart and possibly Eleanor and Marion too, to live with her mother, Mrs. Gartside in rented rooms at Crow Hill, a large house in Marsden, Hannah then returned to her trade as a seamstress to keep her family.

What effect did the strain in her parents' relationship and her father's departure have on the young Dora? It is difficult to understand contemporary family dynamics let alone those of the 1880s and any response to this question must necessarily be tentative. None the less, it is safe to assume that being a child in an impoverished one-parent family, with an absent alcoholic father must have made some impact on Dora. At the very least, it must have helped to shape her attitude to men. Her fa-

---

[1]   Marion married Tom Dyson (no relation of Rev. James Dyson, the future husband of Eleanor Marsden). He also made his money out of textiles, particularly through working for the US government during the First World War. He also owned land in Florida where, according to one family legend, he named mountains and lakes Eleanor, Marion and Dora (Mount Dora is in Florida). T. E. Marsden to Garner, 22 April 1985. There is no local evidence to support this claim.

ther was hardly a reliable and trustworthy patriarch but a feckless man who eventually deserted his wife and children, forcing them to leave home and Hannah to return to paid work. Conversely, Dora's mother became a pillar of strength and reliability, the saviour of the family. Certainly, the importance of the economic independence of women was obvious to Dora through her own family experience. It is perhaps not surprising that she held this belief throughout her adult life[1].

The prospects for the young Dora did not look bright, yet like so many women of her time education was to provide a lifeline. Feminists for many years had pressed for an improvement in the education of women and girls and had argued that this was the key to equality in other areas. Already some of the leading girls' schools, such as the North London Collegiate, had been established and universities were slowly opening their doors to women. More importantly for women like Dora, the 1870 Education Act ensured that all girls would receive some education. This was to have a profound effect.

Dora was already attending the village school when her father left for the USA. Interestingly, her parents (probably her mother) had sent her to the nondenominational Town School rather than the Church School. The Town School had been set up in 1820, and was financed by local businessmen and other notables. It was strictly non-denominational (no clergymen were allowed to be

---

[1] For further information on the Village of Marsden see Marsden History Group, marsdenhistory.co.uk. Members record that weak men within Dora's family throughout several generations were not uncommon.

trustees) and reflected the strong presence of Non-conformism in the area. The school suffered from competition from the Church School but due to a growing population it prospered, so much so that it had to move to new buildings in 1878, with three major classrooms designed to cater for over one hundred children[1].

The pupils were divided into Standards which corresponded to national criteria for particular age groups. Schools such as these received financial help according to progress made, as assessed by Inspectors who would arrive on the premises without notice. Their early reports indicated reasonable satisfaction with the school although they often noted that "half-timers" were a problem[2]. Indeed, attendance was a continual worry for the headmaster W. H. Griffiths, who noted with typical Victorian attention to accuracy and detail, that the average daily roll in 1890 was 127.7. Other problems were the weather which could be particularly severe in winter, and more seriously still, outbreaks of smallpox (1893) and scarlet fever (1895, 1896). Regular attenders were rewarded by annual trips to the sea, with Blackpool being a favourite choice[3].

In 1890 Griffiths' staff were Mr. G. F. Hague (who earned £50 p.a., £10 less than the Head) one pupil-teacher, Miss E. K. Coates (£30 p.a. and one "candidate," Annie Holroyd (£20 p.a.). Staff, as elsewhere,

---

[1] See Robinson (1878) and Pearson (1982).
[2] These were children who spent some of their time working in local industry. See, for example, the report of 25 August 1890. This, as with all the Town School records quoted, are currently held at Huddersfield Public Library.
[3] Marsden Town School Reports, 1890 – 1896.

could be recruited from the pupils themselves. Promising boys and girls (quite often the latter) became "monitors," then "candidates" for a pupil-teacher post, and finally pupil-teachers. Apprentices to the job of teaching in a school like Griffiths' were thus a candidate for one year and a pupil-teacher for four, and had to sit annual exams before being awarded their Elementary Teacher's Certificate. It was a long and laborious process but one that was to provide new opportunities for many women; to Dora Marsden it ultimately led to change the direction of her whole life.

Dora's chance came out of the school's growth, her own ability, and to some extent, luck. The Inspectors were constantly calling for more teachers for the school, one remarking, in 1891, that "a reasonably wide and intelligent style of teaching cannot be maintained without a stronger staff[1]." Another pupil-teacher was taken on but the staff was still too small for a school which, according to Griffiths, could take up to two hundred pupils. It was at this point that a candidate, Lilian Cockerham, resigned and, in the words of the *Report*: "D. Marsden is recognised under Article 33 of the Code," that is to say she was appointed, at the age of thirteen, a candidate on probation, and her long apprenticeship had begun. Her appointment reflected the school's recognition of her abilities. According to Dora herself (again in her unpublished autobiographical notes) she had "proved to be a good diligent pupil," yet there is a feeling that she already saw herself as apart from (or superior to?) her fellow pupils. Many of them probably did

---

[1]   11 August 1891.

not approve of one of their peers deserting their ranks to join the other side, but it seems that Dora did not mix easily anyway. Over forty years later, it was confirmed that "at school Miss Marsden was very clever... meticulous, highly moral and cheerful" but "not sociable[1]."

Mr. Griffiths' staff were predominantly female: the only other man was Mr. Gledhill who worked with Annie Whitehead and Annie Holroyd (both pupil-teachers), Miss Hague and, of course, Dora herself. Dora's duties as a candidate and later as a pupil-teacher included assisting the more senior staff and taking lessons herself. One stressful aspect of her training was the "criticism lessons" when other teachers sat in the class with her, criticizing her performance after the lesson had finished. The resignation of Mr. Gledhill in August 1895 necessitated a reorganization of the staff and Dora was employed in the Infants School for the next few years. She must have performed well for one Inspector's Report, of July 1897, was full of praise: "The Infants," the Inspector noted, "have been taught in temporary premises during the latter part of the school year. The order is good and the children very well advanced in the elementary subjects. The object lessons also deserve great praise." The temporary premises were in fact rooms in the nearby Mechanics Institute. Dora later realized, in her autobiographical notes, that this led to a curious family coincidence for, according to her, she taught "in the very room in which my grandfather had – with others – es-

---

[1] Records on Dora Marsden held at Crichton Royal Dumfries, 26 November 1935. It is likely that this information originated from Dora's sister, Eleanor.

tablished a library for his fellow workmen at the foundry." She further claimed that he had helped to establish the Institute itself, "in which he (and others) conducted night classes for the education of the men." Dora was thus following a family tradition in teaching in the village and she seemed to be successful at it too. Family circumstances remained strained though. Her brother, Ewart, was not yet working, and her grandmother had died in 1891 leaving Hannah Marsden to support and raise her family single-handed. Though a skilled seamstress she certainly would not have been earning much, and Dora's £20 a year salary as a candidate (£30 p.a. when she became a pupil-teacher) must have been crucial to the family finances. It also gave Dora great responsibility at a very early age.

Though Dora enjoyed being a pupil-teacher it was a hard life. Apart from the lessons and sporadic tests set by Griffiths, Dora also had to sit the annual exams that would ultimately lead to the Elementary Teacher's Certificate. The training for this was held at Huddersfield Technical College, over seven miles away, where she had to attend a "Day Special Teachers Class" on Saturday mornings to study, for example, physiography, including "matter and energy... The Earth and The Atmosphere[1]." She passed the first stage in this and felt so interested and confident in her subject that she offered criticism lessons on "The Atmosphere" and "The Sun" in 1898 and 1899[2]. By now she had achieved a first class pass in the advanced stage of physiography, which in-

---

[1]   Annual Report, Huddersfield Technical Prospectus, 1895-6.
[2]   Marsden Town School Log Book, 20 October 1898, 16 February 1899.

cluded analysis of the solar system, the Earth and the tides.

At the age of sixteen, Dora was leading a full and hectic life. In 1898-9 for example, in addition to her teaching, she had to follow a demanding programme at the College. Monday evenings from 6:30 to 8:00 were spent in the laboratory studying human physiology, followed by a lecture on the same subject the following day, from 7:15 to 8:15 p.m. Wednesday nights, from 7:10 to 9:10, were devoted to geometric drawing, and Friday (7:15 to 8:15) to personal hygiene. Thus most weekdays would begin at around 7:00 a.m. to get ready for school, which began at 8:00 and finished around 4:00 p.m. Then she would probably walk the mile or so to Crow Hill for tea, walk back to the station with her fellow pupil-teachers, Annie Whitehead and Annie Holroyd, to catch the train to Huddersfield, getting home at around 10:00 p.m. This demanding timetable reflected Dora's energy and her determination to succeed as a teacher.

Dora's commitment brought results. She passed Griffiths' tests with high marks even though at this stage of her life she already suffered from illnesses, occasionally being absent sick. Of course, there was nothing unusual in this though it is tempting to speculate that it was not unconnected to the toll of her daily routine. However, Dora had become a valuable and valued member of a thriving and rapidly improving school. The 1899 Annual Report recorded that "well-planned work and useful instruction are the characteristic features of this school and the general condition, as regards tone and attainments, is highly creditable." The following year, at the age of eighteen, she qualified as a teacher. What an achievement lay behind the dry words of the *Annual Report* of that year: "Dora Marsden should be informed that she is now qualified under Articles 50 and 52 of the Code."

However, this achievement was to be followed by an even more dazzling success. It had seemed that Dora Marsden was destined to become an energetic and skillful teacher and a respected member of the community. Yet in the late 1890s she had made the momentous decision to apply to a University. Unfortunately, there is little evidence of why she decided to do so. Her autobiographical notes make a fleeting reference to a meeting with two university graduates who were visiting an aunt, but there is no other information on this. Dora would have become aware of scholarship schemes at the Technical College and it was probably this that was instrumental in the making of her decision. In the years before mandatory grants for university students, there was clearly little chance that a woman from Dora's impoverished background would be able to afford to take a full-time degree course. Dora therefore entered the Queen's Scholarship scheme which was linked to Victoria University. This was composed of colleges in Leeds, Liverpool and Manchester which became separate universities at the turn of the century. Dora achieved a First Class pass which meant that her tuition fees were paid as well as a maintenance grant, on condition that she taught for at least five years after graduation. Hannah Marsden may well have been looking forward to Dora bringing in a regular income as a local teacher but not for first nor the last time, she ignored her own interests in order to support her youngest and most gifted daughter. Neither woman could possibly have foreseen what effect it would have on Dora's life.

Havelock Ellis, the famous sexologist, who was later to welcome Dora's paper *The Freewoman*, once wrote in "An Open Letter to Biographers" that they would be advised to concentrate upon "the curve of life that has its summit at puberty and ends with the completion of adolescence: whatever else there is to make is made then. The machine has been created; during these years it is wound up to perform its work in the world. What follows after counts for something but always less[1]." What was "made then," what can be surmised about the eighteen-year-old Dora as she waited at Marsden station for the train to take her to Manchester? She was clearly intelligent and determined to succeed in spite of the obstacles created by family circumstances. Her father's departure had probably left her with a poor impression of men, while her mother, her friends Whitehead and Holroyd and, indeed, her own success enhanced local radical beliefs in the strength and independence of women. Though there is no evidence of direct involvement by Dora in local politics, it is unlikely that she was untouched by the radical spirit of the valley. But if a determined independence in Dora can be detected, a belief in her own difference from others can be discerned too. After all, few eighteen-year-old women from Marsden had succeeded in getting to university. A ner-

---

[1] Quoted in Grosskurth (1981), pp. 48-9.

vous but excited young woman stood on that railway platform, eager to learn more and, it is suspected, confident of her own ability to do so.

Student and Teacher, 1900 – 1908

Owen's College

Dora became a student at Owen's College in the autumn of 1900. She lived in digs with Mrs. Hindshaw at 210 Greame Street, Moss Side which was within walking distance of the university. Mrs. Hindshaw's daughter, Florence, was a second-year student there and may have befriended the new student from Yorkshire. Dora's choice of Manchester later turned out to be crucial for it was a town with strong radical and suffragist traditions and connections[1]. The National Union of Women's Suffrage Societies was very active there and could trace its origins to a Manchester Suffrage Society set up in 1867[2]. In 1903, Christabel and Emmeline Pankhurst formed the Women's Social and Political Union at 62 Nelson Street, close by the university. Dora later became a harsh and virulent critic of suffragism but for her, as for so many women of the time, it was a major catalyst in the development and growth of her own feminist consciousness.

When Dora went to Manchester, female students were still a small minority although not as uncommon as they had once been. In fact, there had been some progress since John Owen, a local businessman, had left an endowment for the creation of a college in 1846. The endowment had specified that the institution was to exclude women but this restriction was removed by legislation in 1870-71. Even then, under the conservative leadership of Principal Greenwood, the entry of women

---

[1] See Liddington and Norris (1978).
[2] This was set up after the failure of a Woman's Suffrage amendment to a Reform Bill in 1866.

into the College had been limited. Indeed, it was not until 1883 that women were allowed to sit for degrees, the first being awarded in 1886. Even then, women were taught separately from men and their choice of subjects was usually limited to Classics, English and History[1].

The women had originally been taught in the Manchester and Salford College for Women which had opened in Brunswick Street in 1877. In 1883 this became the Women's Department of Owen's College which, with colleges in Liverpool and Leeds, became the Victoria University in the same year. The numbers of women students increased throughout the 1880s and 1890s and by 1900 female undergraduates not only had their own Department but their own Student Union too, with premises at 248 Oxford Street. In 1899 Ashbourne House, a hall of residence for women, was opened, though most students, like Dora, lived in digs or at home. By the turn of the century, there were nearly two hundred women students, most of whom were training to be teachers or were following humanities subjects. Only a small minority – less than twenty – were enrolled on science courses and only two, Catherine Chisholm and Catherine Marshall, were studying medicine.

Dora was one of fifty-three new students in the Women's Department in 1900 and one of twenty-six women enrolled on the teacher training course held at the Manchester Day Training College. The course was for both men and women. Throughout the three-year programme Dora and her colleagues had instruction in

---

[1]   See Fiddes (1937), also *Manchester Guardian* 1883.

the theory of teaching, practical teaching skills and needlework, music, elocution and drawing. (The men, but not the women, studied woodwork too.) They also had teaching practice in local schools. This proved to be unsatisfactory and under the leadership of Catherine Dodd teaching practice was reorganized in 1902 at St Paul's School, Brunswick Street, a few minutes' walk away from Owen's. There, according to Dodd, "the best methods of the best thinkers on education" were employed in an attempt to fit the students for their profession by giving them continuous teaching in various subjects[1].

Besides the training course, Dora also took a range of options as part of her BA degree. In the first year she studied Latin, English Language, Geography and Pure Maths, later Music, History and Philosophy too. In 1903 she achieved an overall II.1 gaining firsts, with Jessie Clarkson, Lillian Atkinson and Margaret Thomas, in Ancient History, and, with Irene Parker, the Theory of Music[2].

Dora Marsden had done extremely well but her education in Manchester was not limited to what she learned on her course. Her political and feminist awareness were developed throughout her time there beginning, perhaps, with her experience at the University Settlement. This was opened in 1896 in an impoverished working-class area of Manchester. According to the Settlements' fourth Annual Report of 1900, it was:

---

[1] *Manchester Guardian*, 6 March 1903.
[2] *Manchester Guardian*, 5 July 1902.

founded in the hope that it may become common ground on which men and women of various classes may meet in goodwill, sympathy and friendship; that the residents learn something of the conditions of an industrial neighbourhood and share its interests, and endeavour to live among their neighbours a simple and religious life.

The work was shared between the resident workers, segregated in separate men's and women's houses, and students from the University itself. (Perhaps the nearest modern equivalent to the Settlement would be a local community centre.) The Ancoats Settlement organized clubs and societies, lectures on philosophy, art and literature, held literacy classes, organized holidays and supplied free legal advice. It was successful too. In the words of Owen's College Union magazine of March 1901: "the dirty multitudes flock in as if they were at home there." Yet it was a two-way process: the Settlement workers could learn for themselves about the dreary and overcrowded monotony of life in the slums of Manchester. For some like Victor Grayson, who worked there during 1904-6, it taught them too about the vast gulf between those who created wealth and those who owned it[1].

What was important for Dora too was that the Settlement brought her into contact with the burgeoning women's movement and many of its leading activists. This was mainly through the Settlement's Fawcett Debating Society, although its Elizabethan Society, through its prominent members, Christabel Pankhurst and Eva Gore-Booth, played a part too. The Fawcett was set up

---

[1]   See Clark (1985), Chapter 2.

in the autumn of 1900, the same year that Dora joined the University. It was formed partly in honour of the famous suffragist and leader of the NUWSS, Millicent Garrett Fawcett, but also to encourage women to speak in public debate. The Settlement already had the Toynbee Debating Society but it was felt that the women were inhibited by the presence of men, who were thus excluded from the new club.

What is particularly striking about the Fawcett were the issues debated and the women who raised them. Both the issues and the speakers were in most cases to become central to the women's movement of the early Twentieth Century. In the period October 1900 to October 1901, for example, Eva Gore-Booth, an active campaigner for women's rights and an early mentor of Christabel was booked to open a debate on men, while other speakers included E. J. Minton on unhappy marriages, Katherine Bruce Glazier on the state and the home, Sarah Burstall on what have women to do with politics, and E. Rowton on women's suffrage. Between 1901 and 1903, according to the Settlement's Annual Reports, there were talks on equal suffrage, child labour, early marriages, the woman citizen and trade unions (Eva Gore-Booth) and feminine ethics (Isabella O. Ford). The popularity of these debates was reflected in the steady growth in size of the audience which was usually a mix of students, housewives and textile workers.

All of the women speakers were, or were to become, politically active either as socialists or suffragists or in some cases, both. Eva Gore-Booth, for example, was a prominent suffragist who went on to campaign with women textile workers and barmaids. Isabella Ford was also, by 1900, a long-standing fighter for women, both within the ILP and the NUWSS. She too came from Yorkshire and was no stranger to the Colne Valley. Theresa Billington (later Billington-Greig) who had, like Dora, been a pupil-teacher, was also active in the Settlement and was not only to become a suffragette but one of the most fervent and lucid critics of the WSPU. The woman who was to lead that organization, Christabel Pankhurst, needs little introduction though it should be remembered that she too was a student at Owen's College, graduating with a First Class Honours in Law in 1906. Perversely, she was not allowed to practise at the Bar because of her sex. Christabel had joined Owen's at the same time as Dora although they do not seem to have shared classes. However, Florence Hindshaw shared a Philosophy class with her[1].

The young Dora Marsden may not have been a leading or prominent figure in these circles but it is inconceivable that she was not in any contact with them. After all, the women at Owen's were still a small, closely-knit group with their own department, union and societies[2]. Moreover, many women who were to become great friends – as well as enemies – were Dora's con-

---

[1] For further details, see Rylands Library Archives, Manchester University, particularly on Owen's College and the Settlement. These records also include some class registers from the period Dora was at the university (1903).
[2] There was also a Women's Debating Society in Owen's College Women's Union, and Gore-Booth and Pankhurst took part in that too. *Owen's Magazine*, January 1902.

temporaries at Manchester. Christabel, of course, Theresa Billington and Rona Robinson too. In short, Dora's time at university was crucial to her. It not only confirmed her interest and ability in academic work but engendered and strengthened her interest in feminism. It created too a network of friends and sympathizers that was vital to her during her suffrage and *Freewoman* period and indeed, in some cases, right through to the 1920s[1].

One of the conditions of Dora's scholarship was that she had to teach for five years after graduation and thus any other activity in Manchester had to take second place to the necessity of finding employment. Trained graduates like Dora were expected to find good appointments in training colleges, pupil-teacher centres or schools. Dora was eventually accepted for a post in October 1903 at Kepler Senior School, Leeds. This was within commuting distance of Marsden where Dora's mother had moved from Crow Hill to Westleigh but she chose to live in Leeds, at 26 Gathorn Avenue, not far from the school.

Kepler, a new Board School, opened in 1898 under the headship of Thomas Hudson. In 1904 it had over one thousand pupils arranged in three departments, infants, junior and senior, and Dora was appointed to teach in the senior department. The school was in a working-class area surrounded by industrial works (mostly chem-

---

[1] It is remarkable how many graduates of Manchester University from this period were to become politically active. Omitted from the text, for example, are Ellen Wilkinson (later known as 'Red Ellen') the Labour MP and Lillian Williamson (later Forrester) a prominent suffragette. See Leach (1971).

icals, dye and, of course, clothing), close by the Leeds Union Workhouse. The school log book has few references to Dora, the first simply states: "Dora Marsden appointed 11 October 1903 born 5 March 1882, Pupil-Teacher Marsden Town School, Trained Queen's College, Manchester." It inaccurately records Dora's qualifications as "BA Degree 1st, in Parts I and II," even though the Manchester Register of Graduates records Dora as having a II.1[1].

Her first day at school was hardly promising: the log book records, "October 1st, Miss Marsden – appointed this morning – absent this afternoon ill." She was able to return the following day. Though no further absences through illness are recorded Dora did not settle and was soon looking for a job elsewhere. Within a month she had applied for and got a post as Assistant Mistress at the Colchester and Harwich Pupil-Teacher Centre in Colchester. And, on 23 December 1903, in Hudson's words, "Miss Marsden ceases duty at this school."

What can we learn from Dora's short stay in Leeds? Perhaps she had wanted to work and live in familiar territory near to Marsden but clearly she found this job unsuitable. On the other hand, her appointment in October was a little late – had she dithered in Manchester, not wanting to leave, or had she been too demanding in her job applications? Whatever the answer, it does not seem likely that her stay in Leeds was a happy one with the

---

[1] Subsequent school records refer to Dora's appointment as earlier than 11 October 1903, so perhaps the listing of her degree class was another mistake.

stress of teaching in Kepler being too much for the twenty-one-year-old on her first day.

As an Assistant Mistress in Colchester Dora's salary rose to £95 p.a., and compared well to the £20 p.a. she had received as a pupil-teacher in Marsden. She joined a small staff of four under the Headmaster, F. O. Wilson. The centre itself had opened in 1897 and was a branch of the Technical and University Extension College. It was located in the High Street in a cramped building now currently occupied by the Co-op Bank. When Dora taught there, there were over one hundred students, some attending during the day, others, like Dora herself at the Huddersfield Tech, during the evenings and Saturday mornings only. In addition to teaching students how to teach, Dora also instructed them in History, Needlework, Music, Reading and Arithmetic.

In her autobiographical notes, Dora later recalled her time in Essex with affection, claiming that she had "some very happy months there." Her pay, for a twenty-one-year-old woman, was relatively good even when compared to the average wage of a skilled male worker.

However, the Centre clearly had many problems. In the 1900s Michael Sadler, Professor of Education at Manchester University (and possibly known to Dora) was engaged in publishing reports on the service education committees provided in their localities. In 1906 he was in the County of Essex. His report was critical of the education provision in the area in general and of the Pupil-Teacher Centre in particular. While praising the commitment of the staff, Sadler was critical of the service they provided, citing the heavy demand upon them which in turn led to "a heavy strain of work which renders private study on their part almost impossible and, in spite of the loyalty of those concerned, impairs the freshness of their teaching."

The report was published in 1906 and was based on inquiries carried out in 1905 so its observations are clearly applicable to the year of Dora's tenure at the Centre. In particular, Sadler's comments on the building itself must have applied to 1904 too. He recalled, for example, a visit where "a class was being taught in a stuffy room fitted with antiquated desks with a stepped floor sloping up towards the ceiling... only a small laboratory and a mere nucleus of a library." "The toilets," Sadler added, "were wholly insufficient." Perhaps reflecting Manchester University's growing concern over the education of women, Sadler made particular reference to female teachers and students. He was "struck by the pale face of the girls, a great number of whom look overtired and physically below par." Sadler noted that "One of the women teachers is supposed to be in special charge of the girls, but she has no private room. She and her women colleagues share a little attic room with the two men teachers." Sadler argued that the Centre should be moved as quickly as possible to more suitable premises. His conclusion was that, against many difficulties, "the Headmaster had gallantly struggled. He has had in the main poor material to work with, insufficient leisure for study and a staff inadequate for the present complexity of the work[1]."

Dora's year at Colchester must have been demanding but unfortunately no other evidence of her stay there has survived. Perhaps she began to miss the North and her mother and her friends in Manchester for when a job came vacant as Assistant Mistress in Altrincham Pupil-Teacher Centre near Manchester, a short train journey from Marsden, she applied for it and was successful. It proved to be another crucial move for Dora, she was still only twenty-two years old.

The Pupil-Teacher Centre had been set up in the Technical Institute's buildings in George Street, Altrincham, to serve pupils from Altrincham, Knutsford, Ashton-upon-Mersey, and Lynn. Originally it was conceived as a temporary facility until a new secondary school could be built which would also incorporate the training of teachers. The Centre usually employed a small staff of three or four and had a roll of some sixty students. It already enjoyed a good reputation, with the 1905 HMI Report declaring that "the Centre has made a capital start." (Paradoxically, with reorganization, it folded in 1910.)

The headmistress was Frances M. Kirk, a contemporary of Dora at Owen's College, who had gained 1st Class BA in 1902. It is not inconceivable that the two women had become friends in Manchester and that Kirk invited Dora to join her when a post became vacant at the Centre. But joining an old acquaintance was not the only attraction to Dora. Apart from returning home,

---

[1]   Sadler (1906), pp. 244-5.

Dora's pay now rose to £110 p.a., again a relatively good salary for a woman still in her early twenties. And when another friend from Manchester University, the lively science graduate Rona Robinson, joined the Centre in the summer of 1905, the attraction of Dora's new job was complete. Together the three "Owenites" set out to make it a success.

Certainly, the Altrincham and Bowden Sub-Committee of Cheshire County Council's Education Committee seemed pleased with the progress the women made. The HMI Report of 9 October 1905 considered "the headmistress most suitable and the Assistant Mistress supports her very effectively. The relations between the staff and the pupils were pleasant and the tone and atmosphere satisfactory." Most of the sixty-two pupils were girls and the Report added that the Centre would make a good nucleus for a girls' secondary school. In fact, the Centre had a distinctly female environment with only temporary male teachers, and at one stage a female caretaker, Annie Luxton.

Dora taught French and, with Kirk, other literary subjects, and Rona Robinson taught Science, Maths and Drill. Mr. Madden taught Drawing for a time; two other male teachers, Mr. Rothwell and Mr. Meadows were replaced by Rona. Though successful, Kirk and her fellow Manchester graduates were increasingly under pressure as new regulations for the training of pupil-teachers came into effect and as the new secondary school loomed Dora was ill in the spring of 1906 as was Kirk the following year. Dora deputized for her during her absence and clearly did well. Kirk's report on 27 May

1907 states that: "During my absence through illness through the greater part of the month of February, the school was superintended by Miss Marsden... The work seems to have suffered as little as possible." Probably as a result of continuing pressure, Kirk was ill again in May 1908 and finally resigned the following September. At the age of twenty-six, Dora was appointed head-mistress with a salary of £130 p.a.[1]

Dora had come a long way since her early days in Marsden. A promising future in education lay before her and she could also look forward to an income that would provide a reasonable standard of living. Her success was due to her own abilities, allied to the crucial support of her mother. It was also due to the growth of a national education system, that not only stipulated education for girls as well as boys, but ultimately was to lead to greater job opportunities for women. Here, Dora also owed a debt to earlier feminists who had stressed the importance of women's education in general and who had campaigned for their entry into the teaching profession. These pioneers realized that women could not claim equality while they were still held in ignorance, and felt if women could compete equally with men in education they could do so in other areas too. Though it was the state's concern over the potential weakness and danger of an uneducated workforce that lay behind the development of compulsory education, Dora and countless other women were the beneficiaries of their pioneering work.

---

[1] For reports on the Centre, see Cheshire Council Education Committee Records, Vols II-VII, 1904-10.

Yet within a year both Dora and Rona had resigned and left their posts. This was partly over a disagreement with their employers over wages but was also due to their growing involvement in the suffragette movement described in the following chapter. To give up promising careers in order to fight for votes for women not only reflected their courage but their commitment to feminism. In Dora's case this had sprung from her early family experiences but it had been nurtured by her time in Manchester and through her work as a teacher. Manchester was already developing as a major suffragist centre by the turn of the century and many prominent and emerging feminists were drawn to it as to a magnet. Dora was clearly attracted to them and her first contacts with likeminded women were made at the university. Dora's feminist consciousness was bolstered too by her success as a student and a teacher. She, like Rona Robinson, had shown that women were not only capable of achieving a degree but of fulfilling the requirements of a demanding job too. Their very lives and work showed the potential of women, yet women's progress was still being strangled by artificial and illogical restrictions. At the same time, Dora was well aware of the vast gulf between idealized concepts of women's lives and reality. It was these contradictions that fuelled Dora Marsden's feminist consciousness and propelled her, like so many other women, to the suffrage movement. Whether all her qualities of courage, determination, independence and a strong belief in her own abilities would be always welcome there remained to be seen.

Sweetest and Bravest of Suffragettes: Dora's Life in the Women's Social and Political Union, 1908 – 1911

Dora Marsden

My Love to you Dora Marsden, sweetest, gentlest and bravest of suffragettes.

Emmeline Pethick-Lawrence

6 October 1909

Mrs. Pankhurst required at the outset, for the sake of backing, women with money and with some capacity: when she obtained these she drew the limiting line which would keep out women with accepted followings and too much ability: that is unless they came with ashes in their hair, repentance in one hand and passivity in the other. Then on the principle of the Eastern potentate who illustrated the practice of good government by lopping off the heads of all the stalks of grain which grew higher than the rest, she by one means or another rid her group of all its members unlikely by virtue of personality, conspicuous ability, or undocile temper, to prove flexible material in the great cause. The gaps thus made she filled up with units of stock size.

Dora Marsden

The Egoist, 15 June 1914

Dora first became active in the Pankhursts' WSPU in 1908 when she was still a teacher in Altrincham. After her first arrest in the spring of 1909 she quickly rose to become a full-time, paid organizer and something of a national celebrity. Yet though a much admired and loved activist her relationship with the Union's leadership soon became strained. Like so many independent and intelligent suffragettes, Dora baulked at the autocracy of the Pankhursts believing that it had no place in an organization struggling for democratic reform. She felt too that the Pankhursts' control of the WSPU stifled feminist debate within its ranks. In 1911 Dora resigned and became one of the Union's fiercest critics. She nearly killed herself for "the cause" and these dangerous, tumultuous years illustrate much about this "brave and beautiful spirit," and indeed, the organization which she served so well and was subsequently to revile almost until her dying day.

By the time Dora became a student at Manchester and certainly by her return North in 1905, women's suffrage was a potent political issue. It was part of a much wider debate over electoral reform and was, of course, a major though not the sole concern of contemporary feminists. The suffragettes brought new life to the campaign for women's suffrage but the struggle had begun well before the birth of the WSPU and has its origins in the early Nineteenth Century. Women's suffrage amendments had in fact been proposed during the debate over the 1832 Reform Bill which extended the male franchise and, as noted above, women Chartists wanted it included in the Peoples' Charter.

The history of organized suffragism though begins in the mid-1860s when a small group of women pressed John Stuart Mill to try to include women in the franchise Bill which became the second Reform Act 1867. This group included some of the early pioneers of the Victorian Women's Movement. They included Emily Davies, an early campaigner for women's education, Barbara Bodichon, editor of the *Englishwomen's Review*, and Jessie Boucherett who led the Society for Promoting the Employment of Women. They did not call for universal suffrage – that had to wait until 1928 – but they were incensed by the fact that women were excluded from the franchise, however limited, purely because of their sex. They were united too in a belief that the possession of the vote would lead to general improvements in women's position.

Mill's attempt failed but the early suffragists responded by creating suffrage societies in Manchester, London and Edinburgh. In 1867 these formed a loose federation, the National Society for Women's Suffrage, the forerunner to the NUWSS. Manchester, though physically distanced from the political stage at Westminster, became a suffragist centre with Lydia Becker editing the *Women's Suffrage Journal* there from 1870 to 1890. In many ways, as Liddington and Norris argue, Manchester "with its emphasis on Liberalism and the rights of the individual" was a logical place for a women's suffrage movement to flourish[1].

---

[1]   Liddington and Norris (1978), p.68. See also E. S. Pankhurst (1931); Fulford (1957); Garner (1984).

Suffragism in Manchester as elsewhere made steady if unspectacular progress throughout the latter half of Victoria's reign though its own campaigning style tended to be narrow, and by the 1890s it seemed to be running out of steam. In the last decade of the century, however a new factor, with its origins in the labour and socialist movements, emerged. It flourished in the 1900s, developing into a unique form of radical working-class suffragism which, in spite of some links and interconnections, was to stand in sharp contrast to the aims and tactics of the WSPU. Working-class activists like Ada Neild Chew, Selina Cooper and Sarah Reddish were part of this new force which stressed the needs of working class women. The emphasis on class was further emphasized by the leadership of Esther Roper, who had become secretary of the Manchester Women's Suffrage Society in 1893, and by her close friend, Eva Gore-Booth[2].

The WSPU headed by Emmeline Pankhurst, and her daughter Christabel also had its origins in local labour circles. Richard and Emmeline Pankhurst, who had formed the Women's Franchise League in 1889, not only had a longstanding commitment to women's suffrage but had both been active in the political wing of the labour movement. They were both members of the ILP and Richard had stood, unsuccessfully, for them in 1895. Many of the original founders of the WSPU were

---

[2] Chew, Cooper and Reddish were all working-class women and active trade unionists. Chew and Cooper later became organizers for the NUWSS. Gore-Booth and Roper were also involved with women workers. For further details see Liddington and Norris, pp. 288-92; Liddington (1984); Chew (1982).

members of the party and from its formation in October 1903 until its move to London, the Union was largely dependent on the ILP for publicity, platforms and audiences. Emmeline Pankhurst had even wanted to call the new organization the Women's Labour Representation Committee, only changing her mind to avoid confusion with the recently formed Women's Textile Workers Representation Committee[1].

Her daughter Christabel served her political apprenticeship with Roper and Gore-Booth but she quickly became disillusioned with the Union's parochialism and its links with Labour. She wanted an independent national organization that would work for one goal – votes for women. In any case, and not without justification, Christabel was concerned about the attitude of many members of the Labour Movement to women's suffrage. A large number were particularly worried about the suffragist demand for votes for women on the same terms as men. As a property qualification existed at the time, they argued such a demand, if granted, would only enfranchise middle-class women not noted for their sympathy to Labour's cause. Only adult suffrage would do.

Christabel and others realized that this argument was sometimes used to conceal outright opposition to women's suffrage. "Some say," she complained in the *ILP News* of August 1903, "when they [male socialists] are in power, and have nothing better to do, they will give women votes as a finishing touch to their arrangements." Though Christabel was justified in chiding

---

[1]   Liddington and Norris, Ch. 10; E. S. Pankhurst, Book IV, Ch. 2; Rosen (1974), Ch. 3.

some socialists on this issue, she was unwilling to sympathize with those radical suffragists like Ada Neild Chew and Selina Cooper who felt an allegiance to their class as well as their sex, and who wanted to base the suffrage movement on the needs and demands of working women. They were to find a more sympathetic response in the NUWSS[1]. Under Christabel's leadership, the WSPU hastily broke away from its northern Labour roots. The links with the ILP were severed and the headquarters of the Union moved to London. It was quickly to become an autocracy that concentrated on one issue only – votes for women. As such, the WSPU almost from its birth in 1903 to its death in 1917 when it became the Women's Party, was beset with splits and breakaways[2].

However, women flocked to the WSPU and other suffrage societies. The demand for the vote built on and in many ways coalesced the aspirations of various campaigns that had begun in the Nineteenth Century. These ranged from education to employment, women's property rights to Josephine Butler's struggle against the Contagious Diseases Acts[3]. Armed with the vote, suffragists argued, women's demands in all these areas would be much more likely to be met. However, they would also be the first to acknowledge their debt to the Victorian pioneers who had already achieved some suc-

---

[1] See Chew; also Liddington.

[2] Garner, pp. 44-7 for a further discussion of this.

[3] The Contagious Diseases Acts of 1866 and 1869 empowered magistrates to force women – but not men – to undergo a medical examination if suspected of having a venereal disease. After Josephine Butler's campaign, the Acts were repealed in 1886.

cess by the turn of the century. Allied to the growing organization of female workers, women by their actions had already begun to have some effect by the 1900s even though the vote had not been won and they faced many obstacles to further progress.

In fact, early Twentieth-Century suffragists and feminists operated on extremely difficult terrain. The issue of votes for women became embroiled in party politics while growing unemployment put pressure on women workers, especially married women workers, to return to the domestic sphere. Furthermore, concerns over the fitness of the nation and the birth rate led to a cult of motherhood and more pressure again on women to return to the home. At the same time fears about the growing military might of Germany led to an emphasis on the "male Virtues" of power and strength. Any confusion of "natural" sex roles, or any movement that appeared to threaten those roles had, many believed, to be opposed. As Lord Cromer, the leader of the antisuffragists stated in the *Anti-Suffrage Review* of 1910: "can we hope to compete with such a nation as this [Germany] if we war against nature, and endeavour to invert the roles of the sexes? We cannot do so[1]."

Suffragists thus operated in a turbulent environment where, on the one hand, women increasingly began to organize against their oppression yet, on the other hand, had to face open hostility to any attempt to change their "natural" role. Suffragism, of course, only had one public aim but it is hardly surprising that in this context

---

[1]   *Anti-Suffrage Review* 1910. See Garner, pp. 8-9.

their activity generated further examination of other women's issues within their own ranks and society at large. The "Woman Question" became a very popular topic of debate during the 1900s. Yet suffragists, who came from all points of the political spectrum, were far from united in their analysis of women's oppression or their prescriptions for change. Some wanted the vote but wanted generally to retain the political status quo: others were far more radical in their demands, moving on from an examination of women's powerlessness to a wider analysis of power in society as a whole. Some suffragists even based their arguments on an acceptance of women's sphere, but for others, suffragism was a far more radical if not liberating force. Still others accepted the differences within the suffrage movement but wished to keep them submerged in order to concentrate on the winning of the vote. In all it made for an extremely fluid situation with the ability to respond to and accept dissent dependent on the structure of each suffragist organization and the political attitudes of its leaders. The more autocratic and conservative they were, the less likely it was that more radical analyses could develop and flourish or, indeed, be tolerated. It was these factors, among others (most notably the relationship to working women), that help to explain the main differences of the ideological debate within and between the principal suffrage societies, the NUWSS, the WFL and the WSPU[1]. Yet even the most autocratic and conservative suffragist organization could, and often did, act as a

---

[1] The Women's Freedom League, led by Charlotte Despard, was formed in 1907 and was the first split away from the WSPU. See Garner, pp. 28 - 43.

stepping-stone towards a more radical perspective and commitment.

When Dora returned North in 1905 there were already tensions and differences within the local suffrage movement in Manchester. By the end of the year, there were three distinct groups; the staid and respectable North of England Society led by Margaret Ashton; the radical suffragists, who directed their campaign at working women and trade unionists; and the WSPU which had already begun its individualistic protests. Dora knew women in all three parties but it is not difficult to see which she found the most persuasive. Ashton's would have been too genteel, whereas, though acquainted with Roper and Gore-Booth and later, for a time, sharing their aims, she lacked the experience and background of the radical suffragists. On the other hand, the WSPU had attracted many women like herself – young, independent, educated and with a keen consciousness of their oppression. There was Mary Gawthorpe, for example, one year older than Dora and who, like her, had been a pupil-teacher before winning a scholarship to Leeds University. Mary was to become a prominent figure in the WSPU and a loving friend of Dora. Rona Robinson, Dora's colleague at Altrincham, was a bright science graduate, the first woman to get a first in Chemistry from Manchester. Lillian Williamson (later Forrester), also a contemporary of Dora's at Owen's, Helen and Catherine Tolson, Fanny Helliwell and others, were all young and educated, typical of the Manchester group of activists Dora joined[1].

---

[1]   Leech (1971).

One other member of this group deserves mention here – Theresa Billington (later Billington-Greig). She came from an impoverished bourgeois family and, like Gawthorpe, Marsden, Robinson and Williamson, had become a teacher. An early member of the WSPU, she was also a member of the ILP and secretary of the Manchester Teachers Equal Pay League. She was later to break from the WSPU and helped to develop the Women's Freedom League, led by Charlotte Despard. In 1905, Theresa in many ways was typical of "the 'new' young women, who refused to make any pretence of subordinating themselves to others, in thought or deed[1]."

It was therefore not surprising that Dora found herself drawn to these women and the WSPU. Dora already knew Theresa Billington, Christabel Pankhurst and Lillian Williamson and was no doubt attracted to the militant tactics they were beginning to use. Christabel Pankhurst, already assuming the mantle of chief strategist of the Union, thought that the WSPU needed to pursue votes for women in its own way. She was suspicious of labour and socialist support and eschewed the tactics of Ashton's group as ineffectual. Christabel also felt that the tactics of the radical suffragists could not be successfully transferred elsewhere. Recent violent demonstrations of the unemployed[2] seemed to have had a direct national effect and she argued that equally direct (and publicity-gaining) actions were needed to push the issue of women's suffrage.

---

[1]   E. S. Pankhurst, p.188.
[2]   There had been a major riot of the unemployed in Manchester in the summer of 1905. This had gained widespread publicity and some improvement in securing increased relief for the unemployed.

It was in this context that the now notorious Free Trade Hall incident of 13 October 1905 should be seen. Christabel and Annie Kenney had created a furore by interrupting a Liberal election meeting with their persistent demand that their question, "Will the Liberal Government give women the vote?" be answered by the prominent Liberal and future Cabinet minister, Sir Edward Grey. Eventually they were ejected by stewards and the police who arrested the pair for disorderly behaviour, obstruction and, in Christabel's case, assault. They were found guilty, refused to pay their fines and were sent to prison – Annie for three days, Christabel for seven.

The plan had worked extremely well for it gained both local and national publicity and a number of well-attended and successful protest meetings. Other suffragists backed the Union's actions and applauded Christabel and Annie for their bravery, although some of them, including Theresa Billington, had what proved to be justified misgivings. Looking back on October 1905, the Free Trade Hall protest marked the beginning of an individualistic, centrally-controlled militancy that was ultimately to lead to the suffragette exploits of 1910-14. Its goal was publicity to press the government into electoral reform yet when considered alongside Christabel's position in the labour and trade union movement, it clearly eschewed the notion that women's suffrage could be best achieved through the building of a democratic, rank-and-file, class-based organization. Militancy was individualistic, justified secrecy and autocracy, and reflected a limited and narrow political analysis – criticisms that Dora herself was to make within six years.

In 1905, however, Dora was impressed by the vigour and excitement surrounding the WSPU and was willing to defend its actions even within her own family. Some four years later, while addressing a suffragette audience after her own first arrest, she recalled how her mother, Hannah, had described the Free Trade Hall meeting as "a beautiful one, but spoiled by the action of those two women, who were well-meaning no doubt, but whose action was to be deprecated." Hannah clearly supported the cause of women's suffrage but, at this stage at least, probably shared the misgivings of other older women who felt the possibilities of more peaceful persuasion had not yet been exhausted and could only be jeopardized by the new abrasive tactics. According to Dora though, she "stayed up half the night arguing the point with her mother and sisters, defending the action of the two pioneers. Subsequently her mother later changed her mind[1]."

Hannah Marsden was a quiet, gentle, kind woman, who may not have expressed her ideas as forcibly as Dora, and may not have seen herself as a feminist, but her empathy with Dora's growing commitment to feminism and women's suffrage is not difficult to understand.

Dora began to spend more and more time with the local WSPU and by 1908 her activities were regularly reported in the Union's newspaper, *Votes for Women*. By this time, the organization had radically changed. It was

---

[1] *Votes for Women*, 7 May 1909, p. 629.

no longer based in the North but had moved in 1906 to London and it had broken its connections with the ILP. The ILP had, in fact, agreed in 1904 to press for women's suffrage on the same terms as men (i.e. a limited measure) but this was rejected by the Labour Party the following year. The break with the ILP was confirmed in the Cockermouth bye-election of 1906, when the WSPU refused to support its candidate. Emmeline and Christabel resigned from the organization in 1907. These ideological and physical moves were connected, for if the WSPU did not want to be regarded as a Northern labour organization but wished to concentrate on publicity-generating acts of militancy, then relocating to the capital was a logical move.

It could be argued that these changes reflected what Sylvia Pankhurst (Emmeline's second daughter) regarded as Christabel's "incipient Toryism," her conservative and autocratic outlook. This was responsible for the split in 1907 when, after constant refusals by Emmeline and Christabel Pankhurst to agree to the drawing up of a democratic constitution, leading members, such as Theresa Billington and Charlotte Despard, left to form the Women's Freedom League. Not surprisingly, they could not tolerate working for democratic reform in a distinctly undemocratic organization. They were unhappy too about the break with the ILP. The WSPU belonged to Christabel and Emmeline, and their autocratic rule was to lead to many more splits until its demise in 1917.

None the less the WSPU was undoubtedly responsible for a resurgence of interest in the issue of votes for women and it had attracted increasing numbers of women into its ranks. With offices at Clement's Inn, paid organizers, a weekly newspaper and branches throughout Britain, the Union demanded attention and some respect: a large meeting held in the Albert Hall in March 1908, for example, raised the then staggering sum of £7000 for the campaign. The novelty and bravery of the suffragettes, even before the days of the hunger strike and forced feeding, captured public attention too. Perhaps the best example of this was the "Trojan Horse" incident of February 1908 when suffragettes foiled police cordons around Parliament by hiding in furniture vans[1]. Both the Liberal leader, Asquith, and his Tory opponent, Balfour, had asked for proof that women wanted the vote and the Union had responded energetically to their request. The WSPU had helped to put votes for women on to the political agenda and had, through its tactics, destroyed some of the contemporary notions about the abilities of women.

Criticism of militancy by other suffragists was on the whole fairly muted at this time. The charge that it was self-defeating because it relied on novelty, so that each act had to be more outrageous than the last (though always directed at property, not people) was only made later. Young women like Dora flocked to its ranks, spurred, if by nothing else, by the indignity of being denied the vote purely on the grounds of their sex. She first became involved in Manchester, often working with one of the Union's first paid organizers, Mary Gawthorpe. In fact, the first mention of Dora in *Votes*

---

[1] See Wells (1909) for an impressionistic account of this.

for Women refers to her addressing a crowd in Stevenson Square with Mary. The two women quickly became very close friends. As described above, Mary came from a similar background to Dora although she had more links with the Labour Movement. Mary had been a prominent local member of the National Union of Teachers, the Women's Labour League and the ILP. By 1906 she was Vice-President of Leeds ILP and Secretary of the WLL.

Gawthorpe became a paid organizer in 1906 and quickly became one of its leading personalities. She wrote the popular pamphlet *Votes for Men* and was arrested on numerous occasions, the first time during the first year of her appointment. She was popular too, described by Sylvia Pankhurst as "a Yorkshire lass, very tiny with a winsome face, sparkling with animation and with laughing golden eyes [who] had a gift of ready wit and repartee which, linked with imperturbable good humour made her irresistible to the crowd." Somewhat surprisingly, she stayed with the WSPU even after its links with the ILP were severed. She finally left in 1911, partly because of ill health[1]. As the campaign grew throughout 1908, the demands on Dora and her colleague Rona Robinson, who were volunteers and not paid organizers, grew too. Apart from organizing and speaking at various meetings and "At-Homes" (an Edwardian version of women's groups), in early 1908, Dora's help was also enlisted in organizing local demonstrations. These were intended to maintain the pressure on the government following the enormous Hyde Park

---

[1]   E. S. Pankhurst (1911 and 1931) and Mitchell (1967).

rally of 21 June which was attended by over half a million people. The Manchester rally was held at Heaton Park and attracted a crowd of 150,000. Many had come to see and hear Christabel and Emmeline Pankhurst and perhaps Mary Gawthorpe and the WSPU's Treasurer Emmeline Pethick-Lawrence too, but a new name also addressed them – Dora Marsden.

Dora's appearance with the Pankhursts marked her continuing rise within the WSPU. She was spending more and more time on her suffragette work and was becoming prominent in regional and national Union circles. In late September, for example, she and Rona shared a platform with Emmeline and Adela Pankhurst (Emmeline's youngest daughter), Mary Gawthorpe and Flora "General" Drummond before a crowd of fifty thousand in Huddersfield. Dora had been sent there as a "local," and the meeting, according to the local press, was a great success. It was also a personal milestone for Dora for she was asked to write a report on it for *Votes for Women*. In what is almost certainly her first written article, Dora wrote that "the spirit of the crowd was excellent. Knowing, as a native of the district, the strong Liberal bias of the people, I was much astonished at the general consideration and much more than attentive hearing given to us." She added, "almost every argument went home, especially those relating to the industrial position of women[1]."

The following months were largely spent in the Manchester and Altrincham district organizing meetings,

---

[1] *Votes for Women*, 1 October 1908.

At-Homes and debates where Dora was often called upon to defend the WSPU against the growing criticism of its tactics. According to Mary Gawthorpe's reports in *Votes for Women*[1], she defended the Union well and it was evident that she had become an energetic and valued member. Indeed, when Mary was ill in December, Dora temporarily took over her role as Union organizer[2]. It must have been a hectic life for Dora still had a demanding job at the Pupil-Teachers Centre but her commitment was unswerving. Her life was woman-centred although, as in Huddersfield and later too at Walkeden ILP, Dora did not solely address her arguments to young, educated women like herself[3]. Yet though evidently committed to feminism, she was already beginning to have doubts about the leadership of the WSPU. Within the parameters of centrally defined national policy, local organizers had responsibility to organize in their own way, but they were denied the right to define and shape that policy itself. Moreover, it was others, notably the Pankhursts, who were claiming the credit for the WSPU's successes and thus the focus of national attention. The autocracy of the Union was to lead to growing frustration in Manchester and elsewhere. Within three years Dora, Rona and Mary had left.

Nineteen hundred and nine was a traumatic year for both Dora and the WSPU. Militancy reached new heights, impressing the suffragettes on the national consciousness, if not always favourably. Deputations to the

---

[1] See, for example, 28 December 1908.
[2] *Votes for Women*, 17 December 1908.
[3] *Votes for Women*, 24 December 1908.

House of Commons became more frequent and more violent (108 women were arrested in one deputation alone in June) while every major public Liberal meeting became a battleground between stewards, suffragettes and the police. (The WSPU concentrated on the Liberals as there was a Liberal government at this time). Security surrounding the Prime Minister, Asquith, and his Cabinet was stepped up but did not prevent continuous harassment or, in Churchill's case, a horsewhipping. Indeed, the Home Secretary, concerned about rumours that the Women's Freedom League were practising with revolvers on a shooting range in London's Tottenham Court Road, seemed genuinely frightened that Asquith could become the first Prime Minister to be assassinated since Percival in 1812[1]. Stone-throwing at expensive shop windows began, and Marion Dunlop, without the prior knowledge of the Pankhursts, became the first suffragette to go on hunger strike in July. The state's response – forced feeding – began in Winson Green Prison, Birmingham two months later. Whatever the wisdom of these tactics, and there was little evidence of success by the end of the year, they reflected the remarkable courage of suffragette activists while simultaneously shattering some contemporary notions of the physical abilities of women. None the less, *they had not succeeded* – votes for women was certainly an issue but one that palled alongside Lloyd George's People's Budget[2], the ensuing battle between Lords and Commons,

---

[1] Mitchell (1976), p. 146.
[2] Lloyd George had wanted to increase government revenue through taxation in order to pay for an extension of social reform and benefits. The Conservative Party was bitterly opposed to this and through Lloyd

Home Rule for Ireland, and most crucially of all, industrial unrest in the mines, docks and industry which marked a new phase of working-class militancy.

At the beginning of the year, Dora was still very active in the Union, organizing meetings in Manchester, Preston, Hale and Southport, even though she was now Headmistress of the Centre. Yet if any conflict of loyalty between her job and her commitment to women's suffrage existed it was resolved in the spring. By this time, the Union's tactics were concentrating on deputations to Asquith following "Women's Parliaments" held in Caxton Hall. One such deputation in February had led to violence between suffragettes, police and hostile sections of the crowd: twenty-eight women were arrested, including Emmeline Pethick-Lawrence and Lady Constance Lytton. Sprained ankles, dislocated thumbs and general bruising when thrown to the ground by police, were not uncommon injuries and, along with arrest and imprisonment, the inevitable results of partaking in such action[1].

None the less, the WSPU leadership persisted with this tactic and called another Women's Parliament, the seventh, for 30 March, to be followed by a deputation to Parliament. On this occasion, the Pankhursts decided that the deputation should consist mainly of Lancashire women, partly to quell provincial unease in the Union about their leadership. This was particularly evident in

George's "People's Budget" passed through the Commons it was rejected by the Tory majority in the Lords, thus creating a constitutional crisis.

[1] See for example, *Votes for Women*, 26 February 1909.

Manchester where Dora recalled (some five years later, after she had left the WSPU) that there was "at the very kernel of the suffragette community a tiny group which in its intimate moments and as an unholy joke called itself S.O.S. – Sick of Suffrage... weary of the interminable reiteration of threadbare arguments and the unending donkey work of the gutter and the pavement[1]." Even the loyal Mary Gawthorpe complained to her friend, Isabel Seymour, of being left out of the action, of "the joyous combat which once was and ought to be[2]." Thus Emmeline Pankhurst herself spent a week in Lancashire in mid-March drumming up support, ending her tour with a meeting in the Free Trade Hall on 24 March. Here again she pleaded for volunteers willing to risk violence and arrest. Among others who came forward were Dora Marsden and Rona Robinson.

What lay behind their decision to join the deputation? Why did they give up their jobs and a secure future in education by resigning from the Teachers Centre before going to London? Why did they, like so many other women, seem so willing to change all for the WSPU, an organization coming under increasing internal criticism? It was, of course, an opportunity to do something rather more dramatic than leafletting and organizing "At-Homes" but this alone hardly offers a full explanation. After all, for both women their decision was personally and financially risky. Dora certainly had no wealthy family or friends in high places to fall back on. They both knew too from Mary Gawthorpe what a life de-

---

[1]   Raeburn (1973), p. 108.
[2]   Raeburn (1973), p. 108.

voted to "the cause" meant – ceaseless work, incessant strain, increasing danger and little financial reward. On the other hand, it was a logical step for Dora for she had become increasingly concerned about the position of women and, in spite of reservations, working with the WSPU at least offered the possibility of a life devoted to ending their oppression. Thus, fired rather more by a keen sense of prevailing injustice to women than a love of the Pankhursts, or even the vote, Dora and Rona Robinson left for London after having been given a rousing send-off by their friends and students at the Centre. Did Dora realize that, as she waved them good-bye, she was saying farewell too to the possibility of a respectable and secure future[1]?

Dora, Rona Robinson, Helen Tolson and the rest first went to the Women's Parliament at Caxton Hall where they were urged on by Mrs. Pankhurst[2]. Both the generals and the troops – to use the militant terminology favoured by the Union's leaders – knew that a rough reception and possible arrest awaited them. But the meeting was charged with electric excitement, and after Dora and Rona had addressed the hall too, they and the other twenty-seven women chosen to go were sent into battle to the rousing sounds of the *Women's Marseillaise*. The police had been given orders to avoid arrests if possible but they made things worse, by only allowing the women to leave the hall two at a time. When prevented from going further, Dora, who had been given a WSPU banner, Rona, Helen and the others became involved in

---

[1]   Marsden to Weaver, *c.* 1916.
[2]   Caxton Hall is close by the House of Parliament in Westminster.

a fierce struggle, pushing and being pushed by the police and the crowd, not all of whom were sympathetic to the women's cause. "The women squeak like rabbits," one MP remarked from the safety of the area behind police lines as he watched their arms being wrenched and their bodies pushed to the floor. Yet "faint and out of breath they were not to be daunted; they pressed forward in a hopeless attempt; their wonderful bravery, their endurance, their self control will never be forgotten[1]." In the middle of this chaos was "Miss Dora Marsden, a slight girlish figure carrying aloft the purple, green and white tricolour[2]!"

Dora battled on for over an hour trying to get through the police lines yet as *The Times* reported, "about half past four the exertions of the women, most of whom were quite young and of indifferent physique, had told upon them and they were showing signs of exhaustion, which made their attempt to break the police line more pitiable than ever[3]." Dora, along with Rona Robinson, Emily Wilding Davison, Patricia Woodlock, Helen Tolson and six other suffragettes and one male journalist were finally arrested after a two-hour struggle and charged with disorderly behaviour. Dora was also charged with assault on the police (she had supposedly hit a policeman with her banner). Dora claimed this was accidental and that contact was unavoidable during the chaotic struggle. She also refuted the charge of disorderly conduct but was none the less sentenced to a fine

[1]   *Votes for Women*, 2 April 1909.
[2]   *The Daily Mail*, 31 March 1909.
[3]   *The Times*, 31 March, 1909.

or one month's imprisonment. All those arrested (except the male journalist) chose the latter and Dora thus began her first jail sentence[1].

Even though Dora spent most of April in Holloway her arrest and the deputation as a whole had been a success. The Pankhursts were delighted by the press coverage of the event for it showed, for the first time, the effects of the police action on women whose only crime was to demand the vote. Dora Marsden, a picture of frail and hurt innocence, was splashed over the front page of the 31 March issue of the *Daily Mirror* and in the inside pages too. *The Mirror* followed this, two days later, with a picture of Dora in court, peering over the dock pleading her innocence. What her mother, her friends in Manchester or the esteemed members of the Cheshire County Council Education Committee felt about these pictures is hard to tell, but the deputation, if not forcing votes for women on to Asquith's agenda, had kept the issue alive.

The publicity surrounding the deputation also had a tremendous effect on Dora. For a few days at least, she was a national celebrity. It certainly changed her status in the WSPU from that of a respected worker under Mary Gawthorpe in Manchester to what can only be described as a star. After her release and return to Manchester (on 1 May), she was welcomed by a band at London Road station which was followed by a march and rally in honour of Dora and her fellow prisoners. Just under a week later, they received the further honour of

---

[1]   *The Times*, 31 March, 1909.

an Albert Hall meeting in London, convened to congratulate their efforts and to celebrate their return to freedom. Though this meeting was for all those who had suffered on 30 March, *Votes for Women* recorded that of all the released prisoners, "more than ordinary interest centred in the colour-bearer... this girl had been in the forefront of the battle. She had carried the colours, and in spite of the treatment that made those that witnessed it turn sick with horror, had never let them go." Mrs. Pankhurst heaped praise upon her, claiming that Dora "had more courage that day than any other man of the nation."

Though twenty-seven years old, she could pass for several years younger and her diminutive size increased both the pathos and the bravery of her actions. With some bravado, Dora told them that she was only frightened once, at the sight of the Black Maria, but this was only a passing fear. Prison certainly did not scare her but, with other suffragettes, she condemned the conditions in Holloway: "For herself, she was prepared to spend another month, or even half her life if she could only give these women a better chance of a purer and a freer life."

It was an emotionally charged meeting, long on rousing calls to "fight the brave fight," short on any analysis of *why* women wanted the vote. In the middle of a fierce and exciting campaign, perhaps this is understandable even though ultimately it was no substitute for hard political debate as Dora was eventually to realize. In the meantime both she and Rona were caught up in the heady atmosphere of the struggle and, in common with many others in the WSPU, they were content to rely instead on an indefinable, almost spiritual faith to justify their actions. Following Rona's remark that "there was something supernatural about this movement," Dora added, under the admiring gaze of Mrs. Pankhurst, that "the great work was the work of faith. Women could see behind the barriers – behind the veil. Because of faith she had held fast to the colours – faith in the women's movement as the greatest cause the world had ever seen[1]."

Armed with their medals (a silver brooch, designed by Sylvia Pankhurst, a former art student), a life of hectic activity for Dora and Rona began. They both became paid organizers for the WSPU, first temporarily replacing Mary Gawthorpe in Manchester while she organized the hugely successful Women's Exhibition in London during May, and then on a more permanent basis. Dora (and probably Rona too) was now living at 141 Chorlton Road with her mother and initially she and Rona concentrated their energies on the Manchester area. They were much in demand, organizing and attending on average about six or seven meetings a week. The summer months of 1909 were particularly busy – organizing meetings, bazaars, speakers, support for tax-evaders (who refused to pay tax until women got the vote) and publicity in general. In June, their work took them to London – Rona to Peckham and Camberwell, Dora to Fulham and Putney where she acknowledged "the valuable help given us by men supporters[2]."

---

[1] *Votes for Women*, 7 April 1909.
[2] *Votes for Women*, 7 April 1909.

Dora clearly enjoyed this work but wanted to return to the front, and in particular the march on 29 June to present a Bill of Rights to Parliament. Permission was refused as the WSPU HQ in Clement's Inn did not want to lose its organizers through arrest – a wise policy in this case, for over one hundred women were arrested, including Mrs. Pankhurst herself and Emily Wilding Davison. The decision must have rankled the celebrated standard-bearer as militancy reached – as it had to – new heights, most notably window-breaking and the beginning of the hunger strike by Marion Wallace Dunlop in July. (It should perhaps be pointed out here that Dunlop was not trying to secure her release but "1st Division," or political, prisoner status. This the Government consistently refused to concede, regarding suffragette exploits as criminal acts.) Dora was now responsible for the North-West Lancashire Campaign, visiting and organizing in the cotton towns of Oldham, Bury, Blackburn and Bolton, but to her, this was no substitute for direct action[1].

Dora's frustration at not being in the midst of events was exacerbated by Rona Robinson's arrest in August. In spite of elaborate precautions, she had managed to interrupt a speech by Haldane, a Liberal Minister, in Liverpool's Sun Hall on 20 August. She was sentenced to two months' imprisonment on the 24th but was released on the 26th after a hunger and thirst strike which began immediately after her arrest, while on remand. Rona was warmly praised for her courage in *Votes for Women* which also published her photograph

---

[1]   *Votes for Women*, 20 August 1909.

taken on graduation day[1]. Though the leaders of the WSPU had not initiated the hunger strike, nor did they make it mandatory for those arrested, it was of course a marvellous propaganda ploy, increasing the sense of innocent martyrdom while forcing the government into an extremely tricky dilemma. It called for immense determination and courage and a willingness to accept the risk of permanent damage to health.

But if the suffragettes, like Rona Robinson, needed bravery to risk imprisonment and hunger strikes for interrupting Liberal meetings, they needed ingenuity too. Understandably, security at those meetings, whose numbers increased as the People's Budget crisis unfolded and the first general election of 1910 dawned, became extremely tight, to the point, in some cases, of a total ban on women. If suffragettes or their male sympathizers did infiltrate and create a disturbance, the retribution of the stewards was swift and increasingly violent. As the violence increased, as the Liberals became more nervous and the jail sentences longer, it was a brave woman indeed who was still willing to interrupt a minister's speech with "Votes for Women!"

As was now customary, very elaborate precautions against suffragettes had been taken for Mr. Birrel's Budget meeting in early September at the White City, Manchester. The meeting was in the Concert Hall which on one side was divided from the rest of the White City complex by windows. Tickets were strictly limited, two hundred stewards were employed and the building care-

---

[1] *Votes for Women*, 3 September 1909.

fully searched before the meeting began. Birrel arrived early and began his speech without interruption. Then, at 4:15, the peace was literally shattered. Through the glass partition came four or five iron balls one of which was clearly labelled "bomb!" Some glass was sprayed into the hall and one man's hand was slightly cut. Dora and her friends had outwitted the police, partly by using an American "cakewalk" machine that went by the Concert Hall. Like an early comic cops and robbers' film, it was some time before His Majesty's constabulary could catch the women as different sections moved in different directions. According to the *Liverpool Courier* the spectacle "from the point of ludicrousness, must stand unparalleled in the annals of police adventure... the policeman was unable to make his capture owing to the contrary motion of the two platforms. As he cake-walked forward, they cake-walked backwards[1]."

Finally Dora, along with Emily Wilding Davison, Fanny Helliwell and Helen and Catherine Tolson, were caught and charged with criminal damage and disturbing a meeting, contrary to the Public Meeting Act of 1908. They were a fiery group of Manchester-based women willing to risk a great deal for the cause, and none was more fiercely determined than Dora Marsden. Contrary to WSPU policy, she admitted at her trial that their actions could indeed have threatened the lives of some of the audience in the hall. (The Pankhursts always insisted, even during 1913 – when the violence of militant acts reached its peak – that the WSPU would never

---

[1] Quoted in *Votes for Women*, 10 September 1909. This issue carries a full report of the whole incident.

threaten life, only property.) Dora further argued at her trial (and this was in line with WSPU policy) that her actions were political not criminal, but the magistrates were unimpressed and fined her £5 or two months' imprisonment. Like her co-defendants, she refused to pay and defiantly claimed the trial had been unfair. Further, "she wished to know what division they were to be placed, as unless they were treated as political prisoners they would refuse to eat the prison food and thus it meant practically a sentence of death unless the Government acknowledged the justice of their claim by releasing them[1]."

Dora's defiance did not stop in the courtroom. On arriving at Strangeways, she and the others linked arms, refused to be handcuffed or to cooperate in any way with the prison officials. They were eventually forcibly separated and stripped. One of them[2] resisted so fiercely that she had to be put in a straitjacket. They then all broke windows and went on hunger strike. Within two days, they were released. It must have been an horrific ordeal particularly for Helliwell and Catherine Tolson who had not been previously jailed but also for the others who had all been in prison before. Dora certainly suffered and, in a poor state, she had to be collected from Strangeways by her mother[3]. Yet the experience

---

[1]   *Votes for Women*, 10 September 1909. See also the *Southport Visitor*, 7 September 1909.

[2]   It is not certain who this was, although my own guess is that it was Davison who developed a fearless and reckless opposition to prison when jailed.

[3]   Bate to Garner, 15 August 1984. Mrs. Bate, as Elaine Dyson, Dora's niece, recalls Hannah Marsden claiming that Dora had been force-fed, and hence her poor condition. For a discussion of this see p. 96-97.

did not succeed in deterring any of them from future acts of militancy.

Dora and her group had, on the whole, been extremely successful within the terms of current WSPU strategy. Yet with others they would be responsible for a new development in the battle between the suffragettes and the state. Basically, those "common rowdies with a passion for notoriety," as the outraged *Pall Mall Gazette* put it, had not only outwitted the Liberals at the meeting but, by securing their release through the hunger strike, had again embarrassed the government. Would the women, the *Gazette* pondered, "secure their release by the simple expedient of a two-day fast[1]?" That would be an embarrassment; but could the government risk the only alternative, forced feeding? It certainly had to do something as throughout July, August and early September thirty-seven women had secured early release from imprisonment by hunger striking. Even the King wondered why "the existing methods which must obviously exist for dealing with prisoners who refuse nourishment, should not be adopted[2]." He was not alone. *The Southport Visitor*, for example, was outraged by Dora's early release and claimed it was a "particularly flagrant example of the misplaced clemency in which such female hooligans are now treated... the asylum doctors know how to feed them[3]." By the end of September, Mary Leigh and six other suffragettes, were force-fed in Winson Green prison, Birmingham. Nearly eighty years

---

[1]   Quoted in *Votes for Women*, 10 September 1909.
[2]   Quoted in Rosen (1974), p. 123.
[3]   *The Southport Visitor*, 16 September 1909.

later, their accounts of their ordeal still make harrowing reading.

Forced feeding marked another stage in suffragette militancy and was to test the courage and fortitude of suffragette prisoners to the limit. But their bravery should not obscure criticism of militancy as a whole, and the growing unease within the WSPU itself of its limitations. It was individualistic and easily relegated by the government to a "law and order" issue. No attempt was made to link it to a mass class movement and, in the end, apart from keeping the issue of women's suffrage in the nation's eye, it made little impact on a political scene that was becoming more complex by the day. For some women – Billington-Greig, Gawthorpe, Robinson and Marsden herself – it was only a matter of time before they realized the limitations of the Pankhursts' strategy. Yet in the autumn of 1909 Dora and her Manchester friends were in the thick of the battle. Militant action, as she later realized, served to suppress any doubts she may have had.

Her next opportunity to protest came on home ground in October. Lord Morley, the Chancellor of Manchester University, had been asked to open some new and prestigious laboratories there. Though alert to the possibility of suffragette action, the organizers probably believed that such an august occasion, with its robed graduates and professors, would be left in peace by the WSPU. Dora, Rona and Mary Gawthorpe had other ideas. Dressed in University gowns they entered the meeting and just before Morley began, raised the question of the recent forced feeding of women in Winson Green. There was an uproar, and the three were quickly bundled out and arrested on the pavement. Even Lord Morley was said to have blanched at the rough treatment they received.

The story, and especially the photographs of the three dwarfed by burly policemen, made excellent copy and the leadership exploited the incident to the full. "No one," *Votes for Women* declared:

> who knows these three women graduates, or who glances at the numerous photographs which have appeared in the Press can fail to be struck with the pathos of the incident. Mary Gawthorpe, Rona Robinson and Dora Marsden are all slight, *petite* women who made their protest in a perfectly quiet and gentle manner... They are women moreover, who have done great credit to their respective Universities... Yet they are treated as 'hooligans;' treated with such roughness that all 3 had to have medical attention, and hauled before a police magistrate and charged with disorderly behaviour.

Sentimental appeals that relied on the pathetic femininity of women would later be much criticized by Dora and others yet, in terms of current WSPU strategy, the protest was successful, especially when, after pressure from Morley, the University decided not to press charges.

The leadership of the WSPU were very pleased with the Manchester women; Dora and Rona were awarded the Union's Victoria Cross by Mrs. Pankhurst. Emmeline Pethick-Lawrence was particularly lyrical: "My dear, dear brave and beautiful spirit," she wrote to Dora in early October, "I have not words to express what I feel about your wonderful courage and heroism. When I think of your face as I saw it in prison my head is full of reverence for the human spirit." She added, in her now typically spiritual way, "A great force is being generated in this movement. We shall send out stronger and stronger thoughts that will change the course of the world's life... My love to you Dora Marsden, sweetest, gentlest and bravest of suffragettes[1]."

However pleased the WSPU leaders were with Dora and her friends, they were in many ways a troublesome group. Rona and Dora, as educated, independent women, would not always confine themselves to the policy guidelines issued from Clement's Inn. They were restless before the March deputation – the only action they took, it seems, with the full approval of the Union's HQ. They were certainly courageous but reckless too, acting sometimes as uncontrollable freelancers. Emily Wilding Davison, arrested with Dora in March and September 1909, could certainly be seen in this light. She was treated with some suspicion by the Union's leaders for she had acted independently and without official permission many times before her tragic death in 1913. According to Rosen, they were suspicious of her, for she "was regarded by some of the WSPU staff as a self-dramatising individualist insufficiently capable of acting within the confines of official instructions[2]." It is likely that in spite of the praise given her, Dora too began to be

---

[1] E. Pethick-Lawrence to Dora Marsden, 6 October 1909.

[2] Davison was killed when she attempted to grab the King's horse during the Derby. She certainly wanted to create further publicity for the WSPU but whether she intended to kill herself is unclear. Rosen, pp. 198-9.

seen in a similar light.

As 1909 drew to a close, Dora was thrown into the general election campaign. The WSPU's policy continued to be one of harassment of the Liberals and they called on voters not to elect them until they conceded women's suffrage. Billington-Greig and others thought this was suicidal, for the Union had not secured a firm commitment on votes for women from the Tories. As I have pointed out elsewhere, this was yet another indication of the incipient conservatism of Christabel and Emmeline Pankhurst. Certainly, the Union's line stood in marked contrast to that of the National Union of Women's Suffrage Societies and the Women's Freedom League, both of which were moving closer to the labour movement[1].

Dora was sent to Southport, a marginal constituency held by the Liberals with a slender majority of 260. Dora had been to Southport before but not in these circumstances. She was now given the onerous task of organizing the election campaign and all for the grand sum of £2 per week. Mary Gawthorpe appealed for "members to rally round her at once... introductions from sympathisers in other parts of the country would be most helpful[2]." This cry for help only indicated the tough job that lay ahead. Finances were tight and Dora did not even enjoy a permanent base, living at six different addresses between November 1909 and February 1910 alone. Nevertheless she threw herself into her work with typical energy and gusto, organizing meet-

---

[1] Garner, pp. 46-7.
[2] *Votes for Women*, 12 November, 1909.

ings, local workers, publicity and so on. Again, her efforts were crowned with not a little success. However this was mixed with growing tension between Dora and HQ.

Not unreasonably, Clement's Inn insisted that Dora, as a paid official, should avoid arrest, as they did not want to have to replace her at short notice when resources were so stretched. Dora, eager for excitement and action, found this instruction as irksome as the patronizing tone of the correspondence from London. Emmeline Pethick-Lawrence was genuinely concerned about Dora's health, which had begun to deteriorate after her arrests, and she tried to use this to moderate and limit Dora's actions; "I am grieved to hear of your health," she wrote on 24 November 1909:

> We are all so anxious that our organizers should not overwork... I know how carried away you are by your utter devotion and enthusiasm, but I very earnestly beg you to pay all due regard to your health, forgive these little warnings dear, they are prompted by concern and affection for yourself.

This concern about Dora's health also masked apprehension about her style of working. Dora not only wanted to follow an independent line unfettered by the dictates of Clement's Inn but seemed incapable of delegating work to others. But it was her independent streak that was inevitably bound to clash with the WSPU leadership. This surfaced with Dora's wish to stage an action which could involve arrest and, subsequently, a hunger strike and forced feeding. The Union leaders refused her permission: "I know the matter is very difficult for you,"

Emmeline Pethick-Lawrence wrote on 1 December 1909, "and I quite appreciate your perplexity, but you must rest assured that we at the centre can judge these matters in their due relationship and importance with one another." Dora ignored her instructions and within two days of receiving the letter was arrested in an incident destined, as the *Southport Visitor* put it, to be "famous in suffragette annals[1]."

Winston Churchill, the Home Secretary, was due to speak at the Empire Hall, Southport, on 4 December. As a prominent Liberal, and particularly as Home Secretary, he had been the focus of suffragette attention. As a prime target for the WSPU not surprisingly security precautions at the Empire Hall were extremely strict. Only Liberal women were allowed in and they were restricted to seating in the gallery. Stewards checked the building on the Friday and Saturday morning and there was a considerable police presence surrounding the hall. The organizers were nervous but confident that no "female hooligans" would be able to interrupt the Home Secretary, one foolishly remarking just before Churchill's arrival that "The Empire is impregnable." The local press agreed that security for the meeting was unprecedented in the history of the town[2].

Churchill arrived and after a poor speech by the local MP, Baron de Forest, rose to speak. He at first seemed apprehensive and not without cause for, unbeknown to him, he had escaped a soaking by Mrs. Duncan at the Queen's Hotel where, at the last minute, he

---

[1] *The Southport Visitor*, 7 December 1909.
[2] *The Southport Visitor*, 7 December 1909.

had cancelled his pre-meeting lunch, deciding instead to go for a walk. Yet after ten minutes or so without interruptions he relaxed, warming to his theme while the stewards smugly congratulated themselves on their success. He was condemning the Lords for rejecting the People's Budget which had been passed by the Commons, an elected body which represented the wishes of the people, when a voice (where from?) cried out, "But it does not represent the women Mr. Churchill."

Pandemonium! The audience rose shouting and searching and pointing everywhere. Churchill, flabbergasted, sat down, stood up and sat down again. The stewards, so arrogantly confident in their success in securing the Hall from suffragette intervention, were in a blind fury. Eventually:

> peering through one of the great porthole openings in the slope of the ceiling, was seen a strange elfin form with wan, childish face, broad brow and big grey eyes, looking like nothing real or earthly but a dream waif. But for the weary paleness of her, she might have been one of those dainty little child angels the old Italian painters loved to show peeping down from the tops of high clouds or nestling amongst the details of their stately architecture.

It was, of course, Dora Marsden accompanied by Helen Tolson and Winson Etherley (a local activist) who for a full fifteen minutes tried to address Churchill and his audience from her lofty yet hazardous perch. After a quarter of an hour, the stewards, aware that this woman could easily throw a missile made their way on to the roof. Dora calmly told them the safest way down but in their fury they refused her advice, preferring a much more dangerous route across the roof. Dora, who was clinging to a chimney now became frightened as a violent and potentially fatal struggle began. "A dirty hand," Dora later recalled:

> was thrust over my mouth, and a struggle began. Finally I was dropped over a ledge, pushed through the broken window, and we began to roll down the steep sloping roof side. Two stewards, crawling up from the other side, shouted out to the two men who had hold of me, 'stop that you fools: you will all fall over the edge.' The man who was pulling my right arm screamed hysterically, 'I don't care what happens; we'll manage them.' They managed so well that we balanced ourselves skilfully on the water trough. At the police station an inspector said to me, 'You ought to be grateful to me. If I hadn't caught your foot you would have gone to your glory[1].'

The incident generated enormous publicity for Dora and the WSPU, and it became even more astonishing when it emerged how Dora and her companions had got on to the roof. On the Friday prior to the meeting they had hidden in the hall behind some baskets after attending the evening's entertainment. Somehow they had escaped the watchman's search. At 2 a.m. Dora climbed on her friends' shoulders, eventually got on to the roof, and let a rope down for her friends to climb up. Discarding their flasks and sandwiches so they could crawl through an eighteen-inch passage, they finally reached their perch where they waited for over 12 hours without food or drink, in the wet and dark December night, knowing that one false move could at best mean discov-

---

[1]   *Votes for Women*, 10 December 1909. This issue tells the whole story in full.

ery, at worst, death. Whatever criticism of the WSPU's strategy there may be, how can anyone but admire the extraordinary courage of these women?

In spite of Dora's failure to obey their orders, the WSPU's leaders could do little but admire her too and they hailed her latest escapade as another great victory for the cause. Emmeline Pethick-Lawrence praised her "wonderful resources and immense courage and pluck in a piece of strategy that entailed a great deal of hardship and risk. It is," she claimed, "a story worthy of one of the nation's great battlefields[1]." The day after she added, "We are very proud of you[2]."

Dora, Helen and Winson were lucky to escape injury and indeed, imprisonment, for the magistrates, fearing even greater controversy if the prosecution succeeded, dismissed all the charges against them. Dora had gone on hunger strike in Strangeways in September and would certainly have done so again, and so escaped the dreaded possibility of forced feeding. As this was her last arrest, it seems she was spared this torture during her life as a suffragette. Or was she?

There is some confusion over this. Her relatives distinctly recall Hannah Marsden telling them she once had to collect Dora from prison after she had been forcefed. Her daughter, the story goes, was in a terrible state as a result of her treatment in jail[3]. The deterioration in

---

[1]   Emmeline Pethick-Lawrence to Dora Marsden, 7 December 1909.
[2]   Emmeline Pethick-Lawrence to Dora Marsden, 7 December 1909. Rereading this in 2018, I am still struck by the incredible courage and bravery shown by Dora and her two friends. I am also amazed that it remains a suffragette story largely untold.
[3]   Bate to Garner, 15 August 1984.

Dora's health in 1909 is used to support this claim although this could have been due to overwork and imprisonment (including a hunger strike). Hannah's story may in fact refer to her collecting Dora from Strangeways in September. Dora herself never claimed she had been force-fed and there is no contemporary documentary proof that she was. Further, her imprisonments in April and September occurred *before* forced feeding began in Birmingham. Yet one part of the story remains unresolved. Dorothy Pethick, a younger sister of Emmeline Pethick-Lawrence, told Antonia Raeburn that she distinctly recalled being in prison with Dora Marsden in Newcastle in early October. Forced feeding had begun by then and Pethick, along with some of the others arrested with her for various disturbances connected with Lloyd George's visit to the city, were force-fed. They were also pestered by "an awful old chaplain... but when he began mithering Dora Marsden she eyed him without a word, until at last she said. 'If you're not out of my cell within half a minute, you'll find yourself outside[1].'" This certainly sounds like Dora, but again, there is no record of her being arrested in Newcastle along with Lady Constance Lytton, Jane Brailsford, Kitty Marion, Emily Wilding Davison and the rest[2]. When Lytton described her experiences in her book *Prison and Prisoners* there was no reference to Dora and none by Dora in

---

[1] Quoted in Raeburn, p. 139. Raeburn recalls Pethick, whom she interviewed in the 1960s, as "one of the most lucid and well informed of suffragettes" but concurs with the view that it is not certain that "Lily Asquith" was Dora Marsden. Raeburn to Garner, 17 December 1985.

[2] See, for example, *The Times*, 11 October 1909.

her review of Lytton's work[1]. Furthermore, Dora was booked for various meetings, for example, on the 13th with Mary Gawthorpe in Burnley, when she was supposed to be in a Newcastle jail. The only explanation is that she used a false name when charged. Though "Lily Asquith" aged twenty-five, and one of the Newcastle Twelve remains an elusive figure, a desire for anonymity on Dora's behalf seems unlikely and hardly credible. Thus, while Dora did suffer in prison and many of her friends underwent the trauma of the funnel and the tube, it appears that she herself was not force-fed[2].

Meanwhile, back in Southport, Dora enjoyed further success though friction between her and Clement's Inn continued. She covered the whole constituency, including the working-class areas like "The Banks," during the election campaign and became a scourge of the local Liberals. Their fury reached new levels when the result was announced: the Tory, Major White beat the incumbent, Baron de Forest by 419 votes. The campaign had become so highly-charged that Dora brought charges against Arthur Lamont, a Liberal councillor, who, she alleged, had assaulted her and her friends outside a polling booth. Dora lost the case 5:4, all five magistrates finding against her being, not by pure coincidence, Liberal[3]. In spite of losing the case the WSPU

[1] *The Egoist*, 15 May 1914.

[2] I have been unable to trace "Lily Asquith." It would have been a good joke for a suffragette to use this name when arrested, particularly if she was using it to avoid flaunting bail conditions arising from another charge. On balance though it seems that Ms. Asquith was not Dora.

[3] As one local writer put it, "a party whip up had been made... every man of the quitting majority of 5 was a Liberal. I can recall no such scandalous miscarriage of justice in more than forty years residence in

congratulated Dora on the Southport election result claiming it as another victory for, and justification of, their anti-Liberal policy. The fact that neither Major White nor the Tory Party as a whole, the possible beneficiaries of such a policy, had given any commitment to women's suffrage was, of course, overlooked. The result of the January 1910 election was a disappointment for the Liberals but how far their failure to achieve a workable parliamentary majority was due to the WSPU's intervention is very debateable, in spite of Christabel's bombastic claims[1].

Though Dora's standing in the Union after the election (and particularly after the roof-top incident) had never been higher, the inevitable conflict between intelligent, independent women like herself and the autocracy of the Pankhursts was bound to surface. As we have seen, this had already begun in 1909 but became increasingly open the following year. Criticisms at first tended to concentrate on Dora's lack of business sense and poor financial acumen, but at heart, were directed at her unwillingness to accept a centralized system of command, discipline and organization from Clement's Inn. Even at the moment of her great Empire Hall triumph, there were complaints about her hiring a lawyer without seeking prior approval from HQ. Emmeline Pethick-Lawrence in particular seemed worried about Dora's poor financial organization and wrote, "I want to have a good talk with you on this subject." She pointedly added

---

this town." Quoted in *Votes for Women*, 4 March 1910.

[1] The Liberals had won a landslide victory in the 1906 General Election but could now only form a government with the support of the Irish Nationalists.

that the Union could not be strong "without heart and soul co-operation of every one of its organizers[1]."

The following day, though again praising Dora's "cleverness, ingenuity and courage," Emmeline argued that she needed someone with "a very good business head and a person thoroughly trained in business habits." This would then allow Dora to concentrate on general WSPU activity – arranging meetings, fund-raising, selling *Votes for Women*, and so on. After expressing concern over her health and admitting how difficult it was "to impress upon ardent spirits not to overdo it," Pethick-Lawrence, wary of Dora's reaction, pleaded with her "to take time to read this letter carefully and give it due consideration."

Dora may well have read the letter with anger, insulted by its patronizing tone. None the less, Pethick-Lawrence did have a valid point – as a paid Union organizer it was not unreasonable to expect Dora to adhere to instructions and follow agreed procedures. But circumstance and Dora's own personality made this an unrealistic expectation. Dora's independent streak, her individualism, her high self-confidence, her thirst for action, were all admirable qualities but not those necessarily required to make an ideal organizer for the WSPU. The Union needed disciplined as well as energetic workers and, above all, women who could be relied upon to follow orders from HQ to the letter.

The potential for conflict between Dora and the WSPU leadership was increased by the political circum-

---

[1]   Emmeline Pethick-Lawrence to Dora Marsden, 7 December 1909.

stances of 1910. Between February and November, the Union called a halt to militancy in order to give the Conciliation Bill a chance. This would have enfranchized approximately one million, mainly bourgeois women only but it would at least have established that women could not be denied the vote purely because of their sex. The truce came to an end in November due to Prime Minister Asquith's lack of commitment to it but was resumed in January 1911. Hostilities resumed when the Bill was "torpedoed" later in the year. It was a trying time for the WSPU, an impressive national body but one which was inextricably tied to militancy. It meant too that activists like Dora Marsden had to be restrained while the Union's organization had to be strictly maintained, ready at a moment's notice for a renewal of hostilities. These two seeds further strained the relationship between Dora and the WSPU.

Thus, throughout 1910 correspondence between the Union and its Southport organizer was littered with refusals to Dora's requests and proposals for action, along with criticism of her working methods. This was particularly marked in early 1910 when the WSPU was amassing statistics and information for its forthcoming Annual Report. Beatrice Sanders, the financial secretary, had an especially trying time with Dora. She continually had to demand that Dora send in her accounts and, on one occasion, exasperatedly pointed out to her that lists of supporters without their addresses were quite useless. By the end of February, Dora had become "the last of the many laggards we have to deal with[1]." In the end,

---

[1]   Beatrice Sanders to Dora Marsden, 9 and 16 February 1910.

Beatrice went to Southport to sort out the mess for, as Pethick-Lawrence pointed out some months later, "there are certain points about it (the financial system of the WSPU) which you have not grasped[1]."

Nevertheless, Dora's salary was increased in February and she continued to work hard on the Union's behalf throughout the year. Her district was extended to include Blackburn and meetings, addressed by Emmeline Pethick-Lawrence and Emmeline Pankhurst, and fund-raising events (ranging from cake stalls to lectures on palmistry) were organized. She was kept busy too rallying support for demonstrations in London in June and July. Her continuing popularity was reflected by the fact that she was given her own platform at the latter, as well as a photograph and a potted (and inaccurate) biography in *Votes for Women*[2].

Yet in spite of her bustling activity a sense of restlessness and unease surrounds Dora in 1910. Organizing boats bearing *Votes for Women* placards to sail up and down Southport beach, bring-and-buys, cake sales and talks on palmistry were not really her style and were far removed from the White City or the roof of the Empire Hall. Further, when she did suggest schemes of her own, they were invariably turned down by Clement's Inn. "I have consulted others," Christabel wrote, "and we adhere to the decision that a political shooting gallery is not desirable and must not be undertaken[3]." But what really angered Dora was probably the refusal to allow her

---

[1]   Emmeline Pethick-Lawrence to Dora Marsden, 2 November 1910.
[2]   *Votes for Women*, 22 July 1910.
[3]   Christabel Pankhurst to Dora Marsden, 14 November 1910.

to join the June demonstration and the Black Friday protest of 18 November when several women were seriously injured by the police and two later died. One of Dora's friends, Mrs. G. M. Solomon who had led the 30 March 1909 deputation wrote to her of the rough treatment, including sexual assault, which she received from the police. She concluded her letter with "Much love, Gallant Standard Bearer! and may God bless your grand work! Lovingly and in the sisterhood, Mrs. G. M. Solomn[1]."

The simmering conflict with the WSPU's leadership finally came to the boil over what initially seemed an innocuous proposal to hold a bazaar in Southport. Dora wanted to model it on the hugely successful Women's Exhibition which had been organized by Mary Gawthorpe in London in May 1909. She proposed exhibitions of women's work, stalls, entertainment, refreshment and of course, meetings with "star" speakers. She first put forward the proposal in January, envisaging the bazaar opening in March.

Not surprisingly perhaps, the Union's leaders were apprehensive. They felt she was rushing things, that her plans were too grandiose, and that she was, in any case, incapable of efficiently organizing an event on such a scale. Christabel felt a bazaar would be a very good thing" but quickly suggested that it should be delayed until the autumn: "Things can be done in a rush, it is true but if they are other work has to be neglected[2]." Emmeline Pethick-Lawrence was worried from the be-

[1] G. M. Solomon to Dora Marsden, 29 November 1910.
[2] Christabel Pankhurst to Dora Marsden, 27 January, 7 February 1910.

ginning. "I do not think," she wrote, "you have the slightest idea of the immense work involved," and reminded her that the London Exhibition had an executive committee, two full-time secretaries and the whole of the Union to help. She must be careful, Emmeline warned her, "not to work herself to death[1]."

The bazaar (sometimes referred to as the Exhibition) was none the less allowed to proceed even though it became an increasingly ambitious and unwieldy project. Its opening date was constantly being revised in order to cater for Dora's plans. She hoped to have thirty stalls, a *fête*, entertainment, sport and other amusements, a restaurant (with waitresses dressed in "the colours," purple, white and green) and finally a pageant, organized with the help of the famous actress and Women's Freedom Leaguer, Cicely Hamilton. Yet as the Exhibition grew, a note of desperation entered into Dora's appeals for help. "so much to do, so many sources of help yet to be trapped," she wrote at the end of October, "we want thousands of Pounds worth of goods[2]." And this was only five or six weeks before the opening.

Helped only by her friend and secretary Grace Jardine, Dora had, as Pethick-Lawrence feared, taken on too much. Besides all the work for the bazaar, Dora still had regular WSPU duties to perform and, by the end of 1910, had to prepare too for yet another election campaign. (Asquith had called a general election for December 1910.) The scheme had again to be postponed until after Christmas. And, in the end, despite the support

---

[1]   Emmeline Pethick-Lawrence to Dora Marsden, 25 February 1910.
[2]   *Votes for Women*, 28 October 1910.

given to it in *Votes for Women* as late as November[1], it never took place.

The crisis came to a head in December when, according to Clement's Inn, Dora had again acted without permission by booking a hall for the Exhibition for May 1911 and publicizing its opening on that date[2]. Dora was annoyed about the further delay anyway and ignored Mary Gawthorpe's advice not to book the hall without first getting HQ approval[3]. Dora's action, as Pethick-Lawrence argued, put the Union in a very difficult position. On the one hand, they had very serious doubts about the feasibility of the whole project and would have preferred to abandon it altogether. On the other hand, Dora had publicly committed the Union and to cancel now would be an embarrassment. But if Dora had presented the WSPU with a dilemma, she had also incurred their wrath. According to Pethick-Lawrence, the executive committee (in effect, herself, Christabel and Emmeline Pankhurst) was "strongly inclined to abandon the Exhibition and repudiate all responsibility... we have resolved that this will be the last action in which you will deal with us in this way without having to take the consequences further. There is no other organiser in the Union who would assume the responsibility you assume[4]."

This warning and, to Dora, an insulting admonish-

---

[1] *Votes for Women*, 18 November 1910. Even then Pethick-Lawrence called it "this very ambitious scheme."
[2] Emmeline Pethick-Lawrence to Dora Marsden, 22 December 1910, 11 January 1911.
[3] Mary Gawthorpe to Dora Marsden, 13 November 1910.
[4] Emmeline Pethick-Lawrence to Dora Marsden, 22 December 1910.

ment was compounded by a general belittlement of the scheme and by the imposition of a series of conditions, which had to be met if it was to be allowed to proceed. The pageant was to be dropped, the entertainment reduced, and every estimate to be submitted to HQ: "No arrangement must be made without our consent. If we find you transgressing this rule we shall be obliged to send someone else to take your place in Southport to assume charge of the Exhibition arrangements." If that did not make Dora livid, the committee's vision of the scheme merely being "a little Bazaar in a provincial watering place[1]" certainly did.

Dora reacted violently to this letter, which not only cast doubt on her integrity but was in fact a very thinly veiled threat to replace her if she did not obey HQ. Fortunately perhaps, she did not reply immediately but waited until after her Christmas break. Consequently her response, though full of anger, was more calm and considered than it might have been. For its reflections on herself and the WSPU it is worth considering in detail. For the first time too, it reveals her gift for the telling phase.

---

[1] Emmeline Pethick-Lawrence to Dora Marsden, 22 December 1910.

"It is not easy," Dora memorably began:

for I know that words spoken and written become ghosts
which are never laid; a turn of memory and we are face to
face with them again. I will say briefly what I am driven
into saying. You have sent me, an educated talented and
thoughtful woman a lecture couched in tones which the
meekest standards of self-respect could only consider intolerable[1].

She complained that all "the baseless charges" over
the Exhibition had been "erected into a reputation"
which she did not deserve. It transpired that not only had
Clement's Inn disputed Dora's orders and bookings but
there was a rumour too that she had misappropriated Exhibition funds. Dora wrote that every accusation of in-
competence and dishonesty had been disproved yet she
had not received an apology. "The situation is inexplicable to me. It would be a catastrophe to a thousand ideals
to believe that the leaders of this movement, built up as
it has been by the passion of us all, could live in an atmosphere of suspicion respecting the good faith of its
organisers."

---

[1]   Dora Marsden to Emmeline Pethick-Lawrence, 9 January 1911.

Dora felt the accusations were particularly unfair given her unswerving commitment and loyalty to the WSPU. "Your letter, Mrs. Lawrence," she concluded:

> came at the beginning of my holiday – a holiday following a year of strain, the tension of which you will never know. Success (and I have won success in every single venture since I undertook an independent campaign) success is not a happy chance. It is bought at the price of a watchfulness which snatches every opportunity, and I have kept watch in the interests of this Union since I knew it, as few people have the strength, or the brains, or the love to do.

It was an extraordinary reply, full of a hurt anger and not a little arrogance. Dora quite naturally took the whole affair personally. But in a wider context, it reflected on the difficulty independent women like herself had in fitting into a centralized autocracy like the WSPU. The Pankhursts needed Annie Kennies who slavishly followed the leaders' wishes not Dora Marsdens or Billington-Greigs. If the rift had not occurred over the bazaar it would have surely been something else. Pethick-Lawrence's immediate response was muted – just a promise to forward Dora's letter to the committee. The bombshell dropped some weeks later. Mabel Tuke, in a curt letter, informed Dora that the Finance Committee of the WSPU had decided that the Exhibition would be abandoned. She added, as a final insult, that she "was surprised by the very improper tone of your letter to Mrs. Pethick-Lawrence and hopes no letter couched in such extraordinary terms will be submitted to the Committee again from you[1]."

The abandonment of the bazaar by Clement's Inn and the refusal to answer the points covered in the letter were, despite all Dora's faults, a gross insult to her. There could now be only one response: resignation. Accordingly, and ironically on paper headed "Great Northern Exhibition – Pageant, Fair and Fete December 14, 15, 16, 17," Dora, the "bravest and sweetest" of suffragettes, wrote on 27 January: "Dear Mrs. Pankhurst, I beg herewith to tender to you my resignation as organiser of the WSPU. I do this, not on account of the abandonment of the Bazaar (though I consider this to be a serious matter) but because the Committee consider a phrase about 'improper tone' the fitting answer to my letter of January 9th[2]."

An eventful and colourful association had come to a bitter and resentful end. The WSPU had lost one of its more talented and gifted members but its leaders were probably more relieved than upset by her resignation. There was no attempt to persuade her to stay and within days her resignation was accepted. In recognition of Dora's service to the Union however, Mabel Tuke sent her a cheque for two month's salary (£18) and the committee's good wishes for the future. Pointedly though, they hoped Dora would find work "in a direction more suited to your special gifts and qualifications[3]." Dora thanked Tuke and offered to help Beatrice Sanders to organize the takeover of Southport's finances. Her pride,

---

[1]   Mabel Tuke to Dora Marsden, 26 January 1911.
[2]   Dora Marsden to Emmeline Pankhurst, 27 January 1911.
[3]   Mabel Tuke to Dora Marsden, 3 February 1911.

rather than any personal financial security, refused to let her accept the cheque, which was immediately returned. Dora Marsden was now on her own.

In spite of the good wishes for the future, there was little love lost between Dora and the WSPU. Indeed, the row between them would become even more bitter and lasted for several years. It might be argued that Dora never really got over her treatment by the Union, never really worked through her anger at being rejected by them. The rejection was total, no farewell notice appeared in *Votes for Women*, no public recognition given to her services. Worse still, it was accompanied by pernicious rumours that cast doubt on her integrity and, in particular, her honesty. Lillian Williamson, a friend from university days, told Theresa McGrath of the rumours that were still circulating in the Union as late as 1912. McGrath passed these on to Dora: "My dear Dora," she wrote, "are you aware of the rumours that are about concerning your resignation... that you left the accounts for Southport with a deficiency of £500 and that your resignation itself was owing to a request that you should meet the Treasurer for the purpose of going into the matter[1]?" Though there had been quibbles over financial organization, some of which persisted into 1911, Dora had not refused to see Sanders and it is extremely unlikely that she embezzled a single penny of Union funds. What is likely is that the gossip was fomented both by Dora's lifelong inability systematically to organize money and the ever-widening rift between her and the WSPU in the period 1911-13. It was in these years that Dora, as editor

[1]   Theresa McGrath to Dora Marsden, 19 April 1912.

of *The Freewoman* and *The New Freewoman*, published vitriolic attacks on the Pankhursts and their Union. The rumours were perhaps one way in which suffragettes' loyal to Christabel and her mother could retaliate on behalf of their beloved leaders[1].

Dora's life in the WSPU reveals a great deal about herself and the organization she served, even though the ending of this relationship was so bitter and the recriminations so long. Her work in the Union reflected the commitment, bravery, ingenuity and reckless courage needed to become an active suffragette but it also exposed the limitation of working in such an autocratic body. Essentially, the leadership had little time for independent thought and action by its members, especially its organizers, and the results were inevitable; the history of the WSPU is littered with almost annual splits leading to the WFL in 1907 to the Suffragettes of the WSPU during the war. In the WSPU's defence, it could be claimed that Dora was particularly headstrong and that in any case, as an employee, the Union's leaders had every right to expect her to carry out their instructions. Whether blindly obeying these fitted into a call for freedom and independence for women was overlooked and subsumed in the military talk of war, generals and

---

[1] Much later in life, when in hospital, Dora gave another account of why she resigned from the WSPU. This story hinged on some statues which she had borrowed for the Exhibition. They were mislaid and she was summoned to London to explain their loss, the implication being that she had stolen them. They later turned up in a left-luggage locker in Glasgow. I have found no independent evidence to support this story but the account's claim that she also resigned because of the Pankhursts' autocracy is certainly true. (Unpublished autobiographical notes.)

battles. Soldiers have little say, they carry out their orders without question. Finally, Dora's resignation from the WSPU did not signify a rejection of feminism, rather the opposite. Her experience in the Union may have led to fundamental differences with its leadership but it also served to increase her feminist consciousness. Indeed, Dora subsequently argued that she resigned partly because she wanted a freer and more open discussion of feminist issues other than that of women's suffrage. What was needed was a platform for this debate.

Dora's feminism was not solely expressed through her public activity as a suffragette but was reflected too in her personal life which was so clearly woman-centred. With her mother providing a permanent base, Dora developed close and loving relationships with women in this period, primarily Rona Robinson, Grace Jardine and Mary Gawthorpe. Dora's relationship with the brilliant Rona went back to Owen's and was cemented at the Teachers Centre in Altrincham. They resigned their jobs together and, for a time, were joint organizers in Manchester. However, by 1910, Rona had become a Gilchrist postgraduate scholar in Home Science and Economics at Kings' College for Women[1]. Their friendship continued but suffered through being physically distant, with Dora in Southport and Rona in London. By this time though, Dora and Grace Jardine had become close.

Dora probably first met Grace in Burnley in October 1909 and, from then on, and for some years they were to live together in Southport, London and Black-

---

[1] Leech (1971).

burn. There was consequently little need for correspondence between them and it is difficult to be precise about their relationship. Grace however was clearly devoted to Dora and became her personal assistant in Southport in 1910 and for some years afterwards. As for Dora and Mary Gawthorpe there is little ambiguity, they were close and loving friends probably since 1906. They were similar in many ways except in the ability to organize within the WSPU. Mary showed constant concern over Dora's work for the Union and when she had left it. This concern, and the intensity of the relationship it revealed, was most evident during *The Freewoman* period.

Dora never expressed a hatred of men as a sex and had on more than one occasion thanked male supporters of the WSPU. Yet all her close relationships were with women, none with a man. Indeed, how could she have the independence and freedom she so desperately yearned for if she had become involved in an orthodox relationship with a man? Whether any of her friendships with women were sexual cannot be determined – certainly they were close and certainly too, Dora's personality and fragile beauty inspired many endearing comments from her friends. She appeared to have a special and unique quality that inspired devotion, if not awe, in some women. It was this that encouraged the young Tolsons to such extraordinarily brave and reckless acts. Whether Dora was gay in the modern sense is unknown. There is no concrete evidence to support such a claim. Yet if the term is redefined, as suggested by Faderman[1], to include women who derive all their emotional and

---

[1]   Faderman (1985).

loving support from other women without necessarily expressing this sexually, then Dora Marsden was indeed gay. And it was this support, along with growing feminist criticism of orthodox suffragism in general and the WSPU in particular, that was to lead Dora, unemployed, single and twenty-eight years old, from the wilderness that seemed to face her in January 1911.

Bondwomen

by Dora Marsden
The Freewoman. Volume 1 Number 1 (23 November 1911) p. 1.

It is a wholly pertinent matter that the temerarious persons who launch *The Freewoman* should be asked, "Who are the Freewomen?" Where are the women of whom and for whom you write who are free? Can they be pointed out, or named by name? There must be, say, ten in the British Isles. The question is pertinent enough, but it is difficult to answer, because its answer must of necessity become personal. We might, perhaps, hazard the name of one Freewoman who has become a sufficiently national figure to make her mention impersonal — Ellen Terry. There at least is one, and for the rest the inquisitors must be content with being enabled to arrive at the conception of Freewomen by way of a description of Bondwomen.

Bondwomen are distinguished from Freewomen by a spiritual distinction. Bondwomen are the women who are not separate spiritual entities — who are not individuals. They are complements merely. By habit of thought, by form of activity, and largely by preference, they round off the personality of some other individual, rather than create or cultivate their own. Most women, as far back as we have any record, have fitted into this conception, and it has borne itself out in instinctive working practice.

And in the midst of all this there comes a cry that woman is an individual, and that because she is an individual she must be set free. It would be nearer the truth to say that if she is an individual she *is* free, and will act like those who are free. The doubtful aspect in the situation is as to whether women are or can be individuals — that is, free — and whether there is not danger, under the circumstances, in labelling them free, thus giving them the liberty of action which is allowed to the free. It is this doubt and fear which is behind the opposition which is being offered the vanguard of those who are "asking for" freedom. It is the kind of fear which an engineer would have in guaranteeing an arch equal to a strain above its strength. The opponents of the Free-women are not actuated by spleen or by stupidity, but by dread. This dread is founded upon ages of experience with a being who, however well loved, has been known to be an inferior, and who has accepted all the conditions of inferiors. Women, women's intelligence, and women's judgments have always been regarded with more or less secret contempt, and when woman now speaks of "equality" all the natural contempt which a higher order feels for a lower when it presumes bursts out into the open. This contempt rests upon quite honest and sound instinct, so honest, indeed, that it must provide all the charm of an unaccustomed sensation for fine gentlemen like the Curzons and Cromers and Asquiths to feel anything quite so instinctive and primitive. With the women opponents it is another matter. These latter apart, however, it is for would-be Freewomen to realise that for them this contempt is the healthiest thing in the world, and that those who express it honestly feel it; that these opponents have argued quite soundly that women have allowed themselves to be used, ever since there has been any record of them; and that if women had had higher uses of their own they would not have foregone them. They have never known women formulate imperious wants, this in itself implying lack of wants, and this in turn implying lack of ideals. Women as a whole have shown nothing save "servant" attributes. All those activities which presuppose the master qualities, the standard-making, the law-giving, the moral-framing, belong to men. Religions, philosophies, legal codes, standards in morals, canons in art have all issued from men, while women have been the "followers," "believers," the "law-abiding," the "moral," the conventionally admiring. They have been the administrators, the servants, living by borrowed precept, receiving orders, doing hodmen's work. For note, though some men must be servants, all women are servants, and all the masters are men. That is the difference and distinction. The servile condition is common to all women. Consider, for instance, the wife of the politician. She plays round irresponsibly, helping out the politician's work; the parson's wife — she is the hard-working, unpaid assistant of her husband; the working-man's wife ekes out a straitened existence for herself by allocating the modest wages which the workman, and not she, has earned. Women's very virtues are those of a subordinate class. Women are long-suffering, adaptable, dutiful, faithful, and with unlimited capacity for sacrifice. Even if in such matters as sex, where women are considered more "moral" than men, because women recognise intuitively that men *think* more, they pay their homage as from a lower to a higher authority, by allowing men to frame their standards even in morals. It is because woman is thus, and not otherwise, that she is so useful to man — his "comforter." For man, woman has become a kind of human poultice, or, more poetically, the illusion softening reality, This, coupled with the fact that she is also man's "female," accounts for all the poetic adulation which men have offered to women. But it is not to poetry, but to blunt prose, that one must turn to get at man's real estimate of woman's place in the scheme of things. Hear what he says in plain prose, when woman presumes to speak of equality and "freedom." Out of his own experience of her, he knows her to be a follower, one who has always been ready to sacrifice herself to him and his interests. He would have sacrificed himself for nothing, save his own ideas; but she has always revelled sombrely in sacrificing herself for anything or anybody, for duty, for peace, husband, parents, children. And this, after all, is what speaks far more eloquently than a tome of argument to the ordinary man. It tells him that nothing has ever crossed her mind regarding herself which has appeared to her too good to be sacrificed to anything on earth, itself excepting. He therefore quite naturally argues that she has acted like a second because she felt herself a second.

How women have fallen into this position is a moot point. It is yet to be decided whether they ever did fall — where man and woman have not been, from their creation, master and servant. If otherwise, and if woman did "fall," the reason why is yet to be assigned. It is quite beside the point to say women were "crushed" down. If they were not "down" in themselves — i.e., weaker in mind — no equal force could have crushed them "down." There can be no over-reaching *in the long* run with mind. In the long run, mind plays on its own merits. It can neither receive nor give quarter. Those who are "down" are inferior. When change takes place in the thing itself — i.e., when it becomes equal or superior — by the nature of its own being it rises. So woman, if ever equal, must have sunk on the ground of inferiority. Whether this inferiority arose through the disabilities arising out of childbearing, or whether it arose through women giving up the game — i.e., bartering themselves for the sake of the protection of men — it is difficult to say. Probably in her desire for love continued, for protection, for keeping the man near her, she slipped into the rôle of making herself useful to him, serving *him*, giving him always more love and more, more service and more, until, on the one hand, she acquired the complete "servant" mind, and he, on the other, gained the realisation that her "usefulness" was of greater moment to him than the fret of the tie which retained him.

At the present time, when man's adventurous and experimental mind has made much of her "usefulness" useless, woman finds herself cut off from her importantly useful sphere, equipped with the mind of a servant, and with the reputation of one. She thus finds herself in a position in which she is compelled to do one of two things — i.e., remain solely as the man's protected female, or, making what may or may not be a successful effort, endeavour to take her place as a master. It is this effort to find her place among the masters which is behind the feminist movement; and such a statement of the feminist case is a refutation of the arguments of all those who maintain that there is no duality of interest between men and women. At the present time, there is duality, and duality in this connection will cease to exist only when women sink back into the position of females with nothing beyond, or when they stand recognised as "masters" among other "masters," considering their sex just as much an incidental concern as men consider theirs.

But to return to the Bondwomen. It seems difficult to realise how the females of a virile race could have been content to remain in a permanently subordinate position. It can only be accounted for upon an understanding of the stupefying influence of security with irresponsibility. And this is what "protection" always means for the "protected." To begin with, by securing the "protection" of a man, a woman rids herself of the responsibility of earning her own living. Following upon this beginning, so many pleasures accrue that under their influence women are soothed into such a willing acceptance of their position that they are unable to see the unspiritedness of it. Moreover, besides having "protection" and maintenance, they achieve physical maturity; they have the great adventure of having children; they secure companions and avoid the loneliness of existence; they have the flattery which smooths it, and they live easily under a ready-made code and under the sanction of the communal blessing.

For this protected position women give up all first-hand

power. Really, the power to work and to think. All the power they achieve is merely derivative. They allow to slide past them those powerful incentives which keep up the strain of effort — that is, individual public honour, wealth, titles, decorations, the bits of ribbon. These go to men. To women are offered the great soporifics — comfort and protection. How difficult and hard is a woman's choice made! It is almost too hard. Nothing but one thing — the sense of quality, the sense that a woman has gifts, the sense that she is a superior, a master — can give her the strength to slip the comfort and protection and to be content to seize the "love" in passing, to suffer the long strain of effort, and to bear the agony of producing creative work. Having this sense, they will learn that freedom is born in the individual soul, and that no outer force can either give it or take it away; that only Freewomen can be free, or lead the way to freedom. They will learn that their freedom will consist in appraising their own worth, in setting up their own standards and living up to them, and putting behind them for ever their rôle of complacent self-sacrifice. For none can judge of another soul's value. The individual has to record its own. A morality begotten in a community where one-half are born servants may glibly say that it is woman's highest rôle to be the comforter of men and children; but it is the truth, and men and women both must learn it, that while to be a human poultice is to have great utility, it does not offer the conditions under which vivid new life-manifestations are likely to show themselves, either in the "Comforter" or the "Comforted."

Commentary on Bondwomen

by Dora Marsden
The Freewoman. Volume 1 Number 2 (30 November 1911) p. 1.

It turns out that the editorial attitude for this week will have to take the form of a commentary on that of last. According to correspondence, it would appear that in "Bondwomen" we gave the idea that we consider that only those women who are gifted to the extent of genius can be Freewomen, and all the rest, according to our version, must be Bondwomen, i.e., followers, servants. What, asks a very reasonable correspondent, who wishes to remain anonymous — what is to become of the "ordinary women?" Is not your championing of the strong, of the masters, as unnecessary as it is easy, and your postulating the existence of servants as an established fact, as unhelpful as it is cynical? Cannot the gifted take care of themselves? To use your own instance, has not Ellen Terry made herself free by the simple right of her genius? Are you not treating as negligible considerations the only ones where help such as you can give would count? Are you not engendering a revolt against a sphere wherein most "ordinary women" must of necessity spend their lives? Are you not, by depreciating the value of housework, supporting the view that housework is of little worth, and making it less likely that it should be recognised as a properly-paid profession? A sheaf of questions and objections! Let us see. Returning to the first, that we put forward the view that women's freedom is bound up with genius — well, that is a view we are prepared to uphold. To be a Freewoman one must have the essential attribute of genius. Last week we implied it, and this week we state it, and, having more space, we take this opportunity of defining genius. Genius is an individual revelation of life-manifestation, made realisable to others in some outward form. So we hold that anyone who has an individual and personal vision of life in any sphere has the essential attribute of genius, and those who have not this individual realisation are without genius. They are therefore followers — servants, if so preferred. We called them Bondwomen. We maintain that to accept the fact that great numbers of individuals are born without creative power in regard to any sphere of life whatever, argues no more cynicism than it would to accept the fact, and the statement of it, that coal is black and snow is white. It is a fact to be proved by simple observation. Our contention is that life should supply the conditions which would enable this native endowment of vision to make itself communicable to others, and we consider that so many women appear ordinary, not because they are born ordinary, but because they are bundled pell-mell into a sphere in which they can show no special gift; and because they are expected to be so bundled, they are deprived of that training which would enable them to make their individual revelation communicable, that is, of their chance to become artists. Nor for one moment do we wish to support the view that all women will be free, any more than all men are free. It will be difficult enough for Freewomen to be free, and to force women, who neither are nor wish to be free, into the responsibilities of freedom is as futile as endeavouring to make two and two into five. It cannot be done. This explains why a feminist must make her appeal to Freewomen, and not to "ordinary" women. The doctrine of feminism is one so hard on women that, at the outset, we can only appeal to those who have already shown signs of individuality and strength, and it is just here that the cult of the Freewoman becomes plainly distinguishable from that of the Suffragist. If it is the work of the Suffragist women to guard the rear, it is that of the Freewomen to cheer the van. The cult of the Suffragist takes its stand upon the weakness and dejectedness of the conditions of women. The cult of the Suffragist would say, "Are women not weak? Are women not crushed down? Are women not in need of protection? Therefore, give them the means wherewith they may be protected." Those of the cult of the Freewoman, however, while granting this in part, would go on to say, "In spite of our position, we feel within us the stirrings of new powers and of growing strength. If we can secure scope, opportunity, and responsibility, we feel we can make realisable to the world a new revelation of spiritual consciousness. We feel we can produce new evidence of creative force, which, when allowed its course, will encompass developments sufficiently great to constitute a higher development in the evolution of the human race and of human achievement." We believe that it is to the Freewomen we have to look for the conscious setting towards a higher race, for which their achievements will help to make ready, and their strivings and aspirations help to mould. For this they do not require protection; they need liberty. They do not require ease; they need strenuous effort. They do not wish, by law or by any other means, to fasten their responsibilities on others. They themselves are prepared to shoulder their own. They bear no grudge and claim no exemption because of the greater burdens which Nature has made theirs. They accept them willingly, because of their added opportunity and power.

In the attainment of all these things the vote will lend its small quota — small because it is of the letter and not of the spirit. The spirit comes from within. It can be fostered, but it cannot be created before its time, and when its time has come it cannot be unduly repressed, oh Suffragists!

It is not so long as it seems, but from these hopes and dreams of the future it appears a long cry back to the problems of the domestic questions of to-day. If the Freewoman is not going to be the protected woman, but is to carve out an independence for herself, she must produce within herself strength sufficient to provide for herself and for those of whom Nature has made her the natural guardian, her children.

To this end she must open up resources of wealth for herself. She must work, earn money. She must seize upon the incentives which have spurred on men to strenuous effort — wealth, power, titles, and public honour. To this end she will have to strive, and that she should so strive will be well for her children. Many will say that this responsibility on the mother is too hard. What are the responsibilities of the father? Well, that is *his* business. Perhaps the State will have something to say to him, but the Freewoman's concern is to see to it that she shall be in a position to bear children if she wants them without soliciting maintenance from any man, whoever he may be; and this she can only do if she is earning money for herself, or is provided for out of some common fund for a limited time. Some women and men here suggest a compromise. They suggest, in order that the women shall at once retain dignity and receive maintenance, that they shall act as housekeepers to the men who provide this maintenance, and receive money for their domestic services. There are endless objections to this, even as a voluntary arrangement. In the first place, a growing number of women, while hoping to have children, refuse to sacrifice their career to domestic work, much as they like it. In the second place, many women detest domestic work, which is wholly alien to their natural capabilities. Many of them think that they have capabilities of an order which make them regard domestic work as inferior work. To surmount this difficulty, well-intentioned people have been trying, by artificial adjuncts, to raise the status of domestic work. To these we would point out that the distaste felt is not due to the social estimation in which it is held, high or low as this may be, but is due to a temperamental distaste for it. The well-intentioned people, now utterly bewildered, are pretending that housework has fallen into disrepute because it is unpaid work, forgetting that the best of the worker's work is always unpaid. In their bewilderment they have gone so far as to set up a monstrous theory that wives should become the paid employees of their husbands! Beyond this, folly can no further go!

And yet Suffragists, and advanced persons among women generally, make use of this theory. Imagine the circumstances! The man would be compelled by law to pay a portion of his salary to a person whom he is prevented by law from dismissing, and who is prevented by law from securing release. The paid person may be satisfactory or not. If unsatisfactory, what redress is there for the employer? No redress! but a possible remedy in corporal punishment, such as is administered to soldiers in barracks under similar circumstances. And the employee against a tyrannical employer? No power to refuse to sell her labour! power only to form a trade union of paid wives! The entire theory is ludicrous in its absurdity. No! Personal relationships between equals must be entered into on terms of equality. And this brings us to the real feeling which is expressed in the animus against domestic occupation for so large a proportion of women. The feeling has its roots in the elementary fact that, in order to attend to a house, a woman has to give up the work which represents to her, at most, independence and self-expression, and, at least, self-support. In giving up her work the woman gives up the obvious means of support over which she has control, and she becomes dependent upon the energy and work of some other individual. Feminism would hold that it is neither desirable nor necessary for women, when they are mothers, to leave their chosen, money-earning work for any length of time. The fact that they so often do so largely rests on tradition which has to be worn down. In wearing it down vast changes must take place in social conditions, in housing, nursing, kindergarten, education, cooking, cleaning, in the industrial world, and in the professions. These changes will have for their motive the accommodation of such conditions as will enable women to choose and follow a life-work, apart from, and in addition to, their natural function of reproduction.

So it is from a full recognition of the fact that the feminist doctrine is a hard one for women, that the path of the Freewoman will be beset with difficulties, with temptations both from without and within, that we are led to the further recognition of the futility of preaching it to the women who are essentially ordinary women, who do not already bear in themselves the stamp of the individual.

We are convinced that, at the present time, our interpretation of the doctrine has merely to be stated clearly to be frankly rejected by, at least, three women in every four.

Probably these replies will raise more objections than those they were put forward to meet, but if such is the case it will be not merely what was expected, but what is hoped.

The Freewoman, 1911 – 1921

THE

FREEWOMAN

A WEEKLY FEMINIST REVIEW

No. 1. Vol. I. THURSDAY, NOVEMBER 23, 1911 THREEPENCE

[Registered at G.P.O. as a Newspaper.]

Joint Editors:
DORA MARSDEN, B.A.
MARY GAWTHORPE

CONTENTS

	Page
1. Bondwomen	1
2. Notes of the Week	3
3. A Definition of Marriage. By Edmund B. d'Auvergne ...	5
4. Der Bund für Mutterschutz. By Bessie Drysdale ...	6
5. Feminism Under the Republic and the Early Empire. By Amy Haughton	7
6. Contemporary Recognition of Polygamy. By E. S. P. H.	9
7. The Spinster. By One ...	10
8. The Fashioning of Florence Isabel. By E. Ayrton Zangwill	11
9. The Illusion of Propagandist Drama. By Ashley Dukes	13
10. The Psychology of Sex. By J. M. Kennedy	14
11. A University Degree for Housewives? By Educationist	16
12. The Sheltered Life. By W. H.	18

BONDWOMEN.

IT is a wholly pertinent matter that the temerarious persons who launch THE FREEWOMAN should be asked, "Who are the Freewomen?" Where are the women of whom and for whom you write who are free? Can they be pointed out, or named by name? There must be, say, ten in the British Isles. The question is pertinent enough, but it is difficult to answer, because its answer must of necessity become personal. We might, perhaps, hazard the name of one Freewoman who has become a sufficiently national figure to make her mention impersonal—Ellen Terry. There at least is one, and for the rest the inquisitors must be content with being enabled to arrive at the conception of Freewomen by way of a description of Bondwomen.

Bondwomen are distinguished from Freewomen by a spiritual distinction. Bondwomen are the women who are not separate spiritual entities—who are not individuals. They are complements merely. By habit of thought, by form of activity, and largely by preference, they round off the personality of some other individual, rather than create or cultivate their own. Most women, as far back as we have any record, have fitted into this conception, and it has borne itself out in instinctive working practice.

And in the midst of all this there comes a cry that woman is an individual, and that because she is an individual she must be set free. It would be nearer the truth to say that if she is an individual she *is* free, and will act like those who are free. The doubtful aspect in the situation is as to whether women are or can be individuals—that is, free—and whether there is not danger, under the circumstances, in labelling them free, thus giving them the liberty of action which is allowed to the free. It is this doubt and fear which is behind the opposition which is being offered the vanguard of those who are "asking for" freedom. It is the kind of fear which an engineer would have in guaranteeing an arch equal to a strain above its strength. The opponents of the Freewomen are not actuated by spleen or by stupidity, but by dread. This dread is founded upon ages of experience with a being who, however well loved, has been known to be an inferior, and who has accepted all the conditions of inferiors. Women, women's intelligence, and women's judgments have always been regarded with more or less secret contempt, and when woman now speaks of "equality" all the natural contempt which a higher order feels for a lower when it presumes bursts out into the open. This contempt rests upon quite honest and sound instinct, so honest, indeed, that it must provide all the charm of an unaccustomed sensation for fine gentlemen like the Curzons and Cromers and Asquiths to feel anything quite so instinctive and primitive. With the women opponents it is another matter. These latter apart, however, it is for would-be Freewomen to realise that for them this contempt is the healthiest thing in the world, and that those who express it honestly feel it; that these opponents have argued quite soundly that women have allowed themselves to be used, ever since there has been any record of them; and that if women had had higher uses of their own they would not have foregone them. They have never known women formulate imperious wants, this in itself implying lack of wants, and this in turn implying lack of ideals. Women as a whole have shown nothing save "servant" attributes. All those activities which presuppose the master qualities, the standard-making, the law-giving, the moral-framing, belong to men. Religions, philosophies, legal codes, standards in morals, canons in art have all issued from men, while women have been the "followers," "believers," the "law-abiding," the "moral," the conventionally admiring. They have been the administrators, the servants, living by borrowed precept, receiving orders, doing hodmen's work. For note, though some men must be

A disgusting publication... indecent, immoral and filthy.

Edgar Ansell to Dora Marsden

14 July 1912

Until *The Freewoman* came, I had to lie about the feminist movement. I lied loyally and hopefully, but I could not have held out much longer. Your paper proves that feminism has a future as well as a past.

Floyd Dell, Editor, "Friday Literary Review"
Chicago Evening Post, 1912

A valuable medium of self-expression for a clever set of young men and women.

Charlotte Payne-Townshend

1912

The WSPU and the suffragette movement had, for over three years, been central to Dora Marsden's life, giving her purpose and recognition. She had risked financial and personal security, even life itself, for the cause of woman's suffrage but now she was on her own. For the second time in three years she had resigned from paid employment and in January 1911 Dora had no money, no job, no income. What Dora did have, though, was a highly developed sense of her own worth and ability and a keen determination to succeed. She also enjoyed what turned out to be the crucial support of Rona Robinson, Grace Jardine and above all, Mary Gawthorpe. Allied to the growing criticism of the Pankhursts and an emerging frustration with the limitations of orthodox suffragist thought, these factors were to lead to the birth of the outstanding feminist journal of the 1900s, that "nauseous publication[1]," *The Free-woman.*

The idea for a new feminist publication had been germinating in Dora's mind for some time and was first expressed during her ill-fated attempt, in early 1911, to join the Women's Freedom League (WFL). The League was set up in 1907 by leading members of the WSPU like Theresa Billington-Greig and Charlotte Despard, women who could no longer tolerate the autocracy and conservatism of Emmeline and Christabel Pankhurst. Though small it became an important suffragist organization with its own weekly paper, *The Vote.* The WFL

---

[1] Agnes Maude Royden, *The Times,* 22 June 1912.

described itself as a militant organization but though members risked arrest, the League was unwilling to adopt the same tactics as the WSPU, preferring acts of passive resistance. Under Charlotte Despard, a member of the ILP who later stood for Labour in the General Election of 1918, the League developed a sympathetic and supportive attitude to the Labour Movement and was certainly more progressive than the WSPU. It was also a democratic organization and one which Dora felt would be responsive to her requests[1].

It appears that Mary Gawthorpe suggested to Dora in the spring of 1911 that she should contact the League. Charlotte Despard, the League's President, certainly seemed eager to enroll her. "We have all heard of your courage and capacity," she wrote. "It would give me the greatest pleasure to welcome you," and she wanted Dora to meet the League's executive committee[2].

There was some excitement in WFL circles about the possibility of capturing Dora from the WSPU, and Edith How-Martyn and Margaret Nevinson, both prominent members of the League, were especially warm in welcoming her to their fold. But even they must have been a little taken aback by Dora's insistence on an increase on her old WSPU salary and her request for a post for Grace Jardine, "Martha to her Mary," too[3].

What eventually emerged in the spring was that

---

[1]   See Garner, pp. 28-30, Linklater (1980).
[2]   Despard to Marsden, 7 February 1911.
[3]   Nievinson to Marsden, 13 February 1911; How-Martyn to Marsden, 26 March 1911. The description of Jardine and Marsden's relationship comes from *The Freewoman* by Rebecca West, in *Time and Tide*, 16 July 1926.

Dora was to work on *The Vote*. Dora felt that a more analytical input into the paper, and indeed suffragism as a whole, was needed, a feeling shared by others in the League and elsewhere. Edith How-Martyn, who had helped on the League's short-lived magazine *Woman and the Hour* a few years previously, wrote, for example, "I feel sure that you can supply something the Women's Movement needs." She added that "it would be a joy to me to work to make the WFL the intellectual leader of the Suffrage Societies[1]." More specifically, Dora suggested to the League's executive committee a three-point plan, viz.: "I. A practical cessation of toy militancy. II. An allowing of an influx of ideas from outside the movement and consequently an independent platform. III. A preparedness to be the cause of dissension etc.[2]"

In essence, Dora wanted an independent supplement to *The Vote*, to be financed by the League but under her total editorial control. *The Freewoman* had been conceived but, not surprisingly perhaps, the WFL was not going to be its mother. Despard was not only jealous of her power within the WFL but, like other suffragist leaders, concerned that open discussion of controversial issues, particularly those connected with sex, would severely damage the cause of woman's suffrage. Thus the supplement proposal was quashed and Dora invited instead to work on new ways of increasing the circulation of *The Vote*. This was unsatisfactory to her and, in spite of the temptation of a weekly salary, negotiations closed

---

[1]   How-Martyn to Marsden, 26 March 1911.
[2]   Marsden notes, n.d.

in April. Curiously, she also left this suffrage organization under a cloud and again it was partly connected to finance. "I see," Constance Tite, treasurer to the League, complained, "that you know nothing of the spirit of the League but you evidently never had the least intention of adjusting yourself to it. Your account partly shows this, no true Freedom Leaguer would spend 2/6d on lunch[1]."

Dora must have left the League still convinced that her proposal for an independent platform for a wider and unlimited discussion of issues relating to women was not only needed but could succeed. Yet her failure illustrated a major problem for more radical thinkers within the suffrage movement. The very demand for the vote inevitably brought up all kinds of questions about the relations between the sexes and many suffragists wanted an open discussion of these issues. But they faced two major obstacles. First, though the moral code was often honoured more in the breach than the observance, to be seen to be demanding new rules of conduct (particularly if they did not put a premium on chastity and monogamy for all) would be to invite massive opposition. Indeed, opponents of women's suffrage – the antis – constantly claimed that votes for women would lead to a loosening of moral standards. Secondly, suffragist leaders such as Despard and Fawcett argued that if the WFL and NUWSS adopted radical positions on sex and morality, it would severely affect the cause of women's enfranchisement. In any case, suffragist leaders, includ-

---

[1]   Tite to Marsden, 26 April 1911. At around £14 in 2018 this would indeed be a not inconsiderable sum.

ing Emmeline and Christabel Pankhurst, wanted the contemporary moral code upheld, not broken.

None the less, by 1911, with the vote still not won there was growing frustration within the ranks of the suffrage movement and a feeling that open discussion was being stifled. In the WSPU this was exacerbated by the Union's autocratic structure and by its renewed truce with the government over a revised Conciliation Bill. This would still only enfranchise one million propertied women, but partly because it was such a narrow measure, it looked like it might succeed. The Pankhursts thus maintained the cessation of hostilities as they did not want to impede the progress of the Bill. Thus militancy, as we have already seen, was more or less suspended throughout 1910 and 1911. This left many of their members restless and perhaps more ready to question the wider issues of women's oppression beyond the fact of their being denied a vote. It could also be argued that the suspension of militancy gave many suffragettes time to ponder about the nature of the WSPU itself.

Certainly, by 1911 frustration with and within the WSPU and mainstream suffragism generally, was becoming increasingly evident. One of the first women publicly to express this was Theresa Billington-Greig who, as described above, had left the WSPU in 1907 to form, with others, the WFL. She felt that the emphasis on the vote tended to obscure wider visions of what emancipation meant and involved; like many others Theresa became disillusioned with suffragism. She resigned from the WFL in January 1911, partly to develop her career as a writer but also because "the greater emancipation of women is being sacrificed in the haste for immediate enfranchisement[1]."

Theresa reserved most of her venom, however, for the WSPU which she began to criticize in a series of articles in the radical weekly, *The New Age*[2]. These became *The Militant Suffrage Movement – Emancipation in a Hurry*, published in 1911. In this marvellous tirade against Christabel and Emmeline Pankhurst's WSPU, she described herself as "a feminist, a rebel and a suffragist" who wanted emancipation from "all shackles of law and custom, from all chains of sentiment and superstition[3]." She expressed the disappointment of many suffragettes who had joined the Union as part of a fundamental struggle for liberation. "Gradually," she complained:

> the movement has lost status as a serious rebellion and become a mere emotional obsession, a conventional campaign for a limited measure of legislation, with militancy as its instrument of publicity and the expression of its hurry. The leaders of the militant movement do not want a revolution; we were mistaken who believed that they did; they would be afraid of one.

It was sentiments such as these which help to explain a major part of the initial support that was given to *The Freewoman*.

Dora Marsden certainly would have responded favourably to Billington-Greig's comments and not surprisingly she went to see her in the spring of 1911.

---

[1]   *The Vote*, 21 January 1911.
[2]   For further information on *The New Age*, see Alpers (1982).
[3]   Billington-Greig, pp. 1-2.

Theresa had just called, in *The New Age*, for "a new statement of the feminist position... I suggest," she continued, "that discontented and disgusted feminists – and those who are merely truth seekers! – should combine to provide a feminist platform in every town and city in the country[1]." Billington-Greig agreed to contribute to the paper occasionally but was unable to do much more. Dora must have been disappointed by this and again had to rely on Mary Gawthorpe for further advice and support. Mary suggested numerous women for Dora to contact, including the Duchess of Marlborough, but her "dear hustler" enjoyed little success[2]. A Mrs. Lowry of Hampstead did express interest but withdrew, partly on the grounds that Dora's constant pressure on Mary would adversely affect her already poor state of health: "I am very sorry," Lowry wrote in May, "that we shall have to withdraw our little support to your paper[3]."

Dora had made no progress by May and the prospects looked bleak. By this time she was probably surviving on loans from Mary Gawthorpe, who even suggested that Dora should register for work at the local labour exchange. Mary was desperately keen to help but was restricted by her own ill health. "I wish to God I were on my feet little one," she wrote in early May. "How long can you hold out failing immediate temporary remuneration of some kind?" At last she suggested Dora might go to a Fabian summer school to "make the personal acquaintance of the leading women" and pre-

---

[1] *The New Age*, 16 March 1911.
[2] Gawthorpe to Marsden, 9 April 1911.
[3] Lowry to Marsden, 4 May 1911.

sumably persuade them to back her scheme[1]. "I can see", she added two days later, "you will *have* to go to Fabian school[2]."

The Fabians were a moderate left-wing group who believed Socialism could be achieved through education and piecemeal reform. Leading members included Beatrice and Sidney Webb and George Bernard Shaw. Though reformist, the Fabians had many contacts with other Socialists and they had increasingly concerned themselves with women's issues. For example, Fabian women were active within the British section of the Women's International which had been set up in the 1900s as part of the international Socialist movement and they had formed their own women's group in 1908. Moreover, Charlotte Wilson, the first secretary of the Fabian Women's Group, had an anarchist past and had helped to produce the anarchist paper, *Freedom*[3]. The Fabian Women's Group supported women's suffrage but concerned themselves with other issues too, primarily the position of working-class women[4]. By 1911, the Fabians were experiencing a renaissance and Mary Gawthorpe's suggestion was clearly an excellent idea for two reasons. First, these women ought to be receptive to a proposal for a new radical journal; and secondly, some of them, for example Charlotte Payne-Townshend (wife of George Bernard Shaw), might also have the money to back it. Certainly, Mary was keen to

---

[1]   Gawthorpe to Marsden, 13 May 1911.
[2]   Gawthorpe to Marsden, 15 May 1911.
[3]   Wilson founded the paper in 1886 with the anarcho-communist, Kropotkin.
[4]   For further information on the Fabians, see McKenzie N. and J. (1977).

know the result of Dora's contact with them in late May: "Dearest Dora, let me know without delay how the Bentinck-Shaw-Wilson combination has affected you or has been affected by you? What are the prospects[1]?"

Dora had written to Charlotte Wilson in May and her letter clearly shows the direction of her thoughts at this time. First, Dora wanted to emphasize the importance of involving working-class women in the struggle for emancipation. She wanted to stress also the importance of economic independence and proposed a new society: "The Society for the Promotion of the Economic Independence of Women." As for the suffrage movement, this, Dora argued, was limited both in tactics and philosophy. "What is really needed," she claimed:

> is a popular demand. Neither Mr. Asquith or any other can withstand a really popular agitation and the Women's Suffrage agitation is not popular because the women have not been taught the connexion between abstract political rights and concrete matters such as work and wages. To make it a natural movement the philosophy of the women's movement will have to be worked out in terms of everyday life... The Suffrage Societies are trying the short cut to Women's freedom and there are no short cuts.

Though Wilson, Townshend and others did express an interest (and in Townshend's case at least, gave financial support to *The Freewoman* when it came out later) nothing concrete came of Dora's discussions with the Fabian women. Perhaps they could not respond with the urgency Dora wanted or, like Despard, they were unwilling to give her a free hand. Dora wrote to Mary in

---

[1] Gawthorpe to Marsden, May 1911.

early June of her disappointment of the "special women" who have "ceased to judge" and this probably referred to the Fabians, although it could also refer to others who had refused to help[1]. None the less, Dora remained convinced that the time was ripe for a radical feminist journal and Mary agreed, for there was a "lot to be done on the constructive side of ideas and there is *ground waiting too...* a critical controversial paper will always be in order and would ultimately be a blessing all round." She was unsure whether this could be turned into a movement though, for "a critical *movement* postulates a pretty problem in psychology. Work it out sweetheart and let me know[2]."

Mary Gawthorpe's support and friendship throughout this period was crucial to Dora and it is clear that they enjoyed a close, affectionate and loving relationship, in spite of their differences over the WSPU (Dora was continually bitter, Mary surprisingly loyal). Mary had for some time suffered physically as a result of her suffragette activity and had internal injuries as well as a dislocated neck. As a result she had not been active for at least a year, though her concern was always for Dora's health and well-being. "Now look sweetheart!," she wrote in May. "Write to me as often as you please while the pressure and uncertainty is with you... We must take care of you as the first means to the desired end." Further, though having little money of her own, she was constantly offering small "loans" and regretted not being able to finance the paper herself. "At the risk

[1]   Marsden to Gawthorpe, June 1911.
[2]   Gawthorpe to Marsden, 11 June 1911.

of repeating myself I say that if I had the cash you should start that paper at once... Love always, Mary[1]." Their letters, written almost daily, were couched in endearing and affectionate terms, with "sweetheart," "dear little one," and "my dearest girl" not being uncommon.

By the summer of 1911, Dora did not seem to be having any success. She had by now moved to London and was living in temporary accommodation with Grace Jardine. Mary suggested that A. R. Orage, the editor of *The New Age*, might be able to help, for even though he seemed hostile to the WSPU, he had carried the articles by Billington-Greig. Pompously, Orage argued that "there are not enough writers who understand feminism to run a paper and there are not enough to keep it going. No new magazine ought to be started unless it can be shown to be clearly necessary[2]." Yet Dora's determined persistence and Mary's unstinting support eventually paid off when Charles Grenville, the owner of the radical publishers Stephen Swift came to the rescue. Swift already had a reputation for publishing advanced material – "books that compel" – and their list included Katherine Mansfield and Reginald Wright Kauffman, author of *Daughters of Ishmael*, a controversial work on the white slave traffic. Grenville himself was a radical poet, publishing several works between 1907 and 1911, before being jailed in 1913 for bigamy and fraud[3]. Initially, he was extremely keen on Dora's proposal though he came to regret his decision to back her. But in the au-

---

[1]   Gawthorpe to Marsden, 30 May 1911.
[2]   Quoted in Gawthorpe to Marsden, 8 September 1911.
[3]   Rebecca West, "The Freewoman," in *Time and Tide*, 16 July 1926.

tumn of 1911, he was Dora's saviour and Mary wrote to Grace, "It's excellent. Grenville is an angel. I'm just waiting to tell him so[1]."

Once a backer had been secured, events moved swiftly. Printers and offices were found, adverts placed in the suffrage press, leaflets and circulars distributed. All these made the radical tone of the new paper clear. For example, the advertisement placed in *Votes for Women* stated that it would encourage "a full and frank discussion of feminism in all its aspects... the subject of sex morality... will be dealt with in an unreservedly fair and straightforward way[2]."

Dora herself made the aim and the scope of her paper explicit in an interview with the *Evening Standard* and *St. James Gazette* in October. After apologizing for using the word "feminism" (for, to Dora, this was currently and wrongly limited to the struggle for the vote), she argued that *The Freewoman* was going to expand its terms and "give it new significance... the great change which the Feminist Movement seeks to bring about is not merely a matter of political readjustment... carried to success, it would accomplish a vast revolution in the entire field of human affairs, intellectual sexual, domestic, economic, legal and political." Hinting at potential controversy she added: "it will be an open paper and will not be afraid to publish anything which has behind it thought and knowledge." Finally, she concluded with a comment that illustrated the breadth of her own feminism:

---

[1]   Mary Gawthorpe to Grace Jardine, n.d., *c*. summer 1911.
[2]   *Votes for Women*, 17 November 1911.

Woman is a distinct entity... she must be taught that she is not an adjunct to man... in an ideal condition she would be released from the narrow conditions of the household and free to make her contribution to the labour of mankind in that sphere to which she had a bent[1].

The launch of *The Freewoman* in the Autumn was unfortunately marred by a bitter, acrimonious yet telling row between Mary and Dora. It centred on Dora's insistence that Mary, still a much respected and well-known suffragette, take an active and prominent role in the paper as co-editor. This certainly would have given the paper much needed respect and credibility, at least in suffrage (and particularly WSPU) circles. Mary, however, resisted Dora's attempts to recruit her to the editorial staff, not least because of her poor health. She was also concerned that Dora alone should receive all the credit for the paper but was worried about the possibility of attacks on the WSPU. Mary insisted that the latter should not take place for at least a year after the beginning of publication. Though critical of the Pankhursts herself, Mary still had affection for the WSPU and was still committed to the cause of women's suffrage.

Mary wrote to Dora in early September and expressed the hope that the project would "bring forth fruit 1. for you personally: a sound reputation 2. for the feminist ideal: whereby women shall be helped to know themselves," but she herself could only take a quiet role in the background as a reservist[2]. Her wish for Dora

---

[1] *Evening Standard* and *St. James Gazette*, 25 October 1911. This is interesting given that in less than two years, Marsden clearly disputed the notion that "woman is a distinct entity."

[2] Gawthorpe to Marsden, 9 September 1911 and 23 September 1911.

alone to enjoy the anticipated success of *The Free-woman* was, like her ill health, a sincere and genuine objection to the suggestion that she become co-editor, but Mary was especially concerned by Dora's attitude to the WSPU. Dora was still bitter about her break with the Union and Mary, not without a little justification, felt it affected her judgement: "I want you to keep your mind free from bitterness," Mary had written earlier about Dora and her departure from the Union. "There are a few little clouds no bigger than D. M.'s small hand[1]." Moreover, Mary still had respect for many suffragettes, if not the leaders who she felt had not treated her well for some time, particularly since becoming an invalid. Yet she had yet to resign and if she assented to becoming co-editor, "it would savour of intrigue and that isn't my line... I haven't left the WSPU. I have something to say before I do[2]."

Dora continued to persist, ignoring her pleas and objections. For example, she authorized a circular for *The Freewoman* which listed Mary as co-editor even though Mary had specifically forbidden her to do so. Mary had neither the fitness to cope with co-editing a weekly – a controversial, radical weekly at that – or to cope with attacks on an organization she had helped to build and in which many of her friends were still actively involved. Mary was almost begging Dora to find someone else, even though "my natural impulse is to come to you at once when you want me." Reluctantly she said she could only agree "if I had your certain word

---

[1]   Gawthorpe to Marsden, 9 September 1911 and 23 September 1911.
[2]   Gawthorpe to Marsden, 15 September 1911.

that for a year there shall be no *editorial attacks on the demand for the vote*." She felt that "the vote must be won and the fight must go on alongside with education and constructive thought[1]."

Dora must have given Mary this assurance for she left the Union in September and Emmeline Pankhurst, in accepting her resignation, said that she realized "the necessity of perfect freedom before entering in a co-partnership with an editor of a review." The Union gave Mary a cheque to cover debts caused by her illness and convalescence though Dora felt that after five years, this was hardly a gracious or full acknowledgment of her services to the WSPU. "Dearest girl," Mary tried to assure Dora, "you *shall* understand me. I DO NOT MIND. THE JOY HAS BEEN MINE. THEY DO NO INJURY." But though now willing to help, Mary still resisted the post of co-editor, offering instead "suffrage notes of the week (theory not movements you know)." Again she emphasized her desire that Dora seize her chance for herself. "Your offer has never been a temptation to me because I have honestly and consistently been seeking your individual and personal welfare... Dora – I want you to win. That is TRUTH[2]."

Mary did appear willing to help but only on a strictly temporary basis until someone else was found and even then if the paper was monthly, not weekly. But the bullying continued, with Dora complaining that Mary's "vacillations" were inexplicable to her. "Downright refusal I could have understood... I wished you

[1]   Gawthorpe to Marsden, 18 September 1911.
[2]   Gawthorpe to Marsden, 20 September 1911.

could have taken the courageous course and risked the consequences... you might have given the weekly a chance." Astonishingly accusing Mary of cowardice, Dora continued that what she really wanted from her "was the use of your name to give it a preliminary and quite artificial kick-off... Well you have decided you cannot take that risk with your reputation[1]."

Mary was dumbfounded by the insensitivity of this letter, the downright refusal to consider her oft-repeated objections and, by no means least, the grossly insulting accusation of cowardice. It certainly reflected the ruthless, darker side of Dora, so unwilling to let others' reasoned arguments stand in the way of her chosen course. Not surprisingly, it led to a full-scale row between them. Mary furiously rejected the charge of cowardice and declared: "I will give loyally, unsparingly and as self-sacrificingly as you please and without any fuss; but any other sort of giving (that is forced giving) is to my mind but another form of prostitution. I am neither prostitute nor commercial seller." She concluded bitterly: "If I seem to fail you it will be rather unfortunate for any generalisation you may be tempted to make, that you are the great exception of years. It should give you furiously to think. Yours in acute humiliation but in no wise unashamed, Mary[2]."

Having cooled down a little, Mary sent a second, conciliatory letter the same day wondering: "Little One, is it over? What has happened? Where am I?" and apologized to Dora for having written in anger. The tempera-

---

[1]   Marsden to Gawthorpe, 24 September 1911.
[2]   Marsden to Gawthorpe, 7 October 1911.

ture dropped, if only because Mary seemed to give in to Dora's demands. Mary began to draft circulars, see people on the paper's behalf and most crucially of all, agreed to support the paper. Mary's anger shook Dora, who confessed she did not fully understand the reasons for it. None the less, Dora was keen to emphasize her love for her: "Mark one thing. Among all the acquaintances, friends and the like which you will ever make, you will find none ever, who will be as faithfully your admirer and firm champion when you are absent, than I have been[1]." Dora followed this the next day with a plea that they "mustn't become strangers in spirit over this matter no matter what it takes. With much love, Dora[2]."

The row ended, albeit temporarily, with a remarkably restrained and loving response from Mary. Again refusing the post of co-editor, she advised her not to write so harshly when "ever face to face with personal disappointment," but she emphasized she did not doubt Dora's loyalty: "Bless you dearest Dora... why should I doubt one whose intellectual sponsor I have consented to be? ... No we haven't become strangers. We shall know each other better... all this is between your soul and my soul, and through it all I say it in no name but that of love[3]."

The heated correspondence between Mary and Dora in the autumn of 1911 reflected a great deal about them both, particularly Dora. Dora clearly held Gawthorpe in great affection but was willing to ride

---

[1]   Marsden to Gawthorpe, 7 October 1911.
[2]   Marsden to Gawthorpe, 8 October 1911.
[3]   Gawthorpe to Marsden, 9 October 1911.

ruthlessly roughshod over her objections. She ignored her illness, her unease about the WSPU, her justified misgivings about making *The Freewoman* weekly. What lay behind this ultimately was a fierce self-confidence and arrogance. ("Do not fear for my writings," Dora once wrote to Mary. "Believe me you have no need. For one thing they are good[1].") On Mary's part, they showed that her love for Dora was so powerful and strong that she felt she had to submit to her pressure, eventually accepting the post of co-editor on a temporary basis only. It was a powerful relationship, based on mutual affection and admiration but it was not equal in terms of giving and taking. It had been repaired by October, but it could never be the same again.

❦

"The Freewoman, a Weekly Feminist Review," proprietor C. J. Grenville of Stephen Swift, joint-editors Dora Marsden and Mary Gawthorpe, issued its first number on 23 November 1911. Born during a row, burdened by a commitment to being a weekly and by its relatively high price of 3d (the suffrage weeklies were a penny), it was hardly an auspicious start. It lasted only eleven months (in its original form as a "feminist weekly" only six) and yet was never far from controversy. *The Freewoman* evoked strong feelings, it was either loved or loathed, there was no middle way. To the writer and leading anti-suffragist, Mrs. Humphrey Ward, it represented "the dark and dangerous side of the 'Woman Movement[2];'" to Agnes Maude Royden, a

---

[1] Marsden to Gawthorpe, 7 October 1911.
[2] *The Times*, 19 June 1912.

prominent member of the NUWSS, it was a "nauseous publication[1]." The President of the National Union, Millicent Fawcett, read one copy and "thought it so objectionable and mischievous that she tore it up into small pieces[2]."

But to others, like the radical suffragist Ada Neild Chew, for example, *The Freewoman* was "meat and drink to the sincere student who is out to learn the truth, however unpalatable that truth may be[3]." Certainly, the journal was open to a remarkable number of controversial writers and thinkers, some already famous, others about to become so. Billington-Greig and Chew, both feminist critics of mainstream suffragism, wrote for the paper alongside the famous novelist H. G. Wells and the young woman with whom he was to have a tempestuous affair, Rebecca West[4]. The Socialist Edward Carpenter and the sex psychologist Havelock Ellis were committed supporters, as were the anarchists Guy Aldred and Rose Witcup. Stella Browne, who later formed the Abortion Law Reform Association, also wrote for the paper, originally under the *nom de plume*, "A New Subscriber."

These and other contributors raised crucial questions about the connections between personal and sexual life and radical social change. It was a discussion that was as described above, fuelled by contemporary feminism and frustrations within the suffrage movement but it also built on a small yet significant radical tradition

---

[1]   *The Times*, 22 June 1912.
[2]   Strachey, p. 235.
[3]   *The Freewoman*, 18 April 1912.
[4]   See Glendinning (1987).

within the left. This had its origins in the late Eighteenth and early Nineteenth Centuries and it re-emerged forcefully in the 1880s with the resurgence of the socialist movement.

Thorny issues surrounding sex began to be debated and, as in the Colne Valley Labour clubs, visions of a "New Life" created.

Socialists, as today, were hardly united in this discussion, with some, like Hyndman and Bax of the SDF, dismissing analyses of the family and sexuality as being irrelevant to Marxism, and others wishing to uphold contemporary moral values not change them. Indeed, Blatchford reassured his followers that Socialists did not want to "destroy home life, abolish marriage... and establish 'Free Love[1].'" Socialists were also divided on the issue of contraception with many regarding birth control as part of a capitalist plot to limit the swelling ranks of the working class. In doing so, the potential benefits to women were overlooked or ignored. Yet others – women in the SDF, rank-and-file members of the ILP and other socialist groups inspired by Carpenter's *Love's Coming of Age* and anarchists like Aldred – though always in a minority, were not willing to let these issues be submerged and forgotten[2]. To them and growing numbers of feminists, *The Freewoman* would become, in the writer Reginald Wright Kauffman's words, "a torch in the night[3]."

---

[1]   Quoted in Rowbotham (1970), p. 73.
[2]   Quoted in Rowbotham (1970), p. 73. See also, Rowbotham and Weeks (1977).
[3]   *The New Freewoman* circular, n.d., *c.* 1913.

Radicals such as Kauffman were clearly overjoyed by the launch of the paper and the American anarchist, Benjamin R. Tucker, was moved to declare that it was "the most important publication in existence[1]." Others showered praise on *The Freewoman*'s editor. Frances Bjorkman, writing in the *American Review of Reviews*, for example, was moved to declare:

> The writer of *The Freewoman* editorials has shot into the literary and philosophical firmament as a star of the first magnitude. Although practically unknown before the advent of *The Freewoman*... she speaks always with the quietly authoritative air of the writer who has arrived. Her style has beauty as well as force and clarity[2].

Whether her style was as lucid as Bjorkman claimed is debatable, but her writings in 1911 and 1912 were certainly powerful and at the beginning at least, mainly concerned with women. Marsden's own analysis eventually went beyond feminism but the origins of *The Freewoman* can clearly and primarily be located in the contemporary feminist movement. *The Freewoman* was its child. Certainly, Dora saw its purpose as thoughtfully to examine not "the fight" but what women were fighting *for*. Not without modesty or, indeed, some justification, she declared in the first issue that:

---

[1] *The New Freewoman* circular, n.d., *c.* 1913.

[2] *The New Freewoman* circular, n.d., *c.* 1913. Frances Maude Bjorkman was a prominent suffragist in New York and a member of the National Women's Suffrage Society. A member too of the 'Heterodoxy' women's group which, like *The Freewoman*, embraced a wider discussion of feminism beyond the limits of suffragism. Clearly, feminists in the USA were also concerned by the restrictions of the campaign for the vote.

163

the chief event of the week is our own appearance. The publication of *The Freewoman* marks an epoch. It marks the point at which feminism in England ceases to be impulsive and unaware of its own features and becomes definitely self-conscious and introspective. For the first time, feminists themselves make the attempt to reflect the 'feminist movement in the mirror of thought[1].'

This aim led to a wide-ranging and fearless debate about the oppression of women which suffragist papers were unwilling or unable to publish[2]. Dora welcomed disagreement, although she did attempt to lay down some guidelines for the policy of the paper. Her chief concern was "what [women] may become. Our interest is in the Freewoman herself, her psychology, philosophy, morality and achievements[3]." From the beginning, Dora made her own position on where the responsibility for women's liberation lay – with *themselves*. This was particularly emphasized in her first two editorials entitled "Bondwomen" [and "Commentary on Bondwomen"].

Dora claimed that prejudice and women's own fears of freedom were responsible for their continuing oppression, but she did not ignore the role of men. To her, they presented themselves as "masters," who made the laws, determined morals and standards and, most significantly of all, created the notion of women as a weaker sex, in need of their masculine protection. Dora,

---

[1]   *The Freewoman*, 23 November 1911.

[2]   The debate in the suffrage press did become wider after 1910 but on the whole it avoided controversial criticism of contemporary moral values claiming only that men should live up to them.

[3]   *The Freewoman*, 23 November 1911.

at this stage, accepted that there was a difference in power between men too yet "though some men are servants, all women are servants, and all the masters are men." Woman's role was to be "a kind of human poultice" shielding and comforting him at home from the horrors of the outside world[1].

How this division of sexual roles developed Marsden conceded was a "moot point" but implied that it was connected to childrearing along with "women giving up the game – i.e. bartering themselves for the sake of the protection of men."

It was at this juncture that some readers would perhaps have stopped nodding their heads in general agreement and sat up, startled. Bluntly, Dora stated that a woman had a choice – to accept her fate without complaining or "take her place as master. It is this effort to find her place among the masters which is behind the feminist movement." Women could take men's protection but in doing so "give up all first-hand power. Really, the power to work and think"; or they could accept a belief in their own worth as individuals, seizing freedom and responsibility for themselves. "Nothing," Dora argued, "but one thing – the sense of quality, the sense that a woman has gifts, the sense that she is a superior, a master – can give her the strength to slip the comfort and protection and to be content to seize the 'love' in passing, to suffer the long strain of effort and to bear the agony of producing creative work."

It is hardly necessary to point out that Dora was de-

---

[1] See Zaretsky (1976) for an examination of this role.

scribing herself here, almost justifying her own personal and social position. It was perhaps an individualistic stance yet she realized that for all women to become Freewomen a whole series of changes were required, most notably the creation of economic independence from men. That women might achieve this, as some suffragists claimed, through wages for housework was to Dora laughably ludicrous; "that wives should become paid employees of their husbands! Beyond this folly can no further go!" Even women with children must continue to work outside the home and to achieve these "vast changes in housing, nursing, kindergarten, education, cooking, cleaning, in the industrial world and in the professions were necessary[1]."

"Bondwomen" was an excellent start, setting the paper on its path to expose the customs, morals and conventions that suppressed women, but it also illustrated some of Marsden's own weaknesses. First, the changes required to allow all women access to economic independence were not fully explained, while second, it was an individualistic argument that was perhaps based too far on her own, unique experience. And third, there was an element of elitism in her approach. Dora had already dismissed complaints about the high price of the paper by airily replying that "we are not proposing writing for women whose highest journalistic needs are realised by a penny[2]," and she seemed to accept she was only appealing to a minority. "A feminist," she argued, "must

---

[1] *The Freewoman*, 30 November 1911. In many ways this approach mirrors classic "radical feminism."
[2] *The Freewoman*, 23 November 1911.

make her appeal to freewomen, and not to 'ordinary' women... to those who have already shown signs of individuality and strength[1]."

As Dora wished, "Bondwomen" precipitated a torrent of correspondence and debate, much of which rejected her views. Though often stubborn, she welcomed criticism and usually was prepared to publish it as a means of furthering the discussion. She probably welcomed it too as a challenge to her intellectual prowess. However, one particular criticism was to overshadow the rest and was to lead to a furious row which dominated *The Freewoman* for some time. Briefly, Dora had implied that women must assert their own strength and independence instead of accepting their weakness and demanding protection. In other words, if a woman demanded protection, she accepted she needed it because she was weak. To Dora, this is exactly what many suffragists did, pleading: "Are not women weak? Are women not crushed down? Are women not in need of protection? Therefore, give them the means wherewith they may be protected." Real Freewomen had to reject this subservience to the notion of the inherent, unchangeable weakness of the female sex and struggle for a new, stronger ideal: "they do not need protection: they need liberty[2]."

Dora stressed that "the vote should be like the air and a pure water supply, be free to all" but it could not bring liberation to women. Bondwomen might need it "as a means of protection" but "their robust sisters" less

---

[1]   *The Freewoman*, 30 November 1911.
[2]   *The Freewoman*, 30 November 1911.

so. The vote was not even a symbol of freedom, and stringent calls for it were "culled out of an unthought out and nebulous feminism and its half-hearted and sentimental allusions to prostitution, sweating, child assault, race deterioration and what not." To Dora, therefore, at this stage in late 1911, "feminism is the whole issue, political enfranchisement a branch issue and methods, militant or otherwise, are merely accidental[1]."

It was, however, the specific attacks on the Pankhursts and the WSPU that was to lead to a furore in the paper. It began with an attack on the Union's decision to resume militant tactics at the end of 1911[2]. To Dora this decision showed that Christabel had lost her "political balance" and reflected her lack of "political insight and even common sense[3]." Dora's criticism continued in the second issue and, not surprisingly, prompted a torrent of abuse from outraged suffragettes who, in Dora's words, informed the joint editors of "our unworthiness, our caddishness, our black treachery[4]." They felt they had been deceived into buying and supporting a paper that they had been led to believe would be at least sympathetic to the suffrage movement generally and, in particular, the WSPU[5].

[1] *The Freewoman*, 23 November 1911.
[2] Asquith had "torpedoed" the Conciliation Bill with a proposal of a new Franchise Bill. He appeared to promise that an amendment permitting an element of women's suffrage would be allowed. The WSPU – rightly in the end – did not trust this and resumed militancy.
[3] *The Freewoman*, 23 November 1911.
[4] *The Freewoman*, 30 November 1911.
[5] See, for example, Hertha Ayrton to Mary Gawthorpe, 19 March 1911.

The row spilled over to the third issue, delaying further Dora's proposed series on morality so as to provide space for a reply from Mary Gawthorpe. Mary had been deeply hurt, partly by Dora but also by other friends in the WSPU. She informed readers that she had not written any of the attacks and remained loyal to the women's suffrage. She complained that "the comrades and friends of one hour are the degraded beings of the next. What forms of friendship are these that suffer ship-wreck at the first seeming assault[1]." Mary was over-whelmed by the torrent of criticism and was only spared from despair by the odd letter of encouragement[2]. She remained loyal to the WSPU and, after an attack in the *New Age*, even defended the Pankhursts as "a hero fam-ily, and posterity will attest it[3]." But the whole episode affected her badly, further straining her relationship with Dora. Eventually she resigned her co-editorship in the spring of 1912.

Dora's attacks on the WSPU were in many respects ill-advised, as they alienated many potential readers from the paper. Her criticism even led to estrangement from some of her former friends in Manchester who, as a result of Dora's articles passed a resolution the day af-ter the first issue that "this meeting totally disapproves of *The Freewoman* because of its attitude on the suffrage question, and the spirit of the editorial attack on Mrs.

---

[1] *The Freewoman*, 7 December 1911.
[2] See for example, E. H. Vink to Mary Gawthorpe, 1 December 1911. Vink thought "*The Freewoman* is really great. Be proud of it." Gawthorpe wrote on his letter that she "nearly broke down when this arrived... now I fear nothing."
[3] *The New Age*, 21 March 1912.

Pankhurst; it resolves to boycott the paper and it regrets the strenuous work done by Manchester members in advertising the paper[1]." Certainly, some of Dora's venom was personally-based but Manchester's response clearly reflected many suffragette's inability to allow, let alone condone, criticism of the leaders; to them, as Muriel Nelson put it, "the Voice of Clement's Inn[2]" was unchallengeable, above criticism.

Dora, though, continued to criticize the autocracy of the Pankhursts throughout the life of the paper. Their leadership prevented independent thought and encouraged followers to become "bondwomen" unable to seize independence and emancipation for themselves. To ask for the vote anyway was a sign of weakness, a request for protection. Of course, other suffragists were criticized too for creating "the illusion of [the vote's] invincibility[3]" yet she conceded that the NUWSS and WFL, as democratic organizations, had a potential role to play. Their task was "to find momentum in the thought, the philosophy, the tendency, which suffragism represents." Yet in a long attack on suffragism, she claimed that "there was no idea behind English suffragism" and its leaders, at the least, stood ultimately to "defend the Capitalist monopoly and the marriage monopoly... all things considered suffragists are safer without a programme. To want a vote, and want it now, is a small affair. But it

---

[1]   *The Freewoman*, 7 December 1911. Resolution passed on 24 November 1911.
[2]   *The Freewoman*. Mary N. Murray in the same issue described the Pankhursts as "the blind leaders of the blind."
[3]   *The Freewoman*, 28 December 1911.

has the merit of sincerity[1]."

Dora's fire though was usually aimed at Clement's Inn. By the spring of 1912 she was even claiming that "the paramount interest of the WSPU was neither the emancipation of women, nor the vote, but the increase in power of their own organisation[2]." Dora's vitriolic attacks were, both on a personal and a general level, not without justification and they touched the same raw nerve in the Union as had Billington-Greig in her *Emancipation in a Hurry*. On the other hand, they could be counter-productive and blind others to the positive aspects of the struggle for the vote. As Amy Houghton, an old friend from Manchester put it, they even encouraged the anti-feminists who liked "to see us at each other's throats[3]." Moreover, she pleaded with Dora to see the WSPU as a "forcing house of feminism. You have been through it and others are going through it[4]." Finally, Dora's tirade was, from a financial point of view, also ill-advised. Her natural audience would, of course, be feminists, many of whom would be suffragists too, hence the adverts in the suffrage press. Any debate on the value of the vote would therefore have to be treated sensitively. This Dora would not do and in the WSPU case at least, she aimed straight for the jugular. It may well have been justified but it led to a fall in circulation by the spring when financial difficulties began.

---

[1]   *The Freewoman*, 4 July 1912.
[2]   *The Freewoman*, 7 March 1912.
[3]   Amy Houghton to Marsden, n.d., *c.* December 1911.
[4]   Amy Houghton to Marsden, n.d., *c.* December 1911.

In many ways, the argument over the WSPU was an additional, if avoidable burden on a new paper whose outspokenness on other controversial issues was to lead directly to threats of censorship and prosecution. But nothing would prevent Dora Marsden from expressing her views, least of all respect for contemporary moral values and conventions. This was made abundantly clear in her five-part series on morality which appeared in the winter of 1911 / 12. Briefly, Dora argued that in the past women had been encouraged to restrain their senses and passion for life while "dutifully keeping alive and repro-ducing the species." Part of this process led to the notion of female purity and the chaste ideal, so beloved of suf-fragists. To Dora this had to be broken if women were to be free to lead an independent life.

Marsden made clear that she was not demanding mindless sexual promiscuity for "to anyone who has ever got any meaning out of sexual passion the aggra-vated emphasis which is bestowed upon physical sexual intercourse is more absurd than wicked[1]." None the less, she went on to condemn the current notion that "indis-soluble monogamy is right." First, men had always ig-nored it for themselves; while second, it was an "ideal" that was bought by some women at the expense of oth-ers. "Monogamy was always based upon the intellectual apathy and insensitiveness of married women, who ful-filled their own ideal at the expense of the Spinster and the Prostitute." Monogamy's four cornerstones were "men's hypocrisy, the spinster's dumb resignation, the

---

[1] *The Freewoman*, 28 December 1911.

prostitute's unsightly degradation and the married woman's monopoly." Further "indissoluble monogamy is blunderingly stupid, and reacts immorally, producing deceit, sensuality, vice, promiscuity and an unfair monopoly[1]."

This was, of course, an extremely controversial argument that flew in the face of contemporary moral values, not least with regard to sex. Again, Dora was not arguing for promiscuity but "limited monogamy" – a series of monogamous relationships. How far her views were based on her own experience it is difficult to tell. Yet the notion of a passionate but not necessarily sexual relationship would perhaps adequately describe her friendship with Mary Gawthorpe, if not others too. Certainly, her argument would appeal to single women like herself who had sexual desires and feelings but were not allowed to express them – unless, of course, in marriage. Even then, sex, for women at least, was supposed to be reserved for procreation[2].

Dora realized that her views on morality were controversial and had further implications for women in other areas, for example motherhood. Here, she denounced the hypocritical sentimentality surrounding motherhood; first, because it had little relevance to the reality of most mother's lives, and second, the ideal was again based on protection from men – women could not be free if they sought this. "Women," she argued, "will

---

[1] *The Freewoman*, 4 January 1912.
[2] Re-reading Dora's and other contributors' views on sex and monogamy
   – written, note, in 1912 – is still astounding. They remain remarkable over a century later.

have to rise to their responsibilities and not endeavour to slip them by a device (the protection of men) which robs them of the liberty which is the chiefest dignity of the human being[1]." To become Freewomen was not easy; it involved a complete break with convention and organizing life for themselves with all the risks involved. Yet "to Freewomen this conception is becoming clearer. It is to face life unafraid, to welcome its emotions, to try their value, to be alive and capable of living intensely; to seek life, and that more abundantly; and if there is a price to be paid for it, to be ready with the toll[2]."

This wild call for freedom knew no bounds, and would respect no conventions if they prevented the liberation of the individual. To see protection of a man or the state was to forgo responsibility and freedom. Thus, as described in "Bondwomen," to call for wages for housework, for example, showed Dora "how short a distance the Woman Movement has travelled[3]." Even marriage prevented women's freedom for they gave up their own independence in return for the protection of a man. For suffragists, for example, to complain of married women's position without analysing the institution itself was ludicrous, once the bargain had been struck. As Dora memorably put it: "A prostitute even would not haggle about her wares after receiving her money. Why then should a wife[4]?"

One permanent flaw in Marsden's arguments was

---

[1]   *The Freewoman*, 11 January 1912.
[2]   *The Freewoman*, 18 January 1912.
[3]   *The Freewoman*, 8 February 1912.
[4]   *The Freewoman*, 8 February 1912.

that she never fully explained how the necessary changes were to be achieved if women were indeed to realize their freedom. However, she did recognize that her call did present additional, practical problems. For example, women could hardly be free if children remained wholly dependent on their mothers. Dora thus felt that a national system of nurseries, with fully qualified staff, might provide part of the answer, even taking babies only two weeks old. "It seems," she admitted, "drastic but it is the only way." She wanted a situation where women would choose to have children "and motherhood became the honourable province of all women, married and single[1]." Ultimately though, a woman's responsibility was to herself, not necessarily the next generation. Nothing, not even feeding babies, should be allowed to prevent women's quest for freedom: "Frankly if the feeding of babies is to interfere with the development of women, it is the feeding of the babies which will have to give way[2]."

It is not known whether Dora herself, now aged thirty, wanted a child, but she clearly wanted women, single or married, to have a free choice. It hardly needs pointing out how far this flew in the face of contemporary morality and the prevalent cult of motherhood. Briefly, as we have seen, the latter was connected to a fear about the relative size and health of the British population when compared to its competitors, especially Germany. In short, this resulted in increased pressure on women to pursue a maternal role. Certainly the "duty"

---

[1] *The Freewoman,* 8 February 1912.
[2] *The Freewoman,* 22 February 1912.

of women was to have strong and healthy babies, ready and able to work and fight and defend Britain and its empire[1].

One proposal that in part came out of this pressure was the State Endowment of Motherhood (SEM) and many feminists, particularly Eleanor Rathbone, argued for it too. But for Dora it was, like wages for housework, a ludicrous idea that sought protection and surrendered independence, in this case to the state. Again, women had to choose "between the comforts of protection and the harsh responsibilities of freedom... Is the position of paid domestic servant" she wondered in "Woman: Endowed or Free?," "the ideal of the Woman in the Emancipation movement[2]?"

Other contributors, particularly H. G. Wells, disagreed. Wells, already a renowned writer, admired the paper and Dora, although like so many others, he too had suffered from her bullying – "No. When I see you, you make me write articles" was only one exasperated plea to her to stop pestering him[3]. He sometimes found Dora inconsistent but wrote, "I respect your courage and spirit, dear madam[4]" and signed himself "your constant reader[5]." Wells objected to Dora's views on SEM because he felt it put too great a burden on women to argue that they should only have children if they were financially independent and willing alone to pay for them. But Dora, who was extremely pleased by her *coup* of

<hr>

[1]   See Davin (1978).
[2]   *The Freewoman*, 29 February 1912.
[3]   H. G. Wells to Marsden, n.d. *c.* 1912.
[4]   *The Freewoman*, 21 March 1912.
[5]   *The Freewoman*, 7 March 1912.

getting Wells for *The Freewoman*, could not accept this. "We must resist the endowment," she concluded, "because we can affect bolder things[1]."

Already, by the spring of 1912, Dora's leading articles and "Notes of the Week" had, as intended, provoked wide-ranging and controversial debate throughout the paper. It tapped the frustration that many suffragists and feminists felt in not being able freely and openly to discuss issues that affected women. The need for respectability had certainly bottled this up in the suffrage movement, publicly at least. As Florence Harris put it in the second issue: "You have the foresight to cater for a large section of women to whom few or no other women's papers appeal. *The Freewoman* supplies a need of which we Feminists were only subconscious until its appearance[2]." Dora, of course, had her own views, but the paper did not have, nor was it intended to have, a fixed policy or programme. Rather, as Dora's friend from her Manchester days, Amy Houghton, wrote, the discussion was like "a sort of moral taking out of the contents of one's pockets... some things may be put back and others thrown away[3]."

The sorting out of *The Freewoman*'s pockets recognized no limits in its examination of the institutions and values that appeared to oppress women. Marriage, for example, came under scrutiny and many agreed with Dora that it could be seen as another form of prostitu-

---

[1]   *The Freewoman*, 21 March 1912.
[2]   *The Freewoman*, 30 November 1911.
[3]   Amy Houghton to Dora Marsden, n.d., *c.* late 1911.

tion. Edmund B. D'Auvergne, that "dandy of cranks[1]" to Rebecca West, claimed, for example, that marriage:

> had certain commercial advantages. By it the man secures the exclusive right to the woman's body and by it, the woman binds the man to support her during the rest of her life... a more disgraceful bargain was never struck.

Others wanted freer and easier divorce; some, like the anarchists Guy Aldred and Rose Witcup, advocated "free love unions[2]."

Not surprisingly, the discussion also engendered a fascinating debate on sex and sexuality. Some contributors defended the moral code, arguing that sex should only take place within marriage and even then only for procreation[3], but this view was met with much opposition. Many readers felt that women, in or out of marriage, should be able to decide freely, without the risk of disease or unwanted pregnancies, whether to enter a sexual relationship. Even a vicar's wife, "a would-be Freewoman," asserted that women too had a right to enjoy sex[4]. It is important to note that neither Dora Marsden nor any contributor advocated unlicensed promiscuity and the right *not* to enter sexual relationships was also made with some force. But the right of a woman to enjoy her sexuality free from the "duty" of procreation was also emphasized. Isabel Leatham, for example, hoped that "The Freewoman will not enter upon the sex relationship for any such conscious purpose as that of

---

[1] Rebecca West to Dora Marsden, n.d., *c.* winter 1912 / 13.
[2] *The Freewoman*, 18 January 1912.
[3] *The Freewoman*, 28 July 1911.
[4] *The Freewoman*, 21 March 1912.

reproduction; but rather that they will find in passionate love between man and woman, even if that be transient, the only sanction for sex intimacy[1]." Stella Browne summarized a major current in the paper on this issue when she declared that "the sexual experience is the right of every human being not hopelessly afflicted in mind or body and should be entirely a matter of free choice and personal preference, untainted by bargain or compulsion[2]."

A demand for a free choice to enter a physical relationship alongside a call to separate sex from procreation inevitably brought into the discussion the issue of contraception. Quite simply, as Dora realized, there could be few Freewomen if they were continually pregnant. In the second issue, she wrote that passive maternity had been crucial to the subjection of women in the past, but was now no longer inevitable. "The role of passive maternity," she argued, "combined with the economic dependence of women, which is its correlate, instead of leading to the respect for women by men... has had the reverse effect." She looked forward to "the magnificent future when women demand their right as mothers of the race to regulate their families in accordance with the best physical, mental and moral inheritance and environments[3]."

---

[1] *The Freewoman*, 11 January 1912. Leatham was daughter-in-law of James Leatham, founder of the first Scottish socialist newspaper *The Worker's Herald*. Like Isabel, James was a strong advocate of free speech.

[2] *The Freewoman*, 21 March 1912.

[3] *The Freewoman*, 30 November 1911.

Calls for freely available contraception, however, became embroiled in an argument between Malthusians and Socialists. The former, led by Charles Drysdale, argued that the growth of the population would inevitably outstrip the finite resources of the earth and therefore had to be checked by "preventive measures." The Socialists, wary of a plot to curtail the numbers of workers, replied that poverty was not caused by demographic factors but the unequal distribution of wealth. None the less, in spite of this quarrel, and the different motivations involved, the discussion did at least emphasize the importance of birth control and the possibility of divorcing sex from conception. Further, as Drysdale argued, "one of the definite advantages of prevention rather than continence is that it enables women to take the matter into their own hands[1]."

Stella Browne went further:

for us Freewomen the issue is clear. We must secure a decent chance in the material environment for every child born in the world. We must see to it that the woman who is passionately and pre-eminently maternal shall not be condemned to childlessness through economic pressure and medieval conventions, yet our right to refuse maternity is also our invulnerable right. Our wills are ours, our persons are ours[2].

The discussion on sexuality, already way beyond the limits of acceptable behaviour, knew no bounds. Yet even Stella Browne was apprehensive about her letter of 22 February 1912. In this she again asserted the right of

---

[1]   *The Freewoman*, 21 December 1911.
[2]   *The Freewoman*, 1 August 1912.

women to enter or not enter a sexual relationship. Abstinence was perfectly "normal" too, as long as it did not set a precedent for everyone else. But then she wondered how many abstinent or single women resorted to "auto-eroticism." "How many single women," she asked "have refrained from this practice... whose danger to health and sanity has, on the whole, been much overrated?" Stella Browne was right to add that *The Freewoman* was "the only lay publication in English" in which this issue could be raised but even though it cropped up again occasionally it hardly became a mass debate[1].

Finally, and most daringly, sexuality was also defined as including relationships between members of the same sex. In the early issues, the main contributor on homosexuality was Harry J. Birnstingl who congratulated Dora on her courage in raising this issue. Birnstingl tended to derive many of his arguments from the radical Socialist and homosexual, Edward Carpenter, and particularly Carpenter's *Intermediate Sex*[2]. Birnstingl tended to be oversentimental in his approach but at least he had brought the subject into the open, evoking much praise from readers who had until then not dared to speak of or acknowledge "the love that hath no name." Moreover, Birnstingl did not merely defend lesbianism in the women's movement but praised it, refusing to see it as a problem. In reply to the anti-feminist charge that most feminists were abnormal because they

---

[1] For a wider understanding of Stella Browne see S. Rowbotham: *New World for Women: Stella Browne, Socialist Feminist* (London 1977).

[2] Carpenter (1908).

were single and childless, he argued that perhaps they no longer wanted to be defined by their relationships to men. Indeed:

> it apparently has never occurred to them that numbers of these women find their ultimate destiny, as it were, among members of their own sex, working for the good of each other, forming romantic – nay passionate – attachments with each other? [Instead of disgusted horror, Birnstingl expressed his feeling that] it is splendid that these women... should suddenly find their destiny in thus working together for the freedom of their own sex. It is one of the most wonderful things of the Twentieth Century.

Not all readers agreed with Birnstingl or indeed with any of the discussion on sexuality at all, noting, in Dr. Charles Whitby's words, that in Dora Marsden's *Freewoman* "there are no forbidden facts or topics[1]," Frank Watts was moved to write that:

> surely the woman readers of *The Freewoman* do not want to read articles every week upon such subjects as Uranus, syphylis and prostitution. If these are subjects that attract Freewomen then it must be admitted by sane observers that man in the past was exercising a sure instinct in keeping his spouse and girl children within the sheltered walls of ignorance[2].

But there was an audience there ready and willing to discuss these very subjects and their relationship to women. *The Freewoman* was almost their only outlet, the paper itself a permanent memorial to the courage of Dora Marsden[3].

---

[1]   *The Freewoman*, 18 January 1912.
[2]   *The Freewoman*, 1 February 1912.
[3]   For a further discussion of this, placing it within early Twentieth

Some commentators however have criticized the debate on sex in *The Freewoman*. They claim it was heterosexist and ultimately based on furthering the interests of men. Jeffreys, for example, points out the increasing number of male contributors and argues that their call for new sexual mores should be treated with caution[1]. She claims that they were motivated by a concern that the success of feminism would restrict their power over women in general and hence, their bodies in particular. Jeffreys also criticizes Dora and others for their attacks on spinsters who, to her, had made a rational decision to reject sexual relationships with men. Certainly, this could be justified yet while male calls for sexual liberation, whether in the 1900s or the 1960s, have to be looked at with suspicion her analysis overlooks several key points. First, as described above, Marsden, Browne and others were insistent that women had an absolute right to refuse a sexual relationship and should not be condemned for doing so. Second, their call to divorce sex from procreation alongside Dora's demand that sexuality should not be defined purely in terms of intercourse went some way to attacking heterosexist views. This was, of course, furthered by the defence, however limited, of homosexuality. The debate in *The Freewoman* certainly had its weaknesses, and it mirrored and fed on the divisions over sexuality in the women's

Century discussions on sexology, see J. Greenway: "It's What You Do With It That Counts: Interpretations of Otto Wieninger" in Blend and Doan (eds): *Sexology and Culture* (University of Chicago Press 1998) pp. 27 - 43. Birnstingl was a friend of Marsden, and had aunts who were in the WSPU. Ethel 'and her long-time companion Alice Pollard ran a feminist bookshop in London.'

[1]   Jeffreys, S. (1986).

movement and other radical circles. Yet it emphasized that women, independent Freewomen, should have a choice to express their sexuality on their own terms and outside the confines of a restricted moral code[1].

The strain of editorship soon began to take its toll on Dora. This was furthered by conflict with her publisher, Charles Grenville, and by another, terminal row with Mary Gawthorpe. Running such a controversial journal was always going to be difficult, particularly given its financial insecurity. By February 1912, according to a letter Mary wrote to Dora on 13 October 1912, it appears *The Freewoman* was making a considerable loss of about £20 a week. An appeal was launched in the autumn as Grenville began to get cold feet and Dora was forced to seek other backers. Grenville carried on but his relationship with Dora deteriorated. This may have been due to envy of the contributors Dora had brought on to the paper, for he himself had only enjoyed modest success as a poet and writer. But the major reason was that he resented Dora's insistence on total independence even though he had backed her and was paying her and Grace Jardine's wages.

Grenville was also peeved by not being offered the presidency (given to E. S. P. Haynes, a lawyer and friend of H. G. Wells) of The Freewoman Discussion Circle, a group that had spontaneously grown out of

---

[1] For further analysis of the radical debate on sex and gender in the late Nineteenth and early Twentieth Century, see Bland: *Banishing the Beast: Sexuality and the Early Feminists* (London: New Press 1995). The discussion may not have been in the mainstream of British politics but once again, Marsden provided a remarkable space, enabling it to take place.

readers demands further to discuss issues raised in the paper (see below). He also wanted to be consulted fully on any possible changes in editorial policy for, as he reminded Dora at the end of April, "I have now spent a very considerable sum on the paper[1]." Not surprisingly, Dora reacted angrily to this proprietorial interference and replied, "*You* have put money into the paper. I have put in the whole of my brain, power and personality. Without your money I would not have started, without my brain the paper could not have lived and shown the signs of flourishing which it undoubtedly has." She warned him that if he tried to sack her she would not "submit docilely to the forgoing of all return of the investment of my property... indeed I should at once appeal for a return on it from the public which I have created[2]."

Eventually, the row subsided and Grenville calmed down, later expressing on numerous occasions concern over Dora's health. Many years later, in an article written in *Time and Tide* (16 July 1926), Rebecca West recalled that Grenville was an odd man, proprietor of Chesterton's and Belloc's literary paper *Eye Witness* as well as *The Freewoman*. Though not a literary giant himself, he recognized talent, being the first to publish Katherine Mansfield.

West implied that *The Freewoman* collapsed when he embezzled some money and left for Africa with his lover. It is not certain how true this is, yet he was gaoled (as described above) for fraud and bigamy in 1913.

---

[1]   Charles Grenville to Marsden, 28 April 1912.
[2]   Dora Marsden to Charles Grenville, 29 April 1912.

Dora was shocked by this and reacted by publicly praising his contribution to literature and journalism, in particular *The Freewoman* where "he gave his help freely and graciously and without any reservations." Perhaps forgetting the arguments of spring 1912, she added: "he occupied the truly unique position of financing journals without attempting to control them[1]." *The Freewoman* could not have existed without Dora Marsden but it could not have begun without Grenville, and for that alone, he too deserves some credit for this remarkable journal[2].

Dora's conflict with Grenville came just after a furious and final battle with Mary, a fight that marked the end of their relationship. The issues remained the same as the previous Autumn – Dora's incessant bullying and an unbridgeable difference over the WSPU. Mary still retained some loyalty to the latter and, though ill, even risked imprisonment again in a protest over the forced feeding of William Ball. Ball himself had been protesting about the treatment given to suffragettes yet sadly he was driven insane while in jail[3]. Dora too condemned the government's action in this case but her denunciation of the WSPU, in spite of Mary's pleas, continued unabated.

---

[1]   *The New Freewoman*, 15 July 1913.
[2]   Grenville almost certainly lost money on *The Freewoman*. None of Marsden's works shows a profit. Dora seemed to like him initially, writing to Mary Gawthorpe on 14 October 1911: "Mr. Grenville is a very dear man and the essence of niceness to us – although he does flirt about!"
[3]   *The Freewoman*, 29 February 1912.

A blistering attack, "A Militant Psychology," appeared in 7 March issue. "The Pankhurst party," she wrote, "have lost their forthright desire for enfranchisement in their outbalancing desire to raise their own organisation to a position of dictatorship amongst all women's organisations." The vote was only "of secondary importance to the leaders... before every other consideration, political, social or moral comes the aggrandisement of the WSPU itself [and] the increase of power of their own organisation, absolutely limited in authority to three leaders and one male outsider[1]."

For Mary this was the last straw and in the following issue (14 March) in which Dora again labelled the Union as "the meanest, sharpest and most cynical of working organisations," a bland statement was issued. "We regret to have to announce that Miss Gawthorpe has decided to resign from her nominal co-editorship of *The Freewoman*. We earnestly hope that the coming months will see her restored to health." But Mary, though ill, had not resigned on health grounds, but because of Dora's bullying and her ferocious attack on the WSPU. In a series of furious letters, Mary made her position absolutely clear. She sent Dora two letters on the 22 March 1912, the first being six pages of sheer anger. Mary complained of Dora's "bullying note" and her attacks on the Union which she saw as hypocritical:

---

[1]   *The Freewoman*, 7 March 1912. Dora was referring to Christabel and
Emmeline Pankhurst, Emmeline and Fred Pethick-Lawrence.

Moreover, the very day you begin attacks of the kind you suggest *before you have in your own case removed the mote from your eye...* that day I will tell 'truths' about *The Freewoman from my point of view*. I will tell everything from the initial bullying to the unscrupulous interpolation of a misleading sentence in my WSPU article following on your statement that Friday.

She then went on to offer Dora a public debate on their quarrel over the WSPU and *The Freewoman* and, cooling down a little, wondered whether "perhaps we have all been cruel. Very well, let us mend our ways. Respectfully but critically, Mary."

The second letter of 22 March was calmer, as "last night I wrote in a black (or white) anger. This morning I write in cold blood." She again refused to reconsider her decision to resign. "*I am not coming*! I am in total disagreement with some of your methods." Ill and tired of squabbling, Mary hoped that "this will be our last quarrel about *The Freewoman* and its works. On my part it is final severance, and I do not propose to write to you again thereon." Coldly, she ended with "sincere good wishes for a fair future." It was a long way from "my dear little one."

Gawthorpe was clearly livid, and returned all Dora's letters to her, a significant act of angry rejection. Further, she asked Dora not to write to her, for "the sight of your letters I am obliged to confess turns me white with emotion and I have acute heart attacks following on from that[1]." Dora did not stop attacking the WSPU but she did at last give up trying to make Mary stay on the

---
[1]   Mary Gawthorpe to Dora Marsden, 24 March 1912.

paper. Neither was Dora unmoved by her friend's angry tirade for, alongside all the other pressures upon her, it made her ill. At the end of March, she was forced to go home to her mother, now in Southport, to recuperate. Mary softened a little at this, advocating to "dear Mammy Marsden" that Dora be given "a light nourishing diet and definite regular relaxation[1]." Yet the hurt was permanent, and Mary never fully forgave Dora: their old affection and love had died[2].

The change in their relationship was a sad blow to Dora and only bearable through the support of others – principally her mother and Grace Jardine. Without this, and the admiration of her readers, it is difficult to see how she could have survived. Even so, Dora's health suffered, as it did throughout the whole *Freewoman* period. Partly the legacy of her suffragette days, it was of course compounded by the strain of running the paper and her own inability to relax. Headaches were a continual problem. Throughout this period there were references to these and her general health. Friends constantly advised her to relax and take a holiday which, with Grace, she did do, in May. Yet Dora believed she was indispensable to the paper, refused to delegate and soon the effects of overwork again became apparent. As her friend from university days, Winifred Hindshaw, put it after her holiday with Grace, "I hope you are getting better again, though I am afraid that you will not be better long at your rate of living[3]." Dora also suffered from

---

[1] Mary Gawthorpe to Hannah Marsden, 2 April 1912.
[2] A sad note to both and surely a cause of Marsden's illness at this time.
[3] Winifred Hindshaw to Dora Marsden, 10 June 1912.

the struggle of being a single, independent woman, determined to lead her own life and be judged by her own merits and abilities. Not surprisingly, women like her in her circle were often ill, or as Rebecca West once put it in August 1913 to Dora Marsden, "Good God, what a lot of crocks we Freewomen are!" And finally the strain of these years was increased by the problem of accommodation. Dora and Grace were living in an unfurnished flat in Endsleigh Street at the end of November 1911 but had to move in the New Year, eventually settling together at 22 Grove Place, Christchurch Road, Hampstead. Neither place seemed more than temporary and the two would scuttle back to "mammy Marsden" in Southport. Thus, even the comfort of a permanent home was denied them.

Another burden, though a welcome one, was the development of The Freewoman Discussion Circles. The support for these came from readers eager to discuss issues raised in their paper. The first call was made in February 1912 and "of this suggestion," Dora wrote, "we highly approve[1]." The idea snowballed throughout the spring and many readers (for example, Ethel Bradshaw, secretary of the Bristol Fabian Women's Group)[2] wanted to form circles in their own towns. Eventually, Dora suggested a meeting on 18 April at the International Women's Suffrage Shop in London to discuss how "the circle (or possibly several circles) can best be carried on... Already in the Provinces and Scotland peo-

---

[1] *The Freewoman*, 15 February 1912.
[2] *The Freewoman*, 7 March 1912.

ple are anxious to form such associations[1]." Barbara Low, E. S. P. Haynes and Harry Birnstingl, all regular contributors (Haynes on divorce) agreed to act as a preliminary organizing committee.

The meeting took place on 25 April with, to Grenville's disgust, Haynes taking the chair. It was a remarkable success. "It was," Dora wrote to her aggrieved proprietor, "to my great amazement that instead of the 12 or 15 people expected, 100 people crowded into the room to hold half that number, all immensely interested and eager to accept responsibility in regard to the Clubs[2]." They decided to form a central circle in London, meeting fortnightly, and to organize regional circles too. The next meeting was fixed for 8 May when Dora was to speak on "Women and Evolution."

The rules for the Circles were established. The Circles was open to men and women, subscriptions were to be five shillings a year, meetings were to be fortnightly and talks from eight to ten p.m., with half an hour at the end for free discussion. Charles Grenville was appeased through his election to the Chair: and Barbara Low became Secretary. Under their and Dora's guidance, a whole range of fascinating lectures were arranged, even if Grenville's on "Thought Mists – Some Earthly Suggestions" was somewhat obscure. Birnstingl lectured on "Interpretations of Life," Selwyn Watson, an anarchist, on "Ideas of Freedom," Guy Aldred "Sex Oppression and the Way Out," Mrs. Havelock Ellis "Some Problems

---

[1] *The Freewoman*, 28 March 1912.
[2] Dora Marsden to Charles Grenville, 29 April 1912. See also *The Freewoman*, 2 May 1912.

of Eugenics," Mrs. Gallichan "The Problems of Celibacy" and Charles Drysdale on "Neo-Malthusianism." Other talks were held on Prostitution, the Abolition of Domestic Drudgery (Rona Robinson) and Divorce. Barbara Low and others realized these huge subjects could only be touched on in one evening and suggested that smaller groups might wish to carry the discussion on in members' homes. Low even hoped that the Circle would one day have its own meeting house[1].

Though largely a discussion group, some members wanted action, suggesting an "Actionist Group" in June[2]. Others felt a synopsis of the talk should appear in the issue of the paper that preceded the meeting. The success of the scheme was obvious as the reaction to Guy Aldred's lecture on "Sex Oppression and The Way Out" illustrates. Typically arriving late, Aldred enthralled the audience, his main point being "that the existing social system, whose centre is the family, must be overturned before man can be freed from sex oppression, which is mainly due to the family system and the economic system[3]." So successful was this meeting that the discussion, with twenty-eight people, was continued at the home of the photographer, G. C. Beresford. Here the benefits of smaller groups became apparent to Barbara Low who argued that "much which is impossible in the large meetings can be achieved in the sub-groups. It is in the development of local sub-groups that the most useful work of the Circle, probably, can be done." Low

---

[1] *The Freewoman*, 13 June 1912.
[2] *The Freewoman*, 27 June 1912.
[3] *The Freewoman*, 11 July 1912.

even offered her own house with room for twelve[1].

The Circle was a marvellous innovation and a great triumph for *The Freewoman* and its subscribers. It was certainly welcomed by readers eager to escape their feeling of isolation and who wanted to share their views with others. Laura Greenland probably expressed the opinion of many when she wrote to Dora that she was "anxious to meet with people of 'freer' views on social and moral questions[2]," though others were still apprehensive about such an open discussion. Caroline M. Boord, an original and perceptive contributor to the paper, expressed her shyness to be among such "clever people" yet overcame this and became involved. "You cannot have any idea," she wrote to Dora, "of the absolute lack of opportunity for mental development I have had since I married or indeed before[3]." The Circle encouraged debate, gave mutual support and was later crucial to the revival of the paper when it collapsed in the Autumn. It became a crucial focal point for a varied mixture of feminists, Socialists and anarchists whose vision of emancipation went beyond the question of women's suffrage and who wanted to address sexual as well as economic issues. As such, the Circles reflected on that small yet significant tradition within the Left that against all odds, struggled defiantly to search for and construe a New Life.

The Discussion Circle was not, however, without its tensions and personality clashes. Generally, members

---

[1]   *The Freewoman*, 25 July 1912.
[2]   Laura Greenland to Dora Marsden, 6 July 1912.
[3]   Caroline M. Boord to Dora Marsden, 3 May 1912.

behaved so well that Rebecca West felt it was like being in church[1]. But conflict did arise. For example, a row blew up in May between West and Barbara Low (later an educational psychologist) over the young anarchist and writer for *The Herald of Revolt*, Selwyn Watson. He had become treasurer of the Circle but disappeared, and was accused of absconding with the funds for he was in debt at the time. Low suspected West of having an affair with him and giving him shelter, all of which she reported to West's mother. Rebecca was horrified. "Barbara Low," she wrote to Dora, "ought to be hung, drawn and quartered... at any rate she left my mother with a confused idea of what my relations with Selwyn Watson were. What the blank blank does she mean[2]?" There was little love lost between the two women over this business, West feeling Low's articles were so poor that they were "enough to damn any paper," Low describing Rebecca as "that horrid woman[3]." There were other rivalries too, but on the whole the Discussion Circle was an outstanding triumph, providing both a meeting-place and a supportive centre for the paper's readers.

The pressure of work began to tell further on Dora and this was reflected in the decline in the lucidity of her own work and the increasing number of editorials by others. These were of varying quality, the best perhaps being C. H. Norman's "New Prostitution[4]" (which, of course, was about journalism), the worst Huntley Carter's "The Dances of the Stars." Carter wrote, as Re-

---

[1] Rebecca West to Dora Marsden, n.d., *c.* June 1912.
[2] Rebecca West to Dora Marsden, n.d., *c.* 25 May 1912.
[3] Rebecca West to Dora Marsden, n.d., *c.* June 1912.
[4] *The Freewoman*, 11 April 1912.

becca West and others noted, appalling dross which must have upset many readers. His article began "Man has lost the cosmic impulse and found a piano. He has become erect as an upright grand" and ended with the revelation that "Man will not be permitted to enter Heaven with a piano on his back[1]."

It can only be assumed that Dora was desperate when she published such drivel, though her own tastes had become more esoteric, embracing religion, philosophy and anarchism as well as feminism. Editorials on "Creation and Immortality," "Concerning the Idea of God" and "The Servile State[2]" appeared whose only link appeared to be Marsden's individualism. Crucially, a review of Max Stirner's *The Ego and His Own*, a seminal and aggressive work on individualistic anarchism, also appeared at this time[3]. This clearly impressed her and its significance is discussed in the following chapter. At this time – 1912 – Dora Marsden's thoughts were in a state of flux, so much so that some readers began to complain of her apparent lack of both clarity and direction. H. G. Wells, who we have seen admired Dora, was even moved to complain to her that he "did not believe you have any constructive ideas at all in your head[4]." Wells' frustration was perhaps understandable but this comment was a little exaggerated and unfair.

What was happening in the Summer of 1912 was that Dora was developing her ideas, retaining her inter-

---

[1] *The Freewoman*, 26 September 1912.
[2] *The Freewoman*, 6 June 1912.
[3] *The Freewoman*, 8 August 1912.
[4] *The Freewoman*, 5 September 1912.

est in feminism but taking in the influence of philosophy, religion and to some extent anarchism too. After all, to her it was not such a great intellectual or political leap to move from an analysis of the powerlessness of women to the powerlessness of *all* individuals. Thus Dora began to demand the liberation of all individuals and while a feminist review to her was justified in 1911 it was, a year later, no longer so. Thus *The Freewoman – A Weekly Feminist Review* became *The Freewoman – A Weekly Humanist Review* on 23 May 1912.

Not all readers welcomed this change, regarding it as an important shift away from feminism and an examination of the specific oppression of women. Her call for freedom became directed at both men and women, though a feminist angle remained. Thus, "The Immorality of the Marriage Contract" claimed marriage was immoral because it was a "deliberate abrogation of freedom... a repudiation of freedom." The law was only concerned "with the rights of maintenance on the one hand and rights concerning sexual intercourse on the other." For women, marriage was made even more immoral as it took control of the production of children away from them and tended also to make wives dependent on their men. Indeed, "the marriage contract becomes responsible for the debasing of female human beings to the level of common merchandise which we call prostitution. It is small wonder that Marriage is one of the institutions whose dissolution is already at hand[1]." Dora gave no indication of how the institution of marriage was to be dissolved other than by example, presumably by "Free-

---

[1] *The Freewoman*, 20 June 1912.

women" like herself. "Moral institutions," she exclaimed with more than a hint of elitism, "are dissolved not by the multitude, but by the higher moral consciousness of the few. A handful of moral, thinking articulate freewomen are more than the multitude of the unmoral, inarticulate band. In these things the battle is decided by rank and not by numbers[1]."

Other readers were more realistic in their demands, making comments and prescriptions based on the lives and experiences of the "inarticulate band." Perhaps the best example of this were the lucid articles by the radical suffragist, Ada Neild Chew. She was an avid reader of the paper, and realizing "that *The Freewoman* is too poor to pay[2]," offered her work free. Though she feared, unnecessarily, that they were badly written, as they were scribbled down on trains as she travelled around the North in her role as organizer for the NUWSS, they make stimulating and telling reading. They also strengthened and reemphasized the feminist current within the paper.

Ada's main point was that the emancipation of women depended on their gaining economic independence and rejecting the idea that their natural, lifelong vocation was domestic and maternal. Though sometimes worried about what her friends' reaction might be, she wrote that "a married woman dependent on her husband earns her living by her sex." She continued in slightly

---

1.   *The Freewoman*, 18 July 1912. Does this not have some uncomfortable similarity with Emmeline and Christabel Pankhursts' elitism, so vehemently criticized by Marsden?
2.   Ada Neild Chew to Grace Jardine, 24 June 1912.

less controversial vein: "Why, in the name of reason and common sense, should we condemn a mother to be a life-long parasite because she has had one or more babies to care for?" Ada wanted a national childcare system but noted that this burden decreased once a woman's daughter or son entered school. "And yet we still speak and act as though the 'duties of wife and mother' lasted from the moment a girl baby was born until she dies seventy years later, a great grandmother." More realistic than Dora, Ada conceded that "age-old habits, either of mind or body, are not changed in a day" but to change, women must go out to work and organize, and be no longer "content to fritter their lives away as domestic 'drudge' or 'ornaments[1].'"

The controversial discussions surrounding sexuality also continued within the paper. Not surprisingly, this led to fierce opposition. Mrs. Humphrey Ward even wrote to *The Times* warning readers that *The Freewoman* represented "the dark and dangerous side of the Woman's Movement." Though she conceded it was written well by "women of high education and conscious ability," she condemned its advocacy of "motherhood outside marriage... [and] complete freedom of union, under the guidance of passion between men and women[2]." This was at least good publicity and was in any case motivated by Ward's anti-suffragism. However, leading suffragists also fell over themselves trying to distance themselves from *The Freewoman*; it was Agnes Maude Royden, a leading member of the NUWSS who

[1] *The Freewoman*, 18 June 1912.
[2] *The Times*, 19 June 1912.

dubbed it a "nauseous publication[1]." More serious than the correspondence in *The Times*, was the ban by the distributors, W. H. Smith. In September 1912 they withdrew the paper from their shops because "the nature of certain articles which have been appearing lately are such as to render the paper unsuitable to be exposed on the bookstalls for general sale[2]."

This ban was in part due to the discussion on sex, yet in reality it was politically motivated. Dora thought so. "The animosity we rouse," she argued in the 5 September 1912 issue, "is not roused on the subject of sex discussion. It is aroused on the question of capitalism. The opposition in the capitalist press only broke out when we began to make it clear that the way out of the sex problem was through the door of the economic problem." *The Freewoman* was, and appeared to be, a revolutionary paper and a threat to the economic as well as sexual status quo. It was also a child of the revolutionary times and in Lord Percy's words, part of the "violent agitation against all law and order," which stood in "direct defiance of all authority, human and divine[3]."

Percy and others thought *The Freewoman* was a socialist weekly but even though Socialists contributed regularly this was inaccurate, if only because the paper never officially adopted a single political stance. Much of the debate in the paper was influenced by Socialism but increasingly by Syndicalism and anarchism too. All of these currents reflected the revolutionary situation

[1]   *The Times*, 19 June 1912.
[2]   *The Freewoman*, 5 September 1912.
[3]   *The Morning Post*, 24 July 1912.

that existed in Britain just before the First World War. This is still a matter of historical debate but the early 1900s were surely a time of crisis, and from 1910 onwards, of open and militant class struggle. The relative decline in the economy, due in part to competition from abroad and the refusal to re-invest profits in Britain, was a key factor in creating this conflict. It led ultimately to a fall in the value of real wages, increased unemployment and even sharper divisions of wealth, as exposed by Booth, Rowntree, London and others[1]. The Edwardian Golden Age did not shine equally on everyone and the benefits of the wealth created by the many both at home and overseas were only shared by the few. As Kendall so graphically puts it, "wealth, luxury and indolence was restricted to a small section of society, a well-to-do stratum of society poised above an abyss of poverty, misery and discontent[2]."

Fuelled by the growth of revolutionary Socialism (which in itself was due in part to the inadequacies of the Parliamentary Labour Party) all this resulted in a violent class struggle. From 1910 onwards major sections of the economy – in the docks, the mines, and in transport – were hit, and hit hard, by strike action. In 1912 alone, the year of *The Freewoman*, 38 million working days were lost due to industrial action. One result of this was a polarization of the classes and a naked and vicious conflict between the state and the workers. Many were injured and some died during this struggle which ar-

---

[1] For a further discussion of this see Garner, p. 8-9.
[2] Kendall (1969), p. 24. *Plus ça change, plus c'est la même chose.* The UK 2018.

guably was only suppressed by the outbreak of war in September 1914[1].

Liberal England, especially when the political controversies of Ireland, the House of Lords and women's suffrage are taken into account, was in turmoil. The growth of revolutionary Socialism, the rapid expansion of Syndicalism with its emphasis on the use of a General Strike against capitalism and the more radical elements of the feminist movement created a revolutionary ferment which was reflected in the pages of *The Freewoman*.

Arthur D. Lewis, author of a recent book on Syndicalism and a journalist on the *Daily Herald*, often wrote in the paper. In his attacks on orthodox suffragism and Malthusianism, he constantly stressed that "the dull questions of food and hours of labour are at present the most important questions... what has to be attacked is the private ownership of land and capital and the unequal distribution of the products arising from their use[2]." Isabel Leatham too stressed that Socialism was the only way to guarantee the emancipation of women. Only when "the State has charge of all the national assets and the wealth of the community is properly organised" will this be achieved. Yet she realized that "it

---

[1] Kendall (1969); also Dangerfield (1970); Ensor (1936); Halévy (1952). Many thousands of militant workers were to be slaughtered on the killing fields of the Western Front. Yet radical class action increasingly surfaced as the senseless war continued – in Sylvia Pankhurst's East End, the mining villages of Wales and famously the Red Clyde of Scotland. Emmeline and Christabel Pankhurst of course condemned all such actions as unpatriotic.

[2] *The Freewoman*, 11 January 1912. In the same year he wrote *Syndicalism and The General Strike / An Explanation*.

would be possible to have Socialism with only a shadow of freedom for women" but added that "the complete emancipation of women would be impossible without it[1]."

There was also a strong anarchist and Syndicalist input with contributions, among others, from Lily Gair Wilkinson, Rose Witcup, Selwyn Watson, Guy Bowman and the leading figure in British anarchism, Guy Aldred[2]. Both Bowman, editor of *The Syndicalist* and Aldred, editor of *The Herald of Revolt*, were keen to promote *The Freewoman*. "I think your paper deserves to succeed," Aldred wrote to Dora. "I will use my influence in the anarchist movement to this end[3]." He was also willing to defend it when prosecution seemed likely in the summer of 1912. "Should you ever have to call upon me to stand by *The Freewoman* in time of danger, you may rely on *my doing* so. I like political danger[4]." By this time, Guy, Dora and Grace had developed a less formal relationship, and Aldred had invited them on more than one occasion to his home in Shepherd's Bush where he lived with Rose Witcup. The flavour of his alternative lifestyle was illustrated in his first invitation when he assured them that they "would enjoy things. For we are all friends who live in Bohemia. I do not mean we should have special company for the occa-

---

[1] *The Freewoman*, 21 March 1912.
[2] *The Freewoman*, 11 January 1912. In the same year Arthur D. Lewis wrote *Syndicalism and The General Strike / An Explanation*. Wilkinson was the author of *Revolutionary Socialism and the Women's Movement* (Glasgow: Socialist Labor Party 1910) and *Women's Freedom* (London: Freedom Press 1914).
[3] Guy Aldred to Dora Marsden, 23 January 1912.
[4] Guy Aldred to Grace Jardine, 22 July 1912.

sion... only that my friend, Miss Witcup and myself, whilst believing in freedom and being chums rather than anything else, without being indifferent to each other, live without restraint[1]." Bowman too joined in the anarchist vogue for cordiality, inviting Grace, Dora and Rebecca West for tea in September. He later described *The Freewoman* as "the best feminist paper published... it was the only non-syndicalist paper that understood and could appreciate syndicalist principles[2]."

Aldred, as described above, became an active member of the Discussion Circle and a regular contributor to the paper. He wrote in *The Herald of Revolt* that "the whole tenor of this excellent journal [*The Freewoman*] is Anarchistic": some of his articles appeared in both papers. He would have preferred to write more but he did at least outline some basic aspects of syndicalism and he used *The Freewoman* to defend fellow anarchists. Not surprisingly though, most of his articles in Dora's paper were concerned with women's freedom. In a blistering attack on the WSPU and suffragism, Aldred argued that "it is a woman's duty to be freely equal with man." Suffragists were not seeking genuine emancipation, while "the trouble with militant tactics" he wrote of the WSPU "is that they lack a militant aim." Women ought to "regard man as chum, to insist on her right to be a mother, because of her sex and not of her 'responsibility,' to have some special man friend without losing her identity, to insist on the power of knowledge as knowledge, on the might of Truth standing alone – this is to be

---

[1]   Guy Aldred to Grace Jardine, 22 July 1912.
[2]   Guy Bowman to Dora Marsden, 11 September 1912.

emancipated[1]."

Dora Marsden certainly sympathized with calls for revolutionary change, feeling that "violent or peaceful, the revolution must come[2]." However, it is difficult to categorize her own political position partly because it was continually evolving throughout 1912 and 1913 and also because of the obtuseness of her style, which was carried to appalling lengths during her editorship of *The Egoist*. She was certainly sympathetic to some of Aldred's and Bowman's ideas but it would be a mistake wholly to claim Dora, or indeed *The Freewoman*, for anarchism. None the less, she would have been content in 1912 to be described as revolutionary and anti-capitalist, though from an extremely individual and individualistic point of view.

During the dock strike of 1912, for example, Dora claimed that "the sale of labour is the basis of immorality: it is the contradiction of freedom and the basis of capitalism[3]." The dockers were described as "struggling against the most complete slave system known to the history of the world – a universal slavery of wage earners to capitalists[4]." Fighting for the vote was ludicrous, as was any kind of parliamentary action, for:

---

[1] *The Freewoman*, 8 February 1912.
[2] *The Freewoman*, 6 June 1912.
[3] *The Freewoman*, 6 June 1912.
[4] *The Freewoman*, 20 June 1912.

in any community the politics of the community are a mere superstructure, built upon the economic base ... even though Mr. George Lansbury were Prime Minister and every seat in the House occupied by Socialist deputies, the capitalist system being what it is they would be powerless to effect anything more than the slow paced 'reform' of which the sole aim is to make 'men and masters' settle down in a comfortable but unholy alliance... The capitalists own the states. A handful of private capitalists could make England, or any other country, bankrupt within a week.

Marsden did not consider the revolutionary possibilities of a Socialist government at Westminster alongside equally revolutionary extra-parliamentary action, but she was convinced that voting and legislation were not enough. "The kingdom of heaven has to be seized by force. A cross on a ballot paper will not do the deed[1]."

Dora was emotionally as well as politically drawn to Syndicalism, welcoming its rejection of parliamentary strategies and its emphasis on spontaneous insurrection. In particular, she warmly greeted the revolutionary sentiments in "The Miners' Next Step," published by the South Wales Miners' Federation[2]. This called for a strike in the coal industry and hoped for a more widespread insurrection that would destroy capitalism itself. At this point, Dora was content to describe herself as among the most ardent supporters of the Syndicalists in England. Yet she did not fully accept Syndicalism, for though "we welcome Syndicalism as a method as a final theory our

---

[1] *The Freewoman*, 8 August 1912.
[2] *The Miners' Next Step*, published by the Unofficial Reform Committee of the South Wales Miners Federation, 1912.

views are different[1]."

Dora's "final theory" is difficult to define but it did embrace some elements of anarchism, particularly in its attitude to the state. She explained this in April in "A Servile State." This she described as "a community of which the people are willing to be governed by an external authority for their own good[2]." Allied to this was an aggressive individualism that could be traced back to "Bondwomen" and was furthered by her reading of Stirner. Thus, just as women should not seek the protection of men, individuals should not seek the protection of the state: in both cases it was a denial of freedom and responsibility. Indeed, the responsibility for oppression lay with the individual, or in Dora's memorable phrase: "the person who is responsible for the tyrant is the slave, the person who is responsible for the selfish man is the unselfish man. It is indecent for the slavish to make tyrants and then whine about the result[3]."

Quite clearly, Marsden's position could not be located within Socialism whether of the then fledgling Labour Party or of the more revolutionary kind. "A 'Labour Party' sniffling for 'reform,'" she wrote in September, "for 'arbitration,' for 'nationalisation' and *all by means of the vote*, is a sight before which one would swiftly veil one's eyes[4]." Socialism as a collective theory was, to her, inextricably anti-individual, anti-liberty and would inevitably create a bureaucratic and oppres-

---

[1]   *The Freewoman*, 8 August 1912.
[2]   *The Freewoman*, 18 April 1912.
[3]   *The Freewoman*, 12 September 1912.
[4]   *The Freewoman*, 12 September 1912.

sive state. And to Dora, "a bureaucracy, whether composed of elected representatives in a Parliament, or of elected officers and committees in a vast industrial organisation, constituting a 'government' of masses of men and women is inimical, is contradictory to the full growth of a free people. Socialism, in short, is an impossible form of society save with a servile people." Moreover, "socialism is as immoral as Capitalism... the time is now come when there must be a definite parting of the ways between Individualism and Socialism – when Socialism must be fought as ardently as Capitalism is fought. Indeed, it must be made clear that they are one and the same thing[1]."

Dora's confusion over the alleged similarity of Socialism and capitalism at least illustrated the weaknesses of both her own position and indeed, of anarchism too. How individual liberty was to be gained and guaranteed without the collective ownership and organization of production was never explained. All rested on individual action and the ability of the individual to maintain "his free will [and] his power to follow the inner 'voice' – his only law[2]." Each person must become his or her own master and to this "men and women must have property so that they are not dependent on others." Socialism and Communism, by socializing property for all, prevented this and was thus immoral. Thus "we have no objection to private property; in fact we think it is a necessity, now

---

[1]   *The Freewoman*, 29 August 1912. A classic anarchist view, clearly not shared by myself, that both capitalism and socialism in relying on the State and infringing on individual autonomy, were equally repressive and denied freedom.
[2]   *The Freewoman*, 29 August 1912.

and in the future. We are not communists; we are individualists, and as such find communism an abrogation of, and an intrusion upon, something which is the essence of ourselves[1]."

Dora was sympathetic to revolutionary struggle, particularly what she regarded as the "anarchist, insurrectionist, individualist" nature of Syndicalism. But here she was troubled by its "floundering about with theories of communism" and its demand for some political and industrial organization[2]. Further, she was concerned that, like Socialism and Communism, Syndicalism accepted the need for modern techniques of production. Dora condemned "the machine age" as a further abrogation of individual freedom and she looked forward to a productive system that was based on the use of tools, owned and used solely by their owners. Machines were depersonalizing, demanded servility and were thus immoral[3].

Apart from the fact that *The Freewoman* itself could not have been published without the aid of printing machinery, all this reflected Dora's thinking at its worst. She could not convincingly explain how individuals were to create her machine-less Golden Age or how it would work when it finally dawned. Her whole position relied on intuition (from where?) and a very personal view of morality based on the "soul of Man." It did not explain how conflict would be resolved, or how the weak would be protected or how resources would be organized and distributed other than on a basis of force

---

[1]   *The Freewoman*, 8 August 1912.
[2]   *The Freewoman*, 12 September 1912.
[3]   *The Freewoman*, 22 August 1912.

and strength. It was, of course, connected to her own experience and individual success, yet this on its own hardly constituted conclusive proof of her increasingly odd and quirky theories.

By the autumn of 1912, Dora's views were confusing friend and foe alike, and she felt compelled to write an editorial on "The Policy of *The Freewoman*" in September. This was an attempt to stem the flood of criticism that had begun to spill onto the paper. H. G. Wells, for example, complained to Dora:

> that you do not know what you want in economic and social organization, that the wild cry for freedom which makes me so sympathetic with your paper, and which echoes through every column of it, is unsupported by the ghost of a shadow of an idea how to secure freedom. What is the good of writing that 'economic arrangements will have to be adjusted to the Soul of Man' if you are not prepared with anything remotely resembling a suggestion of how the adjustment is to be affected[1]?

Rachel East, alias Rebecca West, who was just getting to know her future lover Wells, followed up the novelist's attack with mordant criticism of her own. In particular, she ridiculed Dora's machine-less return-to-the-land proposals as impractical. She preferred cooperation and Socialism, and ended mockingly, "Do you think that you will get artists and scientists to produce art and science in the evenings when they have got the asparagus patch on their minds[2]?"

---

[1]   *The Freewoman*, 5 September 1912.

[2]   *The Freewoman*. See also *Time and Tide*, 16 July 1926 for West's account of this argument. Rebecca West, alias Rachel East alias Cicely Fairfield was fond of *nom-de-plumes*. She took the first initially to

Dora's reply to West and Wells was far from satisfactory. She reiterated her opposition to government and claimed rather hazily that only the "soul of Man" can be "the final authority." Machines were morally indefensible and East (West) put far too much faith in agricultural specialists. Land could easily be obtained through an English equivalent of the Irish Land Act or by the force of arms of free individuals. All this was to be achieved through free will: "The core of our religion and our ethics," she concluded, "is the freedom of the will and no socialism... can square with this theory of free will[1]."

Dora's reply was muddied further by the desperate lack of clarity in her style. This in turn probably reflected the strain she was under, especially in the autumn of 1912. Her prose was marvellously parodied by a subscriber, C. E. Bechofer, in *The New Age*. In a satirical sketch Bechofer wrote, in "Freewoman and Politics":

> With reference to the account to and what making exception leads us poor women as we though not so bad as it might be are to deal with politics at all is that we will broke no argument, for none is fitting, denied when all the facts are known. Be that as it were our readers will instantly agree, within all such limits being the same...[2]

Dora could have easily shrugged off such lighthearted fun, but perhaps not the next salvo from Mary Gawthorpe. In September, Mary was forced at last to retaliate and attack Dora personally, and though still ex-

---

shield the fact that she was writing for such an immoral and disgusting paper from her mother.

[1] *Time and Tide*, 16 July 1926.
[2] *The New Age*.

pressing some concern for her, this row was final. It also illustrated major weaknesses in Dora's political position. The argument began over the force feeding of the suffragette Mary Leigh. Gawthorpe condemned this and called for the Home Secretary's resignation, whereas Dora felt Leigh's treatment was inevitable, as all government rests on coercion and force. Replacing one Home Secretary with another would make little difference. It was for individuals to seize power for themselves and to then use it to exercise their own free will.

Mary asked the obvious yet simple question in reply – what happened when one individual's action, based on his or her own free will, affects the free will and action of another? Presumably the stronger wins or, by implication, laws of restraint and thus government are required. Further, Mary ridiculed Dora's description of herself as "a philosophical anarchist" for she "was not really an anarchist at all" but one who believed in rank, with herself at the top. "Intellectually," Mary wrote, "you have signed on as a member of the coming aristocracy. Free individuals you would have us be, but you would have us in our ranks." To Mary, who of course knew Dora and her style of work better than most, the editor of *The Freewoman* did not even behave like an anarchist. "I watch you from week to week governing your paper. You have your subordinates. You say to one go and she goes, to another come, and she comes[1]."

---

[1] *The Freewoman*, 26 September 1912. Stephen T. Byington, an American anarchist, tried at least to resolve some of these issues in a debate, discussed below, in *The New Freewoman*.

Dora must have been hurt by this though she had courageously decided to publish Mary's letter in the correspondence section of the paper. Mary must have realized this for although she too had been hurt, she sent Dora a letter three days later which was full of concern, even of affection. Their relationship, as described above, had gone through irreparable damage and now their political differences were irreconcilable, yet Mary could not completely overcome her feelings for Dora, especially during this time of strain when the paper was on the point of closing. Mary again reiterated her plea to keep *The Freewoman* along feminist lines but was primarily concerned with Dora's health. "You remember from the outset," Mary wrote, "my understanding anxieties for your health's sake, in the conducting of a weekly paper and your warm rejoinder that you were no fool? You were not, and are not. But you are a very tired and overstrained person and you must have rest or your paper will die not from lack of sales but from something else." Mary was in effect implying that her erstwhile friend, through worry and overwork, was on the verge of a breakdown. "To any practical psychologist the signs are many and definite; the diagnosis is certain; the remedy plain." The cure, to Mary, was peace and quiet, for without this "the real Dora Marsden will never come into her own. The real Dora Marsden is a poet and the sooner you realise this aspect of yourself the better[1]."

Unfortunately, Dora did not secure the tranquility she obviously needed, and the paper finally collapsed,

---

[1]   Mary Gawthorpe to Dora Marsden, 29 September 1912.

the last issue being on the 10 October. Grenville had refused to back the paper and the last issue only appeared due to the generosity of G. C. Beresford. Dora realized the paper needed sound backing but was not unduly pessimistic about a re-launch in the near future. However, she did publicly recognize what a great personal strain it had been:

> The editorial work has not been easy. We have been hemmed in on every side by lack of funds. We have, moreover, been promoting a constructive creed, which had not only to be erected as we went along, we had also to deal with the controversy which this constructive creed left in its wake... The entire campaign has been carried on indeed only at the cost of a total expenditure of energy, and we, therefore, do not hold it possible to continue the same amount of work, with diminished resources , if in addition, we have to bear the entire anxiety of securing such resources as are to be at our disposal. If *The Freewoman* is to be resumed, the financial burden must be separated from the editorial[1].

Dora Marsden's *Freewoman* had lasted just eleven months and its influence must not be exaggerated. Perhaps it did only cater for "a clever set of young men and women[2]," perhaps its major function, as Rebecca West put it over sixty years later, was to provide a home for "a bunch of cranks[3]." On the other hand, an appreciation of its limitations should not obscure its importance. It

---

[1] *The Freewoman*, 10 October 1912.
[2] *The New Freewoman* circular, n.d., *c.* summer 1913.
[3] West to Garner, 30 August 1977. In her *Time and Tide* article written in 1926 West was far more complimentary, claiming for example that *The Freewoman* had "an immense effect on its time." *Time and Tide*, 16 July 1926.

began by exposing the limitations of orthodox suffragism and provided an outlet for the discussion of more radical feminist views that went far and beyond a simple demand for a vote. It exposed the political weaknesses of suffragism and in particular, the flawed strategy of the WSPU. Yet it also showed the ideological potential of suffragism – the debate about the vote led, in many cases, to much more thoughtful analysis of the oppression of women. Thus women's roles, sexuality, marriage and morality all came under scrutiny in a way that would not be misplaced in the 1980s, let alone 1911 and 1912. As such, *The Freewoman* in this light acts as testimony to one radical aspect of the British feminist tradition, so long overlooked by mainstream history, and for so long too, overshadowed by the suffragettes and the WSPU.

As *The Freewoman* developed, it attracted Socialists, anarchists, Syndicalists and, as Dora had suggested, it became a "mirror of thought" not only for feminism but other radical currents too. This was reflected in the cross-over with other radical journals and writers. Aldred, Witcup, Bowman and Watson were prominent in the anarchist and Syndicalist press, while many writers in *The Freewoman*, such as West, Lewis and J. M. Kennedy, contributed to the *Socialist Daily Herald* too. There was also a marked connection with *The New Age* and Dora even copied its style and format. Huntley Carter, Edmund B. D'Auvergne, C. J. Whitby, C. H. Norman, Mary Willcocks and Mary Gawthorpe were all regular contributors to both papers. *The New Age* was also concerned with the arts and literature which West and Gawthorpe wanted *The Freewoman* to pursue too. This issue and the literary contacts between the two papers became significant when Dora's journal was relaunched in 1913. When the work of writers like Carpenter and Browne is taken into account, it becomes evident that *The Freewoman* in its short life, became a meeting-place for a remarkable if diverse group of radicals and revolutionaries who wanted to examine and change the Edwardian moral, sexual, economic and political status quo.

On the other hand, the eclectic nature of the discussion in *The Freewoman* resulted in a loss of direction as Wells and West and others noticed, particularly as Dora retreated into her own individualistic philosophy. In a way, this meant that *The Freewoman* became less and less distinctively feminist; indeed it described itself as "A Weekly Humanist Review" on 23 May 1912. This may well have surprised some of its readers and supporters, yet Dora had made her position clear as early as the second issue, on 30 November 1911. Here she described feminism as:

> concerned with the readjustment of the balance of sex relationships, which has been rendered necessary by the age long acceptance of Masculinism... a theory which acknowledges the domination of men in sex relationships and in all various activities... we regard feminism not as a final doctrine, but as a temporary theory of expedients and readjustments. Masculinism and Feminism are relative terms, and when one is strong enough to equate the other, both will become merged in a common doctrine of Humanism.

Whether she thus thought "feminism" and "masculinism" were equal by May 1912 is unclear.

Finally, *The Freewoman* was, of course, a remarkable testimony to the drive, persistence and talent of Dora Marsden. Clearly, both the editor and the paper were children of contemporary political movements yet Dora's personal contribution and achievement must not be understated. She hustled and pushed in 1911, never giving up as one and then another backer withdrew, and then worked herself to a standstill to keep the paper alive. She would publish material deemed untouchable by others and encouraged free debate even if this included outright denunciation of her own opinions. She fought for the paper for eleven months against bans, threats of prosecution and even the loss of loving friends like Mary Gawthorpe.

But if the creation and life of *The Freewoman* showed Dora's positive qualities, her own writings reflected her faults and weaknesses too. The clearest of these were elitism, arrogance and, at times, bullying over-confidence in the validity of her own views. These became less and less defensible as the acute critique of women's powerlessness in "Bondwomen" for example, developed into a general analysis of power within society as a whole. Influenced by anarchism in general and Max Stirner in particular, this degenerated into an extreme yet woolly individualism that, as Gawthorpe, West and others realized was full of contradiction and assertion, relying totally on intangibles like "will," "intuition" and "the Soul of Man." It constituted an individualism that could not recognize the need for collective action to secure liberty for all or the subsequent need for the collective ownership and organization of society's resources in order to preserve it. In this, she perhaps shared the weaknesses of some strands of anarchist thought.

Of course, Marsden's lack of social vision and her individualism was intertwined with her own life and character. Perhaps she had achieved a kind of liberation and autonomy as editor of *The Freewoman*, but it was still difficult to envisage how her own philosophy could be easily applied to others, for example Ada Neild Chew's sisters in the Lancashire cotton towns, or Sylvia Pankhurst's followers in the East End[1]. But by 1912, apart from the Discussion Circles, Dora was no longer involved in direct political work or organization and was, to be harsh, content to assume the role of "the intellectual," to become in Gawthorpe's words "a member of the coming aristocracy." Such isolation has its political and personal dangers, yet in the end Dora Marsden still deserves immense credit for founding and maintaining *The Freewoman*, at great personal cost. "We cannot believe that our common efforts have been wasted," she wrote in the last issue of 10 October 1912; the fading papers of *The Freewoman* in the British Library are permanent testimony they were not.

---

[1] Sylvia Pankhurst had split from her mother and sister in 1914 to form the East London Federation of Suffragettes. This worked with working-class women of the East End and eventually became a Socialist organization.

The New Freewoman, June – December 1913

THE NEW

FREEWOMAN

AN INDIVIDUALIST REVIEW

Published on the 1st and 15th of each month.

No. 1. Vol. 1.   JUNE 15, 1913.   SIXPENCE NET

CONTENTS

Edited by
DORA MARSDEN, B.A.

THE LEAN KIND.

This is the epoch of the gadding mind. The mind 'not at home' but given to something else, occupied with alien 'causes' is of the normal order, and as such must be held accountable for that contemning of the lonely occupant of the home—the Self—which is the characteristic of the common mind. With the lean kind—the antithesis of those 'Fat' with whom latterly we have become so familiarised—the most embarrassing notion is that of the possession of a self having wants. To be selfless is to have attained unto that condition of which leanness is the fitting outcome. Hence, the popularity of the 'Cause' which provides the Idol to which the desired self-sacrifice can be offered. The greater the sacrifice the Idol can accept the greater is it as a 'Cause', whether it be liberty, equality, fraternity, honesty or what not. If ten thousand starving men, with their tens of thousands of dependants, starve in the Cause of Honesty, how great is Honesty! If a woman throws away her life for freedom, how great is freedom! And no mistake.

'Great is the Cause and small are men,' is the creed of the lean kind. Consider the Cause of Honesty—the righteous frenzy for the maintenance of the status quo in regard to property. True it is that all worshippers of honesty have no property, but what of that: the greater the sacrifice: good is it to be a vessel of dishonest if thereby is achieved the greater glory of the Cause.

It is true one may choose one's 'Cause' but choice appears to fall fairly uniformly into classes, and as for the lean kind, they choose honesty. Poor but honest,' is the lean one's epitaph. He makes it his honour to see to it that property shall remain just so.' He will fight and die and play policeman with zeal that property should remain just so! There have been those, however, who have maintained that 'Property was theft.' Monsieur Proudhon said so, and Monsieur Shaw supports him. 'The only true thing which has been said about property,' says Mr.

Shaw. We—and the lean—beg leave to dissent, what though in dissenting, we differ. The lean scout the base notion, for where would the Cause, Honesty be if horribly it should prove true? It is therefore not true for the lean. And for us? If the pick and the shovel are the discovered gold, then property is theft. But if the shovel and pick be as a means to an end—the acquiring of gold—then theft is to property in the same relation. Theft is the time-honoured, success-crowned means to property. All the wholesale acquirements of property have come, do come, will come, in this way. Whether Saxon robs Celt, and Dane robs Saxon, and Norman robs all three: whether William Shortlegs robs the English to give property to his fellow-bandits, or bandits, grown bolder, rob the Church for themselves, or the Trust-maker robs whom he will, the process is one and the same. A constant state of flux (Oh, Cause of Honesty!) flux of property, from hands which yield into hands which seize! Small wonder the lean kind love not this truth, and cover their eyes with their Cause. Hands which seize are not their kind of hands; the spirit of their Cause makes the muscles relax and the grip grow feeble.

Property once seized, the seizers set about to make flux static. They declare a truce. They send forth a proclamation: *Henceforth the possessed—we and our children—must remain possessors; and the dispossessed remain the dispossessed—for ever. These shall not raise disturbing hands against the state of things: should they, the STATE will visit upon them the penalties due.' Yet notice: In the process of proclamation, the victors have taken the proclamation for the deed; they have not merely said 'this state, now established, shall remain,' they have said, without pause for breath, 'this shall be' and 'this is.' The State now is—and we are the State. And so it turns out. The dispossessed—the lean—make answer: You—great conquerors, as you say, so it is.' The STATE

I rejoice beyond all measure in the revival of *The Freewoman*. Its policy even at its worst was a wholesome weekly irritant.

H. G. Wells, *New Freewoman* Circular, *c*. 1913.

The Freewoman did so well during its short career under your editorship, it was so broad-minded and courageous that its cessation has been a real loss to the cause of free and rational discussion of human problems.

E. Carpenter, *ibid.*

The New Freewoman will prepare for the future. It will educate women and men to think in terms of true freedom, and show them that real individuality exists apart from all our accepted standards.

Winnifred W. Leisenring, *ibid.*

I consider your paper the most important publication in existence.

Benjamin R. Tucker, *ibid.*

A mere dumping ground for miscellaneous wits.

Benjamin R. Tucker, *New Freewoman*, December 1913.

The Max Stirner of Feminism.

Floyd Dell, *Women as World Builders*, 1913.

The Freewoman had only a small circulation and, as described above, it died before its first anniversary. Yet it had made a considerable impact both in Britain and the USA and the paper's importance surely lay beyond Payne-Townshend's view that it was merely a valuable outlet for smart men and women. For many, *The Freewoman*'s demise was a sad loss, deeply mourned by its more fervent supporters. However with their help, alongside the fearless and often arrogant determination of Dora Marsden, the paper was relaunched a mere eight months later; a remarkable achievement in itself.

Dora, overworked, often ill and suffering from the deterioration in her relationship with Mary Gawthorpe, had been shattered by *The Freewoman*'s collapse and, with Grace Jardine, soon left London for Southport to rest and recuperate with her mother. Until the very last, she had been hopeful that the paper would somehow survive and that any cessation of publication would be only temporary. Thus, the last issue of 12 October 1912 carried an appeal for support, asking readers to fill in an enclosed slip and return it to the editor. Eventually, forty-five readers did respond, including Theresa Billington-Greig, the author Reginald Wright Kauffman, Mrs. Bernard Shaw and, crucially, Harriet Shaw Weaver of Cedar Lawn, Hampstead.

The response, though, was disappointing. When the list and an appeal for donations was circulated to those on it in late 1912, its composition and size were frequently commented on. One reader, Grace Gladding, wrote: 'Your list surprises me. I imagined some hundreds of comparatively poor women who might contribute a little. I find some score only of (presumably) rich people, evidently able to contribute substantial sums.' She felt her donations to *The Daily Herald* were more important, though she still offered five Pounds[1]. Though some women on the list were wealthy and well known there was no doubting the feeling they all had for the paper. Lily Coppard, "only a working man's wife," enclosed two Pounds[2], while Lilian McErie probably summed up the views of the whole group when she declared: "No paper has given me keener pleasure than yours. Its fearlessness and fairness made all lovers and seekers after truth respect it and love it even while differing from many of the opinions expressed therein[3]."

The fierce loyalty of its supporters, however, was not enough to solve the problems associated with *The Freewoman*'s revival. First, a suitable publisher willing to take the economic and political risks of producing such a radical journal had to be found. Second, given its lack of normal sources of revenue, in particular from advertising, sufficient capital had to be provided to ensure the paper's stability. Third, reasonable and central offices in London had to be located. Alongside the communication and organizational problems created by Dora's removal to Southport, and Swift's contentious claim to the title *Freewoman*, these were indeed daunting obstacles. They could not have been overcome with-

---

[1] Grace Gladding to Dora Marsden, 3 November 1912.
[2] Lily Coppard to Dora Marsden, 5 November 1912.
[3] Lillian McCrie to Dora Marsden, 5 November 1912.

out a small yet crucial nucleus of women. Without the support and care of Hannah Marsden, the help of Grace Jardine, the pugnacity of Dora herself, the energetic canvassing of Rebecca West and, crucially, the capital, determination and organizational ability of Harriet Shaw Weaver, *The New Freewoman* would never have reappeared, certainly not by June 1913. Some men, for example, the contributor Edward Herrin, did help (in this case, by offering free legal advice) but the paper's relaunch, and its subsequent achievements, was largely a result of these women's efforts.

Harriet Shaw Weaver, who played such an important part in the birth of *The New Freewoman*, later becoming the Editor of its successor, *The Egoist*, was to become Dora's life-long friend and benefactor. She was a fascinating woman who led a remarkable life, as Jane Lidderdale and Mary Nicholson's admirable biography of her shows so well. Born into a respectable bourgeois family, Harriet Weaver hardly appeared to be destined to become involved with such controversial projects and people as Marsden, *The New Freewoman*, Joyce and *Ulysses*. From the 1890s onwards she lived in Hampstead in a large house, complete with servants, run by a strict mother and a kindly father who was a doctor and a local JP. However, her biographers record that a combination of her education and her social work encouraged Harriet towards more radical views. Her early influences came from her liberal governess, Marion Spooner, and her own, often secretive, reading. As a young woman she read, for example, Walt Whitman and J. S. Mill, including the latter's *On Liberty* and significantly, *On the*

Subjection of Women. One early incident in her life, when she was caught reading an unsuitable book about an unmarried mother, reflected the growing tension with her parents. It led to a row and the beginning of a conflict between her devotion to her respectable family and her own political convictions.

The latter were furthered in the 1900s by her growing involvement in social work in the East End. Here Weaver learned not only of the appalling conditions within the capital of one of the richest and most powerful nations in the world, but also developed her organizational skills which were to be subsequently so crucial to both Marsden and Joyce. She was influenced too by the teachings of E. J. Urwick, an economist and political philosopher, who attempted to combine individualism with a call for social justice. Significantly, perhaps, one of her tasks in Whitechapel at the time involved trying to train and find skilled work for promising boys and girls. For the first time, "she found scope for the interests and talents that had gradually become articulated: helping underdogs – or underpuppies – with brains to get the chance they deserved[1]." It was a talent that was soon to be stretched to the limit.

By 1912, when *The Freewoman* was in circulation and Harriet was thirty-six, she had become "a confirmed socialist[2]." She had also developed an interest in the position of women and feminism. Indeed, with her friend Eleanor Davies-Colley, she helped to found the London Hospital for Women and Children which was opened be-

---

[1]   Lidderdale and Nicholson, p. 38.
[2]   Lidderdale and Nicholson, p. 39.

fore the war. Harriet also joined the WSPU although she never took part in any direct action herself. In fact, she became dissatisfied with the suffragette leaders, realizing through her work in the East End that the vote was not the cure-all they claimed it to be. Along with others interested in feminism but dismayed by the Pankhursts, she warmed to *The Freewoman* and became a subscriber. She liked its free and open discussion and became a member of the Discussion Circle. Harriet probably saw Dora Marsden for the first time there although they did not formally meet until February 1913.

Their first contact came as a result of Harriet responding to the appeal in the last issue of *The Freewoman*. Dora wrote to thank her, adding: "We hope very shortly to be in a position to make a clear statement of our prospects and this will be at once forwarded to you[1]." It was the beginning of a relationship that was to lead to traumatic changes in Harriet's life. It was the beginning, too, of an unswervingly loyal friendship, often stretched to the utmost limit, which was to last until Dora's death some forty-eight years later.

Weaver, soon to be a major contributor of cash, and organizer in general of *The New Freewoman*, was, along with Rebecca West, vital to the paper's revival. At first though, both women had to work on their own in London. In Southport, Hannah Marsden's quiet support was essential to the restoration of her daughter's mental and physical health. Hannah, Dora and Grace, according to

---

[1] Dora Marsden to Harriet Shaw Weaver, 14 October 1912. The first letter of a correspondence that was to last for forty-eight years.

Grace, made up a "Happy household[1]" sewing and generally relaxing and recuperating. On her return to Southport, to a house sentimentally named "The Hey" in Hatfield Road, Ainsdale, Dora admitted that she had been "far from well and latterly I have had a return of the neurasthenia[2]." Her health was so bad that she had to "confess that for a short spell after leaving London my hopes of reviving *The Freewoman* rested only in the very distant future[3]." It is a tribute to Hannah Marsden's care that this feeling did not last long.

None the less while Dora was away the burden of work largely fell on Weaver and West. West had been introduced originally to Dora and *The Freewoman* through Mary Gawthorpe who Rebecca had met at a WSPU meeting. Rebecca was still a teenager in 1912, but had already made an impact in literary and socialist circles. Besides her contributions to *The Freewoman*, she was also a regular writer in the *Daily Herald* particularly on its "Women's World" series. In this, among other things, she called for communal homes and kitchens as well as for an improvement in the lot of working women in general. She also used the *Herald* to express her own dissatisfaction with the WSPU although she quickly tired of Dora's obsessional attacks on the Pankhursts. But her own feminism remained clear and strong. "Certainly we need rebellion," she wrote in the *Daily Herald*. "Unless woman is going to make trouble she had better not seek her emancipation[4]."

---

[1]   Quoted in Lidderdale and Nicholson, p. 55.
[2]   A general term that usually referred to fatigue, anxiety and depression.
[3]   Dora Marsden to Harriet Shaw Weaver, 2 December 1912.
[4]   *The Daily Herald*, 5 September 1912.

West's major contribution to *The New Freewoman*, however, was to act as a link between the Discussion Circle, still meeting after *The Freewoman*'s demise, and Marsden. In the winter of 1912 / 13 she continually pushed Dora for further information and a statement of policy for the Circle members who were becoming increasingly restless. "Do send me a statement of prospects which can be read to the assembled multitude," she urged, "for lots of people seem quite excited about the re-establishment of *The Freewoman*[1]." West herself wanted the paper to have more literary content, arguing that she could not see "why a movement towards freedom of expression in literature should not be associated with and inspired by your gospel[2]." Rebecca was also responsible for seeking statements of support and for raising money. Her work with the Circle, though, was affected by a lingering personality clash with its secretary, Barbara Low. Rebecca described her as "an honest soul" but "a horrid muddler who has wrecked this series of Discussion Circles[3]."

Rebecca's life was also at this time complicated by her attraction to H. G. Wells, which eventually developed into a stormy and controversial relationship culminating in the birth of a son, Anthony, in 1914[4]. She first met him in September after she had written a hostile review of his work in the 19 September 1912 issue and in a way, it was *The Freewoman* which brought them together for Wells wanted to meet the reviewer. Certainly,

---

[1]   Rebecca West to Dora Marsden, n.d., *c.* winter 1912 / 13.
[2]   Rebecca West to Dora Marsden, n.d. *c.* winter 1912 / 13.
[3]   Rebecca West to Dora Marsden, n.d. *c.* winter 1912 / 13.
[4]   See for example, Ray (1974) and Glendinning (1987).

Rebecca was impressed by the famous author. "I must say I like Wells. He hasn't made love to me and it is from watching his quick mind splashing about in the infinite[1];" though by spring 1913 they had had a row (over Wells' relationship with his wife, Jane) and Rebecca felt "I don't think we shall speak or write again! I'm longing to slaughter him[2]!" She went to Spain with her mother to try to get over him. Wells himself had contributed to *The Freewoman*, entering the still unresolved debate on the State Endowment of Motherhood, but had an ambivalent attitude to the paper. He suffered, like so many others, from Dora's bullying yet he remained a subscriber. He had offered money to *The New Freewoman* too. In fact, West gleefully reported to Dora in the winter of 1912 / 13 that "Wells expatiated at length the other day on your sweetness and brilliance. I think he misses *The Freewoman* very much and appreciates you better now he has to do without you[3]."

However, in spite of West's growing problems with Wells (they became lovers in the autumn of 1913) she never tired of working for the re-launch of the paper. Clearly, Rebecca liked Dora and perhaps her efforts provided further proof of Dora's ability to inspire others. What was remarkable about West, is that she never lost her sense of fun, complaining once, for example, that

---

[1] Rebecca West to Dora Marsden, n.d., also *c*. winter 1912 / 13. The phrase "to make love" did not necessarily have the same meaning then as today. Perhaps "flirting" or "chatting up" would be the nearest equivalent. West and Wells never married. See also McKenzie (1973), p. 285.

[2] Rebecca West to Dora Marsden, n.d. *c*. spring 1913.

[3] Rebecca West to Dora Marsden, n.d. *c*. winter 1912 / 13.

"D'Auvergne is always jumping up [at the Circles] and demanding we should always be kind to illegitimate children, as if we all make a habit of seeking out illegitimate children and insulting them[1]."

In response to West's promptings, Dora finally outlined her plans for the paper's revival in October 1912. The idea at this stage was to set up a Freewoman Publishing Company with capital of £5,000, comprising of 5000 £1 shares. "The sum of £5,000," Dora wrote to Harriet Weaver on 31 October 1912, "would be sufficient to guarantee the paper's existence for 3 or 4 years, during which time we confidently believe, basing our judgement on the success and solidity of its 11 months achievement, that *The Freewoman* would be a self-supporting institution." Dora's proposals were conveyed to the fifty-five people at the Discussion Circle[2] by Rebecca West and were well received. Indeed, Rebecca reported that after she had finished informing the Circle of Dora's plans she was immediately kissed by Mrs. Mc-Donald, Stella Browne, Barbara Low, Helena Greenland and by "a lady in deep mourning with an interest in Eugenics who gives away leaflets on proportional representation." With typical humour, she complained that there was an "epidemic of kissing in the Freewoman Discussion Circle[3]." There were some more tangible results too. Harriet Weaver offered £200 for shares and others offered smaller sums – Beresford, who had taken the photograph of Dora for the special supplement to

---

[1] Rebecca West to Dora Marsden, n.d. *c.* winter 1912 / 13.
[2] Barbara Low to Dora Marsden, 7 December 1912.
[3] Rebecca West to Dora Marsden, *op. cit.*

The Freewoman on 13 June 1912, Payne-Townshend and Bessie Hayes £30 each. However, the total only came to just over £400[1.]

Though the response to the admittedly daunting target of £5,000 had been poor, Dora remained optimistic. She felt that a threepenny fortnightly, with 1,600 subscribers "would enable the paper to pay for itself and according to the circulation already firmly established when publication was suspended, such a subscription should be well within our reach." This was an exaggeration but Dora had been clearly buoyed by "a quite astonishing feature of the situation... the extraordinary amount of interest shown in *The Freewoman*[2]."

This interest was marked abroad too, particularly in America, and to a lesser extent, France. Indeed, Dora later argued that the "emotional push" which landed *The New Freewoman* on its feet came from a tiny group of American women, among them the writers Lucian Cary and Edna Kenton[3]. Certainly, *The Freewoman* had some avid supporters in Chicago and New York. Charles T. Hallinan, for example, an Associate Editor of the *Chicago Evening Post*, wrote that he was "delighted that *The Freewoman* is again to take the field. There is work for it to do here as well as in England." Dr. von Bossini, formerly a probation officer, also wrote from Chicago that there was a ready market for the paper and it could perform "a pioneer service[4]."

---

[1]   Rebecca West to Dora Marsden, n.d. *c.* winter 1912 / 13.
[2]   Rebecca West to Dora Marsden, n.d. *c.* winter 1912 / 13.
[3]   Both Kenton and Cary were novelists and feminists.
[4]   *The New Freewoman* circular 1913.

The most remarkable compliments, though, came from Floyd Dell, the Editor of the "Friday Literary Review" of the *Chicago Evening Post*. Dell devoted a whole chapter to Dora in his *Women as World Builders*, published in 1913. Largely basing his comments on Dora's "Bondwomen," which, as described above, had been published in the USA, Dell emphasized Marsden's individualism and labelled her as the "Max Stirner of feminism." Glowingly, he continued that 'she provokes thought... she stimulates her readers to cast out the devils that inhabit their souls – fear, prejudice, sensitiveness... she liberates them to life." If this were not enough, he concluded:

> Freedom! That is the first and last with Dora Marsden. She makes women understand for the first time what freedom means. She makes them want to be free. She nerves them to the effort of emancipation. She sows in a fertile soil the dragons' teeth which shall spring up as a band of capable females, knowing what they want and taking it, asking no leave from anybody, doing things and enjoying life. Freewoman!

It is not certain whether Dora read these remarkable tributes to her talents, though Dell's publisher certainly hoped she did[1]. If she did the effect on her already keenly developed egoism and confidence can easily be imagined. Dora's belief in herself would also have been increased by an article written by Muriel Ciolkowska, in the 15 February 1913 issue of the French journal, *La Vie*. In this Ciolkowska, who later contributed to *The New Freewoman*, referred to Dora as "a young woman

---

[1] Forbes to Edna Kenton, 2 August 1913. The chances are that Dora did see the book for this letter is in the Dyson collection.

of a remarkably aware intelligence... a journalist [whose paper] fights the current prejudices with a surprising boldness – Miss Marsden does in theory what the militant feminist does in practice[1]." Dora was certainly impressed by the support from abroad although she had originally rejected Mary Gawthorpe's advice in October to seek succour from the USA. By January 1913, Dora had written to Weaver that "the hopeful factor is the attitude and spirit of the Americans[2]," and she was particularly encouraged by their attempts to set up a "Thousand Club" on *The Freewoman*'s behalf. The purpose was to secure a thousand subscribers before the paper was launched in order to give it a sound financial basis. Dora wrote to Harriet suggesting they set up a similar club in England too.

In fact, Dora had become so enthusiastic about starting the paper again that she was becoming impatient at what she regarded as a lack of progress. To her, there was a necessity to speed the process up "if we are to get on a sound working basis by March 27th – the date I have fixed for the Resurrection[3]." This date was hopelessly unrealistic, being only seven months after *The Freewoman*'s collapse and at a time when there was still no solid financial and organizational support. The £5000 appeal had fallen well short of the target and the "Thousand Clubs" had only just begun. And, with a timespan of only six weeks between the date of Marsden's letter

---

[1] *La Vie*, 15 February 1913. With thanks to René Sillet for translation. For article by Ciolkowska see, for example, *New Freewoman*, 15 September 1913.
[2] Dora Marsden to Harriet Shaw Weaver, 13 January 1913.
[3] Dora Marsden to Harriet Shaw Weaver, 13 January 1913.

to Weaver and the proposed launch, there was still no company, no publisher, no capital, no office, no printer. It was another example of Marsden's enthusiasm blinding her to the real obstacles that lay in her path. However, she did concede her "profound ignorance of financial affairs" and the necessity for sound legal advice. All this resulted in her decision in February 1913 to visit London to see, among others, Harriet Shaw Weaver. "Am I too sacrilegious," Dora enquired lightheartedly, "in suggesting a Sunday afternoon[1]?"

At last, in February 1913, Harriet and Dora met. They were in many ways totally unsuited – on the one hand, the rebellious, radical intellectual and on the other, the quiet, modest, unassuming and orderly Weaver. Yet they took an immediate liking towards each other – Weaver impressed by Dora's intelligence and indeed, her beauty, and Dora by Harriet's keen but systematic approach to the re-launch of the paper. Dora had originally just wanted a chat but they ended up in effect having a business meeting while all the time establishing their mutual respect and admiration. For Dora this friendship was to become as important as her relationship with Mary Gawthorpe, in some ways filling the vacuum left by their parting in 1912. Dora had found another woman who, impressed by her talents, seemed willing to help her in her project. Yet it was no cynical abuse of a simple and blind devotee – Harriet was too intelligent for that – and Dora wrote warmly and sincerely to Harriet after their meeting, thanking her for her help. "I must thank you," she wrote:

---

[1]   Dora Marsden to Harriet Shaw Weaver, n.d., *c.* early February 1913.

for the great personal kindness you have shown me while I have been in London. Quite apart from what you have done and are preparing to do to help the paper, your kindness in running about with me in my pursuit of hopes, has been a most valuable thing to me, and I must confess that I entertain feelings of very lively gratitude on that account. Please accept my very warm thanks[1].

Dora's gratitude did not prevent her, though, from sending Harriet a whole string of requests for help, neither did it assuage her irritable impatience. She did apologize for pressing Harriet, but "really if we two do not move, there will be nothing done." Neatly reflecting her distaste for organization and her own impulsive individualism, she continued, "The other people's interest seems to be of such a business-like sort, and the paper is yet in too embryonic a stage to be amenable to business-like treatment. Things are born of faith and belief – not of method and securities[2]!"

Harriet was now as keen as Dora after meeting her, but fortunately she realized the necessity for solid financial and legal organization if the venture was to be a success. She wrote to potential subscribers, opened a bank account and began a British Thousand Club. A Thousand Club committee was formed with Dora in the chair, Mrs. Leisenring as Secretary and Harriet as Treasurer. Leisenring was Secretary of the Blavatsky Institute which was set up for the study of Theosophy, Mystical and Occult Philosophy. (Later Dora secured a notable success in a debate at a Blavatsky summer school in Peebles in July 1913, destroying the arguments of the

[1]   Dora Marsden to Harriet Shaw Weaver, 14 February 1913.
[2]   Dora Marsden to Harriet Shaw Weaver, 25 February 1913.

Theosophists and selling many copies of *The New Free-woman*[1].) More importantly for the paper at the time was that the Institute provided offices in its own headquarters in Oakley House, Bloomsbury. This was a very central and fitting address even though *The New Free-woman* had to share the building with solicitors, Swedenborgians, a teacher of memory and by no means least, a firm of reinforced concrete engineers.

Not surprisingly the demands for money and support were met with further requests for a statement of the paper's policy and eventually, in early 1913, a circular headed *The New Freewoman* was printed. This was drafted by Rebecca West but based on Dora's views. In many respects vague, it did clarify the situation a little, and revealed Dora's continuing interest in individualism. *The New Freewoman*, it declared:

> will be the only journal of recognised standing expounding a doctrine of philosophical individualism either in England or America. Editorially, it will endeavour to lay bare the individual basis of all that is most significant in modern movements including feminism. It will continue *The Freewoman*'s policy of ignoring in its discussions all existing taboos in the realms of morality and religion.

After outlining the financial difficulties of producing a radical paper, the circular emphasized that the "responsibility for its continuance must rest with its readers." It therefore called for a thousand subscribers willing to pay £1 in advance for eighteen months' copies, and that these, if they expressed a willingness to find nine other readers, should go forward onto the Club

---

[1]   Harriet Shaw Weaver to Dora Marsden, 1 August 1913.

committee. The paper was to be fortnightly, priced 6d and was to begin on 15 June, with Rebecca West as assistant editor.

The Thousand Club Membership Fund was not a success. Only 180 had signed up by May and many were reluctant to contribute without the guarantee of a shareholder's vote in any new company to be formed to back the paper. Dora, however, remained adamant that the paper should still come out in June and asked Harriet to establish a company, "The New Freewoman Company Ltd." Harriet was almost working full-time for the paper now, her workload increased by the illness, at various times in this period, of Dora, Jardine and West. By May, the situation looked bleak, with confusion over finance and policy, and still no new company had been formed. Moreover, a new bombshell exploded – the proposed publisher of the paper, A. G. Fifield, backed out.

Rebecca West had originally contacted Fifield after failing to secure the cooperation of another radical publisher, Frank Palmer. Fifield was a well-known anarchist publisher and had brought out a cheap version of Stirner's *The Ego and His Own* in 1912. He was originally extremely keen and offered *The New Freewoman* very generous terms: £1 per week and 5 per cent of sales. This deal, as he must have realized, would not make him a rich man. But almost as soon as negotiations began, difficulties arose which further illuminated the problems of dealing with someone so determined as Dora Marsden.

Fifield was worried over the lack of capital and the structure of the company and by early May was:

> getting sick of the whole affair... I wish I had never heard of the paper. I only agreed at Miss Marsden's urgent request because she said my withdrawal now would injure whatever chances the paper had... I think its possibilities are almost nil and I consider it an unbusiness-like and merely silly decision to go on with it[1].

Fifield's remarks had an element of truth, as did his final comment that "I cannot but think that a certain amount of personal vanity and obstinacy on Miss Marsden's part are among the chief reasons why it will go through."

In fact, Fifield's major objections were concerned with control, politics and Dora. He wrote that he sympathized with the paper's intention to "criticise all conventionalities, sham obstructions and dishonesties in the affairs of life and to endeavour to lay the foundations of a simple emancipated society" but was wary of Dora having total control of content which could lead to trouble with the law. Thus "I would rather Miss Marsden got another publisher. She has a sense of humour and can take things lightly. I can not[2]."

Fifield, it emerged, was seriously concerned about the possibility of being charged with libel and sedition. He reminded Dora that she had advocated the use of violence before[3], and though he supported "philosophical

---

[1]   Fifield to Herrin, 6 May 1913. Herrin was a lawyer who had offered his services to Marsden.
[2]   Fifield to Herrin, 8 May 1913.
[3]   See, for example, *The Freewoman*, 12 September 1912.

anarchism" he could not support this[1]. Not without justification he argued that violent action was "an absurdity for literary people to advocate. The first time a writer saw a bayonet in the side of another man with the blood flowing and agony on his face, he would lose his nerve and faint[2]." In the end, they both agreed to sever the connection. Fifield perceptively wrote: "all told, you are well rid of me[3]"; while Dora noted that "the truth of the matter is that I ought to be my own publisher, or find one who shared my views in relation to such matters as are likely to lead to arrest[4]."

Thus, in early May, *The Freewoman*'s resurrection was far from assured. Fifield had left, finance was still a problem and supporters in London continued to be understandably restless. Even Swifts were giving trouble over the copyright of the title *Freewoman*. Yet at least Dora, somewhat unilaterally and disastrously as it turned out, had found another publisher, F. C. Charles of the Oxford-based and deceptively grand-sounding New International Publishing Company.

Dora was clearly impressed by Charles and she wrote to Harriet, "he is an extremely nice man, enthusiastic in his quiet way for what the paper stands for and, I think, just the right man for us[5]." He also had the added attraction of being cheaper than Fifield. Whether or not she was authorized to do so, Dora immediately offered him the work. At first all went well and Charles became

[1]   Fifield to Dora Marsden, 9 May 1913.
[2]   Fifield to Dora Marsden, 13 May 1913.
[3]   Fifield to Dora Marsden, 16 May 1913.
[4]   Dora Marsden to Fifield, 11 May 1913.
[5]   Dora Marsden to Harriet Shaw Weaver, 20 May 1913.

another legal and financial adviser to Dora and a friendship developed between them. He invited Dora and Grace to visit him in Oxford[1]. He even suggested Dora took up cycling to improve her health. Meanwhile, and only three days before the paper was due out, The New Freewoman Company had been finally set up with a nominal capital of £1,000. There were only fifteen registered shareholders who between them had taken up the total of 359 £1 shares sold. Harriet had the largest number, followed by Bessie Heyes who, along with Dora and Grace, became the directors of the new company.

The New Freewoman appeared in the middle of June 1913 and though this was an achievement in itself, the first issue can only be described as a mess. This was hardly surprising given the events of the 16 June. Dora, staying near Oxford, had finally received the proofs late on Friday, 15 June and went to see Charles on the Saturday. He informed her that the paper could not possibly be printed on that day and a furious row developed. Dora reported to Harriet that "the upshot of it all was that we were stuck there until 7 in the evening, with one man working at their one machine and the manager setting up by hand. They were fuming – utterly outraged." Mr. Charles had asked Dora to excuse the men feeling "'put out' and I replied the only 'putting out' that mattered to me was that of the paper." She concluded that "he *cannot* print *The Freewoman*[2]" – a sentiment with which West, Jardine and Weaver were all heartily agreed. Charles was sacked and professional printers,

---

[1]   F. C. Charles to Dora Marsden, 11 June 1913.
[2]   Dora Marsden to Harriet Shaw Weaver, 17 June 1913.

Johnson & Co. of Southport, were hired by the first directors' meeting held on 21 June at Dora's home in Ainsdale. Here too Harriet Weaver was formally appointed honorary secretary to The New Freewoman Co. and Dora Marsden (editor), Rebecca West (assistant editor) and Grace Jardine (sub-editor and editorial secretary) employed on a salary of £1 a week each.

Thus after a troubled pregnancy and a tiresome labour *The New Freewoman* was born – a scrappy, scrawny child whose survival could not be guaranteed. Only a few months earlier, Dora had agreed that at least £5000 was needed to give it a solid start in life. Yet in June, The New Freewoman Company only had a nominal (not actual) capital of £1,000 with less than two hundred subscribers. Moreover, the infant when it did appear looked extremely odd and unattractive, unlikely to gather many doting admirers. Dora's rashness in appointing Charles was a mistake, the paper had been induced far too early and the chances of a long life looked slim. Yet in spite of all the obstacles, Dora, with more than a little help from her friends, had pulled it off. Given that the paper, and later its successor, *The Egoist*, was subsequently to nurture the likes of Ezra Pound, James Joyce, Richard Aldington, "H. D.", Margaret Storm Jameson, T. S. Eliot and others, Dora Marsden deserves immense and long-overdue credit for her achievement.

The gestation period of *The Freewoman* further reflected upon Dora's ability to inspire diverse types of women to work tirelessly for her. She certainly exploited this but not without expressing warm gratitude. At the beginning of 1914, for example, she told Harriet, "you have been a perfect treasure to me and the paper. It seems odd that a year ago I did not know you[1]. The affection quickly became mutual, with the usually reserved Harriet often ending her letters to Dora "with love, yours very sincerely[2]." Rebecca West was also inspired by Dora, writing to her in 1912 that she was a "wonderful person, you not only write these wonderful first pagers but you inspire other people to write wonderfully... And it's your lead they are following[3]."

Even Mary Gawthorpe – described by West in *The Daily Herald* as "the most brilliant organizer [the WSPU] ever had[4]" – still had a trace of feeling for her former "dear little one." In October 1913, Mary wished Dora "every success for the realisation of your many powers[5]," even though their friendship was over. Mary from this point on (if not earlier) disappeared from Dora's life and indeed public life in the UK. Though ill, she still managed to defend suffragism in the press and she even once called for a national hunger strike in support of votes for women[6]. Eventually she left for America, where she married and wrote her autobiography which unfortunately ends before her *Freewoman* days[7].

---

[1] Dora Marsden to Harriet Shaw Weaver, 4 January 1914.

[2] See for example Weaver / Marsden letters of 12 August, 3 September 1913.

[3] Rebecca West to Dora Marsden, June 1912.

[4] *The Daily Herald*, 11 September 1912. West adored "Lovey Mary" who she met in Leeds at a WSPU meeting.

[5] Mary Gawthorpe to Dora Marsden, 15 October 1913.

[6] *The Daily Herald*, 28 December 1912.

[7] Gawthorpe (1962). In fact, Gawthorpe continued to be politically active. Emigrating to the USA in 1916, she was active in the New York women's suffrage movement and in 1920 became a full-time official of the Amalgamated Clothing Worker's Union. Mary's commitment to

Yet by the end of 1913, Dora's circle of friends and personal support system seemed to be narrowing – even Rona Robinson, who still kept in touch, was busy pursuing her own career in science. In retrospect, this development ran parallel with her own decreasing involvement in direct political action and her pursuit of individualistic philosophy. Grenville had commissioned her to write a book on philosophy in 1911 and she made reference to this project in her correspondence[1]. Dora was hardly social anyway. Amy Haughton, for example, once complained in 1911 that "Dora is a lazy little wretch where any going out is concerned[2]" and her isolation was furthered by her esoteric interests and removal to Southport. Again, she had to rely on the support of Hannah, Grace and now Harriet Shaw Weaver, the latest and, in many respects, most crucial member of the Marsden team.

The first issue of *The New Freewoman* though dated 15 June 1913, did not appear for public sale until the week beginning the 18th. It would have been better if the publishers had waited until the following month. The first issue looked amateurish and bears permanent witness to Dora's rashness, to the inexperience of Mr. Charles and the anger of his workers on that summer's

---

her work in England remained constant throughout her life and perhaps both stands in contrast to Dora's, illuminating their split in 1912. Gawthorpe died in 1973. A full biography is overdue, but Sandra Stanley Holton's *Suffrage Days: Stories from the Women's Suffrage Movement* (Routeledge 1996) is useful.

[1] See Dora Marsden to Mary Gawthorpe, n.d., *c.* September 1911, and Dora Marsden to Harriet Shaw Weaver, 2 December 1912 and 15 April 1913.

[2] Amy Houghton to P. D. (unknown), n.d. *c.* November 1911.

day in Oxford in 1913. The paper suffered from haphazard layout, typographical blunders and too much padding from its predecessor. On the other hand, it reflected well the paths *The New Freewoman* was to follow. It contained Dora's leading article, her views and comments column, a piece by Benjamin R. Tucker on anarchism and, significantly too, a strong literary element represented here by West, Kauffman and the dreadful Huntley Carter[1].

In the first and subsequent issues, Dora continued her exploration of an anarchistic individualism based on Max Stirner's *Ego and His Own*. Stirner, a quiet failure in his own life (1806 – 56), was originally a student of Hegel but had quickly rejected his teachings in favour of an aggressive individualism. His criticisms of the state could be attractive to the Left, but his analysis of power could easily be interpreted as giving succour to the Fascist Right. Stirner's philosophy was amoral, egoistic and highly contemptuous of Socialists in general, and Hegel, Feuerback and Marx in particular. His ideal, according to Woodcock, was "the egoist, the man who realises himself in conflict with collectivity and with other individuals... who judges everything from the viewpoint of his own well being[2]." Everything was based on the interests and needs of the individual, all else, such as "Justice" or "Liberty" or "Humanity," was an abstraction, empty intellectualism. It was almost a nihilistic approach that denied all concepts of reason and common

---

[1] Rebecca West was always complaining about Carter who "seems to me so bad ... his meaninglessness hits you in the face." Rebecca West to Dora Marsden, n.d. *c.* June 1913.

[2] Woodcock (1962), p. 55.

humanity. Only the individual, the Egoist, who ruthlessly judges everything from his own well-being, counts. He may wish ultimately to join a "union of egoists" but only for his own convenience, reserving the right to withdraw at any time.

Man, according to Stirner, was split into two parts – body and mind. In the modern period, the mind dominates, creating fictions like God, Humanity, Morality. But these and other universal ideas were to Stirner empty and illusory outside and apart from the individual. The only way to reality lay through a thoroughgoing analysis of them, revealing that they were nothing but a sham. Again, what really counted was the individual, not the "truth" or a "cause." To Dematteis in fact, Stirner's goal was "To become the 'Unique One' or 'Owner' who guides his conduct according to his realistic appraisal of the situation, including his own abilities and limitations, rather than in accordance with universals and ideals which have no existence save in the mind[1]."

Not surprisingly, Stirner was severely criticized by Marx who denounced "St. Max" in his *German Ideology*. Marx attacked Stirner's subjectivity and his inability to realize that ideas come from reactions to political and social environments. Oppression came not just through individuals' expressing their own egoistic interests and power but through their relationship to the ownership and control of production, distribution and exchange. Liberation could only come through collective action and a collective realization of oppression as a

---

[1] Dematteis (1976), p. 98.

class, not through some magnificent act of individual will. Individual consciousness, Marx argued, could not possibly be abstracted from the social whole; ultimately he condemned Stirner and his philosophy as petit-bourgeois.

Of course, the debate between Marx and Stirner hinged on the conception of human existence as individual or social. Would it be possible to achieve Stirner's goal without collective action, would it be possible to live a totally individual asocial life? Surely the individual is a part of a larger whole whose values, morals and political institutions are ultimately determined by economic forces. Ideas do not simply come from an "empty" mind but from a reaction to the environment. If this is true, what dominates that environment needs analysis and explanation too.

In spite of the weakness of Stirner's arguments, he did become briefly fashionable among anarchist circles in the 1890s and 1900s, though they were, as now, divided in their attitudes to him[1]. A major attraction of Stirner was his criticism of the authoritarian state, and some too would have felt attracted to his violent defence of the use of force in attacks on the state. One major historian of anarchism concludes though that "his influence affected only a few small marginal groups of individualists. It is as the appropriately lonely rhapsodist of the uniqueness of every human being that Stirner claims his

---

[1] For a contemporary defence of Stirner, and a reply to my criticisms, see *The Ego*, privately published magazine by Parker. And of course the current work of the Union of Egoists. For a different analysis of egoism read *Der Geist: The Journal of Egoism 1845 - 1945*, a journal published by the Union of Egoists, also publishers of this book.

place in the history of anarchism[1]."

Stirner's doctrine clearly had its attractions for Dora and she wished to explore its complexities further. In doing so, Dora also suffered from the weaknesses of Stirner's analysis (and unfortunately, the appalling verbosity of his style), but at the same time she made some acute and telling observations of politics in general and of the position of women in particular. She had already emphasized in *The Freewoman* her individualism, her distrust of "causes" and her belief that the possession of property was necessary if an individual was to have power. The responsibility for the individual was not that of the state but of him – or her – self. Thus, in the opening leader, "The Lean Kind," Dora argued that the problem of the poor was not the rich, but *the poor themselves*. In an attack on *The Daily Herald* and Socialists in general she wrote: "None tell 'the worker' the blunt truth that his leanness blights the landscape and that *he is responsible*." Of course:

> The tales of leanness' woes are to the discredit of the fat but they recoil in truth to the discredit of the lean... There is only one thing the downtrodden with retained dignity can do, and that is to Get Up. And there is only one thing for the lean, and that is to get fat; get property.

Individuals had to fight and struggle for themselves, and not for pure figments of the mind such as "movements," "rights" and "freedom":

---

[1] Woodcock, p. 95.

Oh Freedom, subtle deceiver! What chains are forged and riveted in thy Name! .... – Liberty, Equality, Unity, Justice, Truth, Humanity, Law, Mumbo-Jumbo, Mesopotamia, Abracadabra, Om-Tat-Sat. Intellectual concepts all – futile products of men who pursue their own shadow... 'Causes' are the diversion of the feeble – of those who have lost the power of acting strongly from their own nature [for Marsden]... The only fitting description is that of Individual: Ends in themselves; ... Egoists[1].

In the second issue, Marsden emphasized that *The New Freewoman* had no "cause" and would not therefore become a "leader"; clearly that would be a negation of her philosophy. This led many readers to claim that the paper's position was unclear, and even Dora had to concede that "Our quarrel with things in general is difficult to state in words for the precise reason that the biggest part of our quarrel is against words – against thoughts." She continued, echoing Stirner's claim that "I have based my cause on nothing," that:

The New Freewoman has *no* Cause. The nearest approach it has to a Cause it desires to attain, is to destroy Causes ... [indeed] *The New Freewoman* is not for the advancement of Woman, but for the empowering of individuals – men and women; it is not to set women free but to demonstrate the fact that 'freeing' is the individual's affair and must be done first hand, and that individual power is the first step thereto[2].

If notions such as "Equality," "Justice" and "Humanity" were merely "futile products of men who pursue their own shadow," it followed that "the idea of

---

[1]   *The New Freewoman*, 15 June 1913.
[2]   *The New Freewoman*, 1 July 1913.

rights" based on these concepts was equally illusory. "One's claims as Women," Dora argued:

> As Man, as Wife, claims to 'Justice,' 'Right,' to 'Equality' are nothing – so much empty sound. One may claim with sense just what one has the power to get. The emphasis put on claiming is the revelation of the impotence and futility of the complainant. It serves merely as a diversion from the thing which matters, from consideration of the power to get."

In order to have power an individual must have property – "It has become clear that ownership of one's self is impossible in this life, unless one owns *something external to oneself*: owns, that is, material property[1]."

Dora developed this argument to criticize thoughts and ideas which in their anti-intellectualism reflected the thinking of Max Stirner. "Idea, idea, always the idea," she complained, "as though the supremacy of the idea were not the subjection of men, slaves to the idea. Men need no ideas... What men need is power of being, strength in themselves[2]." Ideas, to Marsden, were used to enslave individuals and in reality did not exist. *The New Freewoman*'s task, therefore, was not to create new gods of new ideas, not even "to bring new thoughts to individuals, but to set the thinking mechanism to the task of destroying thoughts; to make plain that thinking has no merit in itself, but is a machine, of which the purpose is not to create something, but to liberate some-

---

[1] *The New Freewoman*, 1 August 1913.
[2] *The New Freewoman*, 15 August 1913.

248

thing: not to create thoughts but to set free life impulses[1]."

These attitudes led to obvious further questions – where did an individual's, or even an Egoist's thoughts come from? What – and how objectively defined – were the "life impulses" that needed to be set free? Typically, Marsden was vague here, arguing that "true" concepts could only be based on something that was felt, for example the Soul[2]. She expounded upon this in the second issue in the leading article "Intellect and Culture." Here Dora argued that the purpose of culture was to act as a map or guide in the conduct of human affairs, yet culture had been established too early for it was based on intellect, not on instinctive and inward-looking analysis. Intellect, in fact, denied the Soul which, to Marsden, should alone shape life and culture[3].

Subsequently, Dora claimed that in fact her analysis was based on "things" – the first and most important "thing" being the Soul. "The first thing of which we can have any knowledge... the only thing of which we can have any knowledge – is the life within ourselves. We call it our soul[4]." The body was different from the soul which is "the general name we would employ to indicate the deeper reaches of the emotional organism. It is the deeper organised complex of all the feelings which the ego – soul and sense combined – has experienced[5]."

---

[1] *The New Freewoman*, 1 July 1913.
[2] *The New Freewoman*, 1 July 1913.
[3] *The New Freewoman*, 1 July 1913.
[4] *The New Freewoman*, 15 October 1913.
[5] *The New Freewoman*, 15 November 1913.

Again, this all slotted in neatly to the Stirnerian belief in the paramount importance of the individual and the Ego. Dora by now was a convinced Egoist claiming in the second issue, for example, that "we are the only self-acknowledged Egoists occupying a place apart[1]." In September she described Stirner's *Ego and His Own* as "the most powerful book that has ever emerged from a single mind[2]." Marsden's analysis, however, shared the strengths and weaknesses of her master. Surely Dora was correct to attack the notion that oppressed people could achieve their liberation merely through an appeal to their oppressors on the grounds of "justice and humanity": to take one contemporary example, this has not achieved anything for the majority of South Africans. That these same people could overthrow oppression individually, through an act of will, seems somewhat ludicrous. It would require collective action and organization for the individual and the common good; it would surely require too the collective organization of society and its resources. But this would be an anathema to Marsden's beliefs for "there is no corporate life. There are only individuals... society is a collection of individuals, that and no more[3]."

This aggressive individualism stood in marked contrast to the reality of contemporary political developments. The growth of sympathy strikes and Syndicalism which culminated, in September 1913, in the creation of the Triple Alliance of miners, railwaymen and transport

---

[1]   *The New Freewoman*, 1 July 1913.
[2]   *The New Freewoman*, 1 September 1913.
[3]   *The New Freewoman*, 1 September 1913.

workers reflected the continuing rise of working-class solidarity and class consciousness. These were especially marked during the Dublin General Strike which began in August and was led by James Larkin.

Dora's reaction to these developments reflected the weakness of her political thinking. She was still sympathetic to Syndicalism and was very clearly on Larkin's side as the dispute dragged on into the winter, but she refused to see the dispute in class terms. Dora hoped the Dubliners would attempt an insurrection but even this was defined as a "self-conscious individualised rising in strength of men who mean to be free[1]." After the success of such a rebellion free individuals would then go their own way; Dora, like Stirner, still rejected Socialism. On the other hand, Marsden's commentary on the Dublin strike included trenchant observations on the nature of power. She was particularly scathing about parliamentary power and dismissed the Labour Party leaders Philip Snowden and Ramsey MacDonald as "dead dogs with an ill odour." Ultimate political power as she had explained in *The Freewoman* did not lie at Westminster. What the workers needed to do was to arm themselves and create a citizens' army. What hope had the worker, Dora asked, when:

---

[1] *The New Freewoman*, 1 December 1913. Five days later (6 December 1913) an advert for the *New Freewoman* was placed in the *The Daily Herald* claiming that the paper was the "only journal which treats of the philosophical base of the insurrectionary movement... it is a philosophical crucible in which all authoritarian morality is dissolved."

he sees himself as the unarmed unit at the apex of a triangle which broadens out to its base in serried rows of armed men, each with his rifle, bludgeon and lash raised at him? ... That an unarmed populace under a government possessing an armed force is a condition of slavery, is a fact which shouts. To be free is to have power to treat with equal terms. The citizen army is the first step in the direction of making these equal. A people will be in the position to say whether they want to be free when every able-bodied man and woman has been enrolled[1].

These sentiments would no doubt be attractive to those Socialists and Syndicalists who still read the paper, yet their involvement with it clearly declined. In all probability they became frustrated by Dora's inflexible and obtuse individualism even though she could still make some telling observations. In spite of a lingering personal bitterness towards Christabel and Emmeline Pankhurst, this also applied towards her analysis of the WSPU.

Nineteen-thirteen was an eventful year for the Union. Though Christabel had fled to Paris to escape arrest (she only returned when the Government announced an amnesty for suffragettes on the outbreak of the Great War in September 1914), her control of the WSPU was complete. The Pethick-Lawrences had been ousted in October 1912 while in early 1914 Sylvia Pankhurst formally left in order to concentrate on her campaign in the East End. Both had gone because of their disagreement over militancy. The Pethick-Lawrences did not want any further escalation to include attacks on property, while

---

[1] *The New Freewoman*, 1 December 1913.

Sylvia objected to its individualistic nature. She wanted the struggle to be more broadly based and specifically to include working-class women.

Under Christabel's unchallenged leadership (and from the safety of Paris) the militant struggle reached new levels of destruction. The window-smashing of 1912 was replaced by a concerted campaign of arson which caused thousands of Pounds of damage. The response of the state was equally dramatic. Forced feeding continued and was augmented by a devious new law, dubbed "The Cat and Mouse Act." This allowed a temporary discharge for a hunger-striking suffragette who would be then re-arrested once her health had recovered. Mrs. Pankhurst was imprisoned and released under this legislation six times during 1913. Not surprisingly it was feared that Emmeline Pankhurst and other hunger strikers might die, although none did. The Union however did get its first martyr when Emily Wilding Davison threw herself under the King's horse in the Derby of June 1913.

Yet in spite of the heroic efforts of the suffragettes the vote had still not been won and their campaign became ever increasingly desperate. Moreover, the very object of their efforts – the vote – was clearly being rejected by other groups, most notably growing sections of the labour movement. Neither the Labour Party nor parliamentary democracy as a whole had satisfied their economic and social demands. Indeed, for some it was incapable of doing so. Dora however criticized the WSPU from a Stirnerist viewpoint. The Pankhursts were now regarded as having dropped to the level of "causists."

They "began to 'lead a cause' and imperceptibly the Cause became Leader – leading where all causes tend – to self-annihilation. Mrs. Pankhurst may die and great is the Cause. What Cause? The Cause of the empty concept – the fount of all insincerity: the Cause of the Symbol – the Nothing worked upon by the Dithyramb[1]."

Dora had been saddened by the death of her old colleague Emily Wilding Davison, and she placed the responsibility for this at Clement's Inn, even though the Pankhursts had no idea what Davison was to do on that fateful day. To Dora, Emily had died for "the cause" but the effect of her death was merely to "give a crowd of degenerate orgiastics [presumably the WSPU] a new sensation… Causes are the diversion of the feeble – of those who have lost the power of acting strongly from their own nature. They are for the titillation of the senses of the herd and a person who can act strongly should shun all Causites and their works."

Dora's attack on the WSPU's treatment of Davison became a thinly-veiled criticism of her own experience as a suffragette activist. Davison, Dora wrote:

> did not understand that the presence of the tiny handful of people like herself in a spectacular affair was a very considerable embarrassment to the situation, which accounted for the suspicion and semi-disgrace in which they were constantly held; that their presence was just tolerated because occasionally the organisation might need to dump them down, one here and one there to act as living beings for an occasion and then to return them to the role of automaton[2].

---

[1]   *The New Freewoman*, 15 June 1913.
[2]   *The New Freewoman*, 15 June 1913.

This ferocious attack on the Pankhursts and the WSPU worried many of *The New Freewoman*'s supporters, who were concerned that it would embroil the paper in a similar row to that of November and December 1911. Rebecca West asked: "Can't we stop attacking the WSPU? The poor dears are weak at metaphysics but they are doing their best to revolt and the discussion concerning the parish pump could be no duller than the discussion of the Pankhurst soul." Rebecca was worried that if Dora continued her barrage of attacks, it "will place us into the same interminable quibbling correspondence as at the beginning of the last *Freewoman*... You have your constructive work before you. It seems a pity to waste the paper on Mama P[1]."

Yet Dora could not resist the temptation to criticize "Mama P" and her daughter, and not surprisingly as "RG" noticed, the paper was "known to excite some antagonism" in suffragette circles[2]." Christabel was likened to a stubborn old woman unable to regard "her pet idea from the outside[3]," while her mother's constant reference to dying for the cause was condemned as pathetic and "To be relying on pity as a main argument is the tactic of the weak[4]." Dora in any case regarded the vote and democracy as a sham, resulting in "the bludgeoning of the individual by the alliance, the majorities[5]," but her opposition to the Union was clearly personally rooted too. Unfortunately, though, some of her

[1]   Rebecca West to Dora Marsden, June 1913.
[2]   *The New Freewoman*, 15 September 1913.
[3]   *The New Freewoman*, 15 September 1913.
[4]   *The New Freewoman*, 15 June 1913.
[5]   *The New Freewoman*, 15 June 1913.

criticisms were so exaggerated that they tended to obscure the positive aspects of the suffragette struggle. As the Canadian feminist R. B. Kerr put it, "the militants have done much to emancipate other women[1]."

Dora's attitude to the Pankhursts would not really have surprised those who knew her and had read her articles in *The Freewoman*. They may, however, have been shocked to discover that, as an individualist, she no longer believed in a Woman's Movement at all. For fear of being found guilty, of supporting the power of another "empty concept," Dora wrote in the first issue:

> we hasten to add that the term 'Woman Movement' is the one which deserves to go the way of all such – freedom, liberty and the rest – to destruction. Accurately speaking, there is *no* 'Woman Movement.' 'Woman' is doing nothing, she has indeed, no existence. A very limited number of individual women are emphasising the fact that the very first thing to be taken into account with regard to them is that they *are* individuals and cannot be lumped together into a class, a sex, or a 'movement.' They – this small number regard themselves neither as wives, mothers, spinsters, women nor men... the only fitting description is that of Individual Ends-in-Themselves. They are Egoists[2].

This bold individualism would have astounded many of her feminist readers, as would the extremely colourful language she used to explain it. "If we take away female reproductive organs from the concept 'Woman,'" Dora asked, "what have we left? Absolutely nothing, save a mountain of sentimental mush." Mars-

[1]   *The New Freewoman*, 15 October 1913.
[2]   *The New Freewoman*, 15 June 1913.

den argued that the concept "Woman" and others associated with it such as mother, wife and so on, were defined from the outside by others – a claim that feminists could to some extent identify with. Yet Dora took it further for, to her, each person, whether man or woman, should define themselves as individuals and not be defined by an external like sex. Indeed to base a "movement" around people because of their sex was ludicrous and invited mockery:

> 'Woman Movement' forsooth. Why does not someone start a 'straight nose movement' or a 'mole movement' or any other movement based upon some accidental physical contournation? Woman? Is there such a thing as woman sensed from the inside? If so, we have got to learn what it is. Never in the course of a long life have we felt 'There, I feel that as a woman[1].'

If this seemed a little odd to the paper's feminist readers, they would have been further confused by the statement in the second issue that "*The New Freewoman* is not for the advancement of Woman, but for the Empowering of individuals." To Marsden, the concepts "Woman" and "Man" were as empty as "Justice" or "Equality," mere intellectualism, ideas and words. Thus, "If men and women would try to turn their attention away from the infinitessimally small differences which distinguish between them... we should have heard the last of Man and Woman spelt with capitals, and the day of the individual would be at hand. And the measure of the individual would not be sex, but individual power[2]."

---

[1] *The New Freewoman*, 1 July 1913.
[2] *The New Freewoman*, 1 July 1913.

The "Max Stirner of feminism" had taken individualism to a point that seemed to subsume feminism itself. It also ignored the specific oppression – whatever its cause – that women faced purely because of their sex[1].

None the less, in spite of this, Dora's writings on women still had feminist implications. Notwithstanding her disclaimers on the notion of a "Woman's Movement" they continued to imply that women were indeed oppressed as a group. How this developed remained unclear, although it was now seen as connected to women's inability to seize property and, therefore, from Marsden's point of view, their inability to exercise power too. This left them with only one thing to sell – their sex. "Women on the whole own little or no property. Automatically therefore the process of bartering begins... for various reasons, but particularly because of the advent of industrialism, there exists a prejudice against the sale of their strength in their arms or in the activities of her brains... Consequently, she sells her sex[2]." As with *The Freewoman*, this led Marsden to a condemnation of current attitudes to sexual morality, claiming again, for example, that there was little difference between marriage and prostitution, it was only a matter of time – the latter wanted cash on the spot.

---

[1] Marsden had been on a rapid journey in four years since 1909 when she had declared "the women's movement the greatest cause the world has ever seen" (*Votes for Women* 7 April 1909). While she claimed "Women is a distinct entity" in October 1911(*Evening Standard* and *St. James Gazette* 25 October 1911), by the following year *The Freewoman* had become a Humanist paper. By 1913, the conversion to Individualism was complete.

[2] *The New Freewoman*, 1 August 1913.

Unfortunately, Dora did not examine in detail how this situation arose although her reference to the effect of "industrialization" echoes some of her earlier condemnation of the Machine Age in *The Freewoman*. Again, it did imply that women as a whole were oppressed although the cause was not necessarily men. Central to her argument were two things – that women were now left with only sex to sell, and that it was up to them to liberate themselves, not as women but as "individuals, ends-in-themselves." Thus instead of attacking men and their sexism, Dora felt the key was for women themselves to see the weakness of their position. They should refuse to sell their sex and assert themselves as free individuals.

Every woman, from the wife to the prostitute to "the respectable 'womanly woman,' her of the modest air, the veil and the pale bonnet," to Dora, played the game and were thus themselves to blame. "It is," she argued:

the hardest thing that can be said of women, the harshest comparison that can be made: but it unhappily can not be denied. The mindlessness of women recoils upon them at every turn: had they more mind, they would not have sunk to the condition of propertylessness; had they had mind, even propertyless, they would not have sunk to the level where it became possible to treat them as mere bodies[1].

This indeed was a harsh argument and somewhat elitist too. Dora clearly regarded herself as a woman who had obviously enough "mind" to avoid such a

---
[1] *The New Freewoman*, 15 August 1913.

predicament. Perhaps her attitude that the responsibility for women's oppression lay with *themselves* and not men would have surprised her feminist readers yet it clearly fit into her individualist position. Further, though she acknowledged that the "hostility of advanced women towards men is a very real thing[1]," the responsibility for this lay with women, too.

Dora felt that hostility between the sexes would continue to grow "until the question of supply and demand on sex matters has been thrashed out." This problem could only be solved when women saw themselves as individuals who, refusing to seek "protection" behind a cloak of respectability and physical apathy, freely and openly accepted their own sexual drives and needs. To her, "Women consciously and subconsciously inflame the sex ardour of men by a simulation of apathy" which is used to attract men in order to put a man's power to a woman's use. This understandably leads to confusion and conflict, for while men look to sex for "physical and mental satisfaction," a woman uses it "to give her power; to win for her a dominion external to herself, to use the man's undisciplined impulses for his own subjection." Clearly a recipe for disaster, for "this difference is the real ground of war between the sexes, because both have expectations based on delusions of each other's motives and in the eventuality both feel defrauded[2]."

Dora's argument led her to continue her attack, begun in *The Freewoman*, on contemporary moral values

---

[1] *The New Freewoman*, 15 September 1913.
[2] *The New Freewoman*, 15 September 1913.

and the ideals in particular of monogamy, purity and chastity. Again, this would place her at odds with many feminists, especially those who supported the views expressed in Christabel Pankhurst's *The Great Scourge and How to End It*, which was also published in 1913. *The Great Scourge* certainly attacked male hypocrisy, blaming the problem of vice on men who, by Christabel's calculations were riddled with venereal disease. Christabel condemned the lust of men and praised the natural purity of women; the only solution was "chastity for men and Votes for Women."

Apart from ridiculing the idea that such an issue could be solved by votes, Dora rejected the notion that women had no responsibility for the problem, that they were just innocent victims of men:

> The rise to power of the protected pure woman represents the most successful swindle on record in history... she stimulates desire in men to an exaggerated need; she holds out promises of satisfaction which she cannot and does not intend to supply; she accepts gifts and binds her victim before she bestows the goods; the business transaction affected, she does as she likes and will make repudiation of claims into a virtue; whereupon the 'prostitute' supplies the needs the pure have created; she pays the pure ones extravagant debts[1].

The "pure woman" was "Irony's Masterpiece" yet it was this concept of womanhood that so many suffragists applauded and revered.

Dora's analysis of women's sexual oppression was not only controversial, it was unique. It was at odds with

---

[1]   *The New Freewoman*, 15 September 1913.

both the more radical views expressed in *The Free-woman* and with mainstream suffragist thinking. The latter, as we have seen, wished to uphold the values of contemporary morality not replace them. It was not the ideals of chastity, monogamy or marriage that were flawed but the refusal of many men to accept them as guidelines for their own sexual behaviour in practice as well as in theory. At its most extreme, and particularly in Christabel's *Great Scourge*, this argument became an explicit acceptance of biological determinism; the natural impulses of men could only be checked by the natural purity of women. This may now appear limited yet it at least emphasized that male sexual behaviour was part of the problem. It also reflected the very real concern about the spread of venereal disease. Dora's views not only tended to ignore the role of men but also gave no practical information on how women were to secure their own individual autonomy other than through an enormous act of will. Once again, she was generalizing from her own experience. Yet Dora and Christabel's analyses did share an unwillingness to accept (or at least examine) the notion that moral values are socially defined and linked to prevailing economic structures. Or in other words, from their own differing political positions they were unwilling to explore the relationship between morality and the needs of contemporary capitalism, with its emphasis on motherhood and the purity of the race[1]. In that way, their arguments were seriously flawed.

In spite of the limitations of Dora's examination of morality it did lead to a remarkable debate within the

---

[1]   See above, Chapter 3.

paper. Much of this was extremely frank, some of it extremely odd. For example, Clarence Lee Swarz agreed with Marsden that "a woman has a right to do whatever she feels with her own body," but then went on to argue that prostitutes should organize themselves into trade unions, for their work was a service like any other. The whole notion was ridiculed, among others, by the American anarchist Benjamin R. Tucker, who envisaged a situation where "the daily papers will teem with bargain counter advertisements offering remainders and shopworn goods at reduced prices. Being a believer in liberty I can not say nay... even liberty has its unpleasant side[1]." Dora herself was against Swartz' idea for though sex was often a woman's only property, to sell that was to accept the inherent weakness of such a position. How women were to get real, substantial property by which they could exercise power was left vague, though Dora suggested that doubtless they would get it through "one of the traditional ways, by buying, begging or thieving[2]."

Theodore Schroeder, a campaigner against the obscenity laws in the USA, was also outspoken on sex, defending "auto-eroticism" and calling for free love in the first issue. He looked forward to the day when "cultural visions of highly refined beings will be free unions of voluntary exclusiveness beside which our present hypocritical pretensions of monogamy, the phallic ceremonials of Christians and the authorised rapes of present le-

---

[1] *The New Freewoman*, 1 September 1913.
[2] *The New Freewoman*, 1 September 1913.

gal history will be shameful to contemplate[1]." Others, for example E. B. Lloyd, in "Intermediate Sexual Types," demanded fairer treatment for homosexuals, while yet others complained of the law which saw "Uranian [i.e. homosexual] love as vice[2]." Dora herself refused to be moved from her individualism and refuted attempts to define new "types" of people. She felt that "men and women should be counted qualified to bespeak their own emotions. We should learn the things of love and friendship from those who feel them as the irresistible expression of an emotion of which they are proud[3]."

However, it was the debate surrounding Stirner and anarchism that increasingly concerned Dora, if not her readers – a debate that sheds light on some of the major problems of anarchism, while reflecting further on her own personality. Dora's biggest argument came with Benjamin R. Tucker who by this time had settled in Paris. Tucker himself had been influenced by Stirner and had published Stirner's *The Ego and His Own*, thus it was hardly surprising that he was attracted to Marsden's "philosophical individualism." He began to write for the paper, generally under "Paris Notes" or "Lego and Penso," a Tuckerian version of Dora's "Views and Comments."

The row between Tucker and Marsden began over the French anarchist Proudhon and centred on whether a future anarchist society would involve a social contract.

---

[1] *The New Freewoman*, 15 June 1913.
[2] *The New Freewoman*, 15 October 1913.
[3] *The New Freewoman*, 15 October 1913.

Tucker argued that Proudhon felt that it should. According to Tucker, Proudhon argued, in his *General Idea of the Revolution in the Nineteenth Century*, that a social contract was crucial where "instead of making oath to God and his prince, the citizen swears upon his conscience, before his brothers and before Humanity." To Marsden, this ran counter to the very principles of individualism and egoism: it was up to each to defend their own interests and certainly not by appeals to such an empty concept as "Humanity." She replied that Proudhon's notion of a social contract was "a dragon, big and very impossible in everything but words." She conceded that he "was a blazing light in a dark age but the passage quoted... shows him at his worst." Rather arrogantly she concluded: "if it were the boyish essay of a youth in his teens with the instinct of a pedagogue, we should put a pencil through half of it as bombast and fustian. The half left would consist of adjectives and propositions. It is," she concluded with unknowing irony given the wanderings of much of her own writing, "the kind of thing that overpowers our mental digestion[1]."

Tucker was outraged by this attack on Proudhon's "style and in part, his sanity" and could not understand why, in her view, it was "insane to suppose that people can associate for mutual protection in the basis of a contract defining the protective sphere." Dora at least accepted that when Proudhon was "looking at things as they exist he is a strong searchlight, but when he is trying to woo his readers to his solutions, he uses methods of cajolery which are positively repellent and makes

---

[1] *The New Freewoman*, 1 October 1913.

style not a thing to be mentioned[1]."

Tucker found some solace in Marsden's partial praise of Proudhon yet he knew that the main issue – "whether it is crazy to think of voluntary cooperation for defence in conformity with a voluntary contract fixing the limits of such co-operation" – was still unresolved. "Miss Marsden," he continued, "still neglects to supply a reason why a person who pursues that ideal will find his proper environment within the confines of a mad house. Until such is forthcoming, the discussion cannot proceed[2]."

Tucker, like an increasing number of others, was becoming exasperated by Dora's inability to define her own or *The New Freewoman*'s position. But, she protested to Tucker, the paper "stands for nothing... It has no 'Cause.' All that we require of it is that it remain flexible and appear with a different air each issue. Should an influence come in to make it rigid, as happens in all other papers, it would drop from our hands imme-diately[3]." Tucker was perplexed by this and threw back at Dora her own words in the issue of July 1913 that the paper did in fact stand "not for the advancement of Woman, but for the empowering of individuals." He continued, "My interest in the paper grows out of my belief that it 'stands for' such empowering... If I am wrong, if in truth the *New Freewoman* is not, or is no longer, a co-ordinated effort towards a definite end, but has become, instead, a mere dumping ground for miscel-

---

[1]   *The New Freewoman*, 15 November 1913.
[2]   *The New Freewoman*, 15 November 1913.
[3]   *The New Freewoman*, 15 November 1913.

laneous wits then... my interest will diminish materially and speedily[1]."

Tucker returned briefly in 1914, when the paper had become *The Egoist* but he could no longer take Marsden's extreme individualism or her refusal to see the necessity for some sort of cooperation in the society of the future. "The egoist," Dora wrote, "stands for nothing; his affair is to see to it that he shall not be compelled to kneel." It was the individual alone that counted, and she ended by deriding Tucker and Proudhon with the call to "Let men cluster together and compound the Holy Unity: as they do, hence Democracy, the Brotherhood of Man, the cult of Humanity and the Race – all holy entities requiring capital letters[2]!"

In spite of Tucker's failure, he had pinpointed a major weakness in Marsden's philosophy and, unwittingly perhaps, that of anarchism in general. How, given their opposition to laws and "the State," was society to be organized? Marsden's vision, as argued above, almost amounted to a survival of the fittest and, at worst, gives a picture of eternal conflict. Others, however, and in particular Stephen T. Byington, readily accepted the problem and attempted to come to some conclusions. Byington courageously tried to do this in his series "On Interference With the Environment" which began on 15 September 1913.

Byington, an American who had helped to translate Stirner into English, quickly realized the enormity of his

---

[1]   *The New Freewoman*, 15 November 1913.
[2]   *The New Freewoman*, 15 November 1913.

task and immediately conceded: "I am in danger of upholding the enforcement of a whole series of laws which friends of liberty have always looked upon with the greatest contempt[1]." By November he had admitted too there were problems with the rule that "one man's wishes were as good as dozens" but to revoke this would necessitate further rules and indeed, law. Byington was, in the end, unable to square the circle, unable to reconcile the anarchist ideal in total individual freedom with the necessity for social organization and the need in particular to accept voluntary limits on freedom for the common good.

Dora was clearly unconcerned by the issues Byington raised. All that mattered to her was the power of the individual and "the means and necessity for self defence[2]." Social contracts with their implicit restriction on that power were anathema to her. All the persuasive powers of Tucker and others could not budge her from this and not surprisingly they drifted away. Though, like feminism, anarchism had many strands, in general it had been attractive to Dora Marsden's views and indeed, had contributed to their development.

Most anarchists shared her criticisms of the vote and parliament and many sympathized with her concern about the sex antagonism the WSPU seemed to encourage. Aldred and Bowman, as described above, particularly welcomed her defence of syndicalism, while Aldred applauded *The Freewoman*'s attempts to explore new relationships between the sexes. Some anarchists

---

[1]   *The New Freewoman*, 15 November 1913.
[2]   *The New Freewoman*, 15 November 1913.

would also have been attracted to the anti-industrialism embodied in her call for a return to a machine-less age. Yet few if any could stand her growing arrogance and her unswerving allegiance to Stirner which led her into further political isolation. Arrogance and isolation are potentially dangerous qualities, but as long as the world (or at least a few hundred readers) listened their pitfalls could be avoided.

❦

By the autumn of 1913 the title *New Freewoman* had become a misnomer. As Dora readily acknowledged the journal had moved rapidly away from the feminist origins of its predecessor and a new title was needed. The final impetus for this came from the growing literary element within the paper. In many ways Dora had appeared indifferent to this as she concentrated on examining individualism and working on her book on philosophy. If anything, she showed a distinct dislike of literary thinking and once, in a reference to the Labour leader George Lansbury, compared the possession of a "literary intellect" to "cultural brain rot[1]." Also, in a discourse against ideas, Dora argued that men should have no use for them "unless they are of the literary breed – then they live upon them by their power to beguile the simple[2]."

None the less, Dora began to comment on both art and literature as part of her exploration of individualism. As already explained above, Dora based the latter on things, the most important of which, "the only thing of

---

[1]   *The New Freewoman*, 15 July 1913.
[2]   *The New Freewoman*, 1 July 1913.

which we have any knowledge," is the soul[1]. To her, it was the artist's job "to make a chart" of the soul which "is not the soundless, unseen thing which common speech makes of it." Though this was admittedly a difficult task, "a good artist" she continued, "could begin by delineating the movements of the soul when it loves, is cruel, shy, joy, courageous, exalted, angry, lustful, repelled, hopeful, fearful, depressed, jealous and when it weeps. He might go further and make clear what is meant by the soul, by those things which we call Beauty, Inspiration, Friendship, Intellect, Sex, God, Good, Evil[2]."

This indeed would be a difficult task, if only because of the woolliness of Dora's own concept of the soul, based as it was on her own subjective belief in "instinct." On the other hand, it could be argued that this would appeal to the writers and artists whose influence on the paper had grown. Apart from the contributions of Rebecca West, there were also articles by Huntley Carter, who described Art as "an activity which is called vibrative force[3]," Hilda Doolittle (H. D.), Richard Aldington, Amy Lowell, William Carlos Williams, Ford Madox Hueffer and Ezra Pound. There were reviews too of Picasso's early works and the work of D. H. Lawrence and Walter de la Mare. Indeed, as Dora herself became preoccupied with other concerns the literary and artistic influence in the paper grew to the point that it occupied nearly half the total number of pages[4]. A new

---

[1]   *The New Freewoman*, 15 October 1913.
[2]   *The New Freewoman*, 1 November 1913.
[3]   *The New Freewoman*, 15 October 1913.
[4]   See, for example, *The New Freewoman*, 1 October 1913. Eight out of

reader could easily have assumed that *The New Free-woman* was a literary review.

Rebecca West had always wanted *The Freewoman* and *The New Freewoman* to be more literary in style and content even though she had understandably found it difficult to attract contributors willing to write without payment. Nevertheless, through the editor of *The English Review*, Ford Madox Hueffer, West succeeded in securing the young poet, Ezra Pound, for the paper. Pound, an American, had arrived in England only a few years previously but had already made a considerable impact on the London literary scene. In this he was aided by his own talent and knack for developing influential contacts and benefactors. By 1909 he had already become a *protégé* of W. B. Yeats as well as Hueffer, who published his work in the *Review*. By 1911, Pound was also writing for Orage's *New Age*.

For Pound and his circle, it was a time of experiment and discovery which culminated in 1912 with his announcement that they were Imagists. With its accent on directness and more realistic rhythmic patterns, Imagism marked a radical break from traditional poetry although it was not welcomed by all literary circles at the time. This did not deter the ambitious Pound from promoting Imagism at any and every opportunity. It was this context that led him gladly to accept the offer of literary editor on *The New Freewoman*. However, he extracted a high price for his contribution: at least a page of his work, or work selected by him, in each issue and

---

nineteen pages were devoted to the arts.

under his total control. The cost of this was to be met by one of his benefactors, John Gould Fletcher, another American poet.

The arrival of Ezra Pound put Dora Marsden in a dilemma. On the one hand, she welcomed his energy and the input of free and controversial material, but on the hand, he constituted a threat to her own control of the paper. She would no doubt have been aware of how he had begun to dominate *The English Review* and she was concerned by his demand in August 1913 that he have "control of all verse[1]." Dora was also apprehensive about Pound's politics and whether they were suitable for an "individualist review." Pound hastily replied that "the seven minutes at my instant disposal is hardly enough to define my philosophical credentials entirely. I suppose I am an individualist, I believe in the arts as the most effective propaganda for a sort of individual liberty that can be developed without public inconvenience." He added, significantly, that he did not believe that "a literary page will queer the editorial columns... I don't want to be 'boss' but if I am to make the page efficient, I must follow my own scheme[2]."

Though not unaware of the dangers of having Pound on the paper, Dora, after a period of indecision, finally agreed, although his position was never formally confirmed. Not surprisingly, Pound promoted Imagism in *The New Freewoman*, writing, for example, "A Few Darts By an Imagist" and seven of his own Imagist poems in the 15 August issue alone. His space and influ-

---

[1]   Ezra Pound to Dora Marsden, August 1913.
[2]   Ezra Pound to Dora Marsden, July 1913.

ence on the paper began to expand beyond a single page and though Dora was perhaps uneasy about this, she had in effect allowed it to happen. She was away in Southport and consumed by her own difficult and tricky work. She preferred to be on her own, to work and think sometimes with energy, sometimes in despair. Such was her isolation from the world outside that she admitted that even after three months, she had not even read any of Pound's material. "As for E. P.'s poems," she confided to Harriet Shaw Weaver, "I haven't read 'em. Speak it not. He is a nice old thing[1]."

Weaver herself seemed to like Pound though she was aware of Dora's concern over his growing influence in the paper. After all, though Dora was increasingly involved with her work on lingual philosophy, where would she be without *The New Freewoman*? She was no longer a famous and much-admired suffragette and it was only the paper that provided her with a platform and an income. What would happen if her control of *The New Freewoman* evaporated? Fortunately, given Pound often appeared to give the impression he was in charge of the paper, West and Weaver remained loyal to Marsden. Pound had talked of finding new American finance but West continued to resist attempts to squeeze Dora out and tried, without success, to find other sources of help. There was some talk of Allen Upward, who had also written for *The New Age*, becoming the business manager but this came to nothing though he did begin to write translations of Confucius for the paper. Pound did not get on well with him and revealingly wrote to Mars-

---

[1]   Dora Marsden to Harriet Shaw Weaver, 19 November 1913.

den, "Allen Upward's translations from the Chinese are, well it's no use scrabbling for adjectives. Will he let me have them for the poetry page in his very own weekly, or your weekly or whose ever it is[1]?"

The uncertainty surrounding the direction and the control of the paper eventually led to Rebecca West's resignation in October. Though she had welcomed, if guardedly, the new literary input, there is some evidence of friction between her and the new arrivals. In the autumn of 1913, for example, she wrote to Dora, "Richard Aldington isn't it? That set has a secret intention of buying us when our money was low, getting rid of me and then of you[2]." Pound's view, expressed many years later, was that "Rebecca West was enthusiastic for the first few weeks of *The New Freewoman* and then saw the impractibility of Dora and the suffragettes as [?] lasts of livelihood[3]." Weaver sent West a month's salary, but with a grace and humour that was to remain with her until her death, she refused. "As Miss Marsden has let me go, I think the least I can do is to go without looting the till[4]."

Many years later, in the 16 July 1926 issue of *Time and Tide*, a feminist magazine she had helped to create, Rebecca gave her own views on why she left. Basically, there were three reasons – political, professional and the pressure from Pound. Rebecca and Dora had already differed over Dora's aggressive individualism and her de-

[1] Ezra Pound to Dora Marsden, n.d. *c.* autumn 1913.
[2] Rebecca West to Dora Marsden, n.d. *c.* August / September 1913.
[3] Ezra Pound to Jane Lidderdale, n.d. *c.* 1962.
[4] Rebecca West to Dora Marsden, n.d. *c.* October 1913.

sire to return to a rustic "Golden Age." "I got no chance to convince her," Rebecca wrote, "for she was already retreated to further remoteness and was developing an egotistic philosophy on the lines foreshadowed by Max Stirner." Second, there was an *arriviste* poet [Ezra Pound] who intended to oust me and his works and those of his friends appeared in the paper without having passed me." As assistant editor, this was difficult for her to accept. Finally, Rebecca felt some of the quality of the work allowed into the paper was appalling: "so I quit. I am quite sure she never understood why. An argument that there is a relation between the expression and what is expressed, and that if one is coarse the other is unlikely to be authentic, seemed to her a far-away babble, for it was becoming less and less imperative for her to express herself. Hers was now to be rather than do." (Rebecca omitted to mention another reason for her departure – the increasingly complex nature of her relationship with H. G. Wells.)

Dora, somewhat arbitrarily, offered Rebecca's job to Richard Aldington who had been writing for the paper since September: "get ready for a shock," Dora wrote to Harriet, "this half of the directors has appointed Mr. Richard Aldington as sub-editor in place of Miss Rebecca West, departed[1]." Pound originally welcomed the appointment, though Dora soon noticed how "'E. P.' and the new 'sub' spit and scratch at each other[2]."

By the end of the year, *The New Freewoman* was evidently sailing into troubled waters, its greatest

[1]   Dora Marsden to Harriet Shaw Weaver, 16 November 1913.
[2]   Dora Marsden to Harriet Shaw Weaver, 19 November 1913.

achievement being its refusal to sink. With an absent editor, a confusion of styles and interests, all of which only appealed to a minority and its shaky finances, it had indeed done well to survive. In August 1913 its guaranteed circulation was a meagre two hundred and sixty-six with twenty-six going to the USA and one (presumably Tucker's) to France. Still suffering from a ban by W. H. Smith, open sales amounted to around one hundred and twenty per issue, making a grand total of around four hundred; hardly a recipe for success[1].

Not for the first or the last time, Harriet Shaw Weaver played a crucial role in keeping an unpopular project alive, in this case through her organization of The New Freewoman Company. Without her, Dora would not have had the security to be able to write. Indeed, without Harriet there may not have been any paper at all. The first shareholders' meeting of the Company held in September 1913, had already revealed a bleak picture. The meeting was held at Oakley House and consisted of Dora, Harriet, Bessie Heyes, Stella Browne, Rebecca West and the solicitor, Edwin Herrin. The accounts revealed that there was probably enough money to finance another six months' copies but *The New Freewoman* was simply not paying its way. They agreed on further advertising and, somewhat optimistically, to leave the print run at two thousand[2].

Finance was not the only problem. For some time, arguably since the first issue, the title *New Freewoman*

---

[1] *The New Freewoman*, Account Book 1913.
[2] *The New Freewoman*, Account Book 1913. Company minutes, and minutes of shareholders' meeting, 11 September 1913.

had become inappropriate for an "individualist review," especially one with such growing literary concerns. Neither Dora nor Ezra Pound liked it and at a directors' meeting in November a change of name was proposed from a short list: *The Egoist*, *The Prophet*, *The Free Voice*, *The Revealer* and *Tomorrow*, none of which implied any concern with feminism[1]. Bessie Heyes, at a further directors' meeting which agreed on *The Egoist*, was particularly concerned about this and the direction of the paper in general. In a letter to Weaver, which was forwarded to Marsden, Heyes complained, not without justification, that "some of the articles begin about nothing, twist and turn through a maze of words, and when I come to the end, I wonder for what purpose it was written. Then the poetry, pages upon pages of it...[2]"

Unfortunately, little detail has surfaced about Heyes, but it is likely that she spoke for many of *The Freewoman*'s original supporters. Bessie charged that to:

Change the paper's name to *The Egoist* seems to be foolish. Such a name would convey nothing to the ordinary practical person. No doubt you will say that *The Freewoman* is not meant for the ordinary practical person. But what is the good of a "gospel" (which Miss Marsden spoke of) if it is only for 20 or 50 people. But there, the "gospel" is hardly seen in the paper now. Don't you yourself think that the paper is not accomplishing what we intended to do? ... I had such hopes of *The Freewoman* and it seems utterly changed.

[1] *The New Freewoman*, Directors' Meeting minutes, 25 November 1913.
[2] Bessie Heyes to Harriet Shaw Weaver, 28 November 1913.

None the less, she conceded that "Miss Marsden said she would do exactly as she liked[1]" and agreed, reluctantly, to the change of title.

Eventually, Pound, Upward, Aldington, Carter and Kauffman drafted a letter which was published in the last issue of *The New Freewoman:*

> We, the undersigned men of letters who are grateful to you for establishing an organ in which men and women of intelligence can express themselves without regard to the public, venture to suggest to you that the present title of the paper causes it to be confounded with organs devoted solely to the advocacy of an unimportant reform in an obsolete political institution. We therefore ask with great respect that you should consider the advisability of adopting another title which will mark the character of your paper as an organ of individualists of both sexes, and of the individualist principle in every department of life[2].

Many years later, Harriet Weaver argued that "The new masculine element which had allied itself with the paper before long raised objections to the title[3]," but though the plea in the last issue was indeed signed by men, it would be extremely fanciful to see the change of name as a male plot against feminism. Dora herself, by no means a meek individual who could be easily swayed by others, wrote that the original title "Can only be regarded as a serious handicap. It contrives to suggest what the paper is not and fails to give any indication of

[1] Bessie Heyes to Harriet Shaw Weaver, 28 November 1913.
[2] *The New Freewoman*, 15 December 1913.
[3] Harriet Shaw Weaver undated notes on the history of *The Egoist* written in response to a request from Patricia Hutchins.

whatsoever it is." The reasons for calling it *The New Freewoman* were no longer valid and "In adopting the neutral title *The Egoist* and thereby obliterating the 'woman character' from the journal, we do not feel that we are abandoning anything there would be wisdom in retaining." She concluded that the titles *Freewoman* and *New Freewoman* had been adopted "more in the nature of a retort than argument. 'Feminism' was the natural reply to Hominism and the intent of these was more to tighten the strings of the controversy than to reveal anything vital in the minds of the controversialists... what women, awakened, emancipated, roused and what not – what they can do, it is open to them to do[1]."

The New Freewoman lived for only seven months and thirteen issues. Its finances were weak, its circulation small, its concerns unlikely to generate a popular following. Even some of the four hundred or so regular readers began to have doubts about the direction the paper was taking. Certainly, many feminist supporters like Bessie Heyes became disillusioned and began to lose interest. Others, for example Catherine Tolson, perhaps Caroline Boord and Stella Browne too, only seemed to remain out of personal loyalty to Dora. Carpenter remained loyal, becoming a (single) shareholder and writing the occasional article in the paper too. Even those who managed to follow her individualist line were put off by the literary input towards the end. As one reader put it, there was a "superficial and ephemeral air about the paper. Most persons appear to know the gang who are running it. Aldington, Hueffer, Pound and others –

---

[1] *The New Freewoman*, 15 December 1913.

none who really matter. They are at their old game... of writing each other up... They have nothing to do with egoism and all it implies[1]."

Though some students of modern literature may dispute this[2], it did appear that by the end of 1913 the paper was divided into two distinct sections around Pound and Marsden. Again, it almost looked like a poor copy of *The New Age*. Of course, the original *Freewoman* was hardly a popular paper yet its appeal was far wider than its successor. Suffragists, other feminists, Socialists, Syndicalists and anarchists could all relate to it and its courageous freethinking style. *The New Freewoman*, however, managed to reduce even this pool of support. The new literary input did secure some new followers but with Dora's increasing concern with individualism, many supporters, like Chew and Aldred, were driven away. Dora tried to contact Aldred in the summer of 1913 but did not seem to get a reply[3]. Even the anarchist support she enjoyed in 1912 withered under her unremitting Stirnerist tirades.

Dora was becoming more and more isolated – physically, politically and intellectually. In Southport, she was no longer at the hub of things, no longer at the centre of the intrigue and gossip that, like any other paper, surrounded *The New Freewoman*. Undoubtedly this made her job as editor more difficult but it was her

---

[1] J. Stephens to Dora Marsden, 7 January 1914.

[2] See, for example, Clarke (1985).

[3] Dora Marsden to Harriet Shaw Weaver, n.d., c. late May / early June 1913. A comparison between *The Freewoman* subscription list and that of *The Egoist* in January 1914 makes interesting reading. The number of suffragists and feminists on the latter is markedly reduced.

choice – there was no reason why she could not return to the capital. Though in almost daily contact with West and Weaver, her decision to stay in Southport made encroachment on her power more possible and subsequently her control over the whole paper declined. However, she wanted to remain in the North to concentrate on her individualism and her book on philosophy, apparently begun at the end of 1911. Yet these concerns only served to increase her isolation. Few wanted to follow Stirner, fewer still the beginnings of her obtuse philosophy, so difficult for readers to follow, so difficult for Dora to explain. Dora had begun to withdraw and to live her life through her writings. In many ways, her life now mirrored that of her hero Stirner. Like "St. Max," Dora combined increasing political and social isolation and powerlessness with a grand and sweeping exposition of the power of the individual. When Dora's quiet life at No. 9 Hatfield Road, Seaside Garden City, Ainsdale, Southport is compared to her articles in *The New Freewoman* the contrast not only becomes marked but almost tragic. Perhaps, as Woodcock argues about the difference between Stirner's pathetic life and his work, it shows "the power of literature as a compensatory daydream[1]."

The key question is, why did Dora withdraw from a more active personal and social life? She argued that it was to enable her to concentrate on her philosophical research and there could, of course, be some truth in this. However, it does not seem to be the complete answer. Was Dora, now thirty-two years old, increasingly with-

---

[1]   Woodcock (1962), p. 59.

drawn because she was both depressed and angry with the outside world, a world that no longer gave her the recognition that she had enjoyed from 1909 to 1911? Does this perhaps help to explain her vitriolic attacks on the Pankhursts and the WSPU, indeed on all "causes" and on all who found it so easy to "join?" If true, combined with the explicit elitism of her individualism, it was a dangerous personal mixture, a recipe for chaos.

The Egoist, January 1914 – December 1919

Published the 1st and 15th of each month.

THE EGOIST

AN INDIVIDUALIST REVIEW.

Formerly the NEW FREEWOMAN.

No. 1.   Vol. I.   THURSDAY, JANUARY 1st, 1914.   SIXPENCE.

Assistant ⟨ RICHARD ALDINGTON.   Editor : DORA MARSDEN, B.A.
Editors : ⟨ LEONARD A. COMPTON-RICKETT.

CONTENTS.

LIBERTY, LAW, AND DEMOCRACY.

THE concepts with which one age will preoccupy itself, and in which it will invest its surplus emotional heat have shown themselves to be so essentially casual as to be now a matter for mirth rather than wonder with its successors. The subject of an age's Master Passion round which its interest rages will be anything accidental and contingent which will serve; stand the heat, that is, and last out until enthusiasm tires. The amount of genuine enthusiasm which Athanasius, Arius and their followers were able to cull from the numerical problems in the concept of the Trinity was—incredible though it may seem—equal to that which this age culls from the figures of the football scores. The Crusaders who were so concerned about the possession of the Tomb of Christ looked forward to finding as much diversion and profit as a Home Ruler expects to get from the possession of a Parliament on Dublin Green. It is only from a distance that these dead dogs look so determinedly dead. Nearer to, one would swear the body had stirred; and we who are so near to an age when the mere mention of " Universal Law " would produce lyrical intoxication, " All's love, All's law," a very swoon of security, do not purpose here to break in upon the belated obsequies of that dead or dying concept. As the sport of the ribald and the mockers " Universal law " is the perquisite of the youth of 1950, not of 1915. And we will not here trespass on the future.

The reference in the title of this article is limited to statutory law, a prosaic and earth-bound branch which not even Apollo himself could have strung to the lyrical note, and it must be allowed that however excellent a run " Universal Law " as a symbol and idealised concept may have been accorded by a generation now settled in obesity, its society representative, so to speak, with which we are here concerned, has never been held in any too high esteem. The increase in its bulk and scope of application, which oddly enough, grows rapidly alongside something called the " Liberty of the people " have proved matters for complexity even when they have not created indignation and alarm. Visions of those not the least penetrating, have seen in the steady advance of the statutory law a devastating plague in which the parchment of the politicians has seemed as capable of devouring the spirit of the people as a swarm of locusts devouring green grass. Proudhon writing in 1850 on the subject says :

" Laws and ordinances fall like hail on the poor populace. After a while the political soil will be covered with a layer of paper, and all the geologists will have to do will be to list it, under the name of *papyraceous formation*, among the epochs of the earth's history. The Convention, in three years one month and four days, issued eleven thousand six hundred laws and decrees; the Constituent and Legislative Assemblies had produced hardly less; the empire and the later governments have wrought as industriously. At present the ' Bulletin des Lois ' contains, they say, more than fifty thousand; if our representatives did their duty this enormous figure would soon be doubled. Do you believe that the populace, or the government itself, can keep its sanity in this labyrinth?"

And yet, while no one would care to dispute these facts or deny they had significance, it is the libertarian interpretation of them which provides the clue

How is it possible that a journal could be popular which possesses no reverence for anything in the world or out of it; which has no use for shut doors, safe harbours, protected causes, established institutions or any other refuge for the timid or humble in mind?

Catherine Wood

The Egoist, 15 December 1914

Like *The Freewoman* and *The New Freewoman*, *The Egoist* had a difficult life. It struggled on for six years surrounded by conflict and rumour of imminent collapse. It enjoyed a readership numbered in hundreds rather than thousands and survived only because of the astounding personal generosity of Harriet Shaw Weaver. When the end did come, in 1919, it was unnoticed except by a handful of devotees. However, *The Egoist*'s importance is great in terms of its contribution to the progress of modern literature and especially in understanding the development of Dora Marsden's life and writing. *The Egoist* not only furthered the careers of Pound, Aldington, H. D. and others but provided a vital outlet for the work of the controversial writer, James Joyce. Joycean scholars have covered this in considerable detail and it is not intended to duplicate their efforts here. However, their work has overlooked Dora Marsden's contribution to his career and, of course, her own work. Too many literary commentators have been too ready to follow Hughes, when he remarked that what Dora wrote "was studiously overlooked by most readers[1]." Finally, it should be emphasized again that what follows is intended to redress this imbalance rather than to make further comments on *The Egoist*'s contribution to modern literature in general and to Joyce's work in particular.

---

[1] Hughes (1931) pp. 31-2. More recent literary historians have in fact tried, not always successfully, to link Imagism with Marsden's philosophy at this time. See, for example, Clarke (1985).

The change in the titles of Dora Marsden's journals clearly baffled many of her readers, especially those with feminist sympathies. Dora herself though had little difficulty in explaining these developments. Writing in *The Egoist* in June 1914, she argued that "far from being erratic the development of *The Freewoman – Egoist* has been in one unbroken line: a line of enquiry which has gnawed its way straight through difficulties where the 'faithful,' the 'loyal,' would have broken down or turned back[1]." She felt that *The Freewoman* "marked the term of an emotion: the militant suffrage enthusiasm" but that the "joy of a good fight" was not enough to explain why men and women became involved in "movements." This led to an examination of causes, of words such as "Morality," "Freedom," "Right" and "Justice" and ultimately as described above, to an attack on these concepts themselves. Thus from looking at "The New Morality," morality itself was examined, similarly with "Freedom" which to her, only existed in relation to the power of the individual. To claim "freedom" and "rights" was to ask for protection, to deny the power of the individual:

> All the suffragists "claims" are of this order, and it was to disentangle the journal from association with these and with the long list of whines, Free Speech, Free Love, Free Assembly and what not, that the "Freewoman" became Egoist, which title is a sign hung about the seat of authority: the centre of power: the self. One has the "freedom" if one has the power, and the measure of one's power is one's own concern[2].

[1] *The Egoist*, 15 June 1914.
[2] *The Egoist*, 15 June 1914.

Dora's explanation of her paper's progress was logical from her own point of view yet it is doubtful whether it would have convinced those who flocked to *The Freewoman* in 1911. In spite of the considerable differences among the contributors to that journal there was considerable agreement that women as a sex constituted an oppressed group. There was a smaller yet significant section that also emphasized the importance of class. Now, Dora's apparent commitment to feminism and her somewhat less certain sympathy towards class analyses of power were clearly subsumed by her overriding individualism. This not only alienated her original devotees but furthered her own political isolation in the troubled times of 1914.

Ever since Dangerfield's brilliant essay on Liberal England[1], there has been considerable debate and furious disagreement over the political climate in England just before the First World War. There is no need to repeat that discussion here, yet even some of the more conservative historians have conceded that there was, at the least, a note of rebellion in the air. The WSPU, for all its faults, carried on an increasingly desperate campaign that continued to give the appearance of a sex war. More substantially, large sections of the suffrage movement, including the NUWSS, the WFL and, as described above, Sylvia Pankhurst, were increasingly moving towards a Labour Movement that was becoming more radical by the day. Faced with intransigent employers and fuelled by increasing frustration with its own leaders in the TUC and Parliament, the working class continued its

---

[1]   Dangerfield (1970).

militant mood of previous years. In the period January to July there were nearly a thousand strikes alone and by the summer there seemed to be disputes across the country. The most significant of these was in the Scottish mines which, given the strength of the Triple Alliance, arguably would have led to a General Strike if the First World War had not intervened. When the revolt of Sir Edward Carson's Unionists (where, along with Conservative leaders, they planned armed resistance to Irish Home Rule) is considered, it is difficult to see the political climate as tranquil or to regard the future of liberal democracy as assured.

Dora's own political analysis was in many ways out of step with these developments but, as before, could still carry some radical appeal. The state, for example, was in reality "The National Repository for Firearms and Batons Company[1]" while liberal democracy was merely "a method of governing the people and in that, it is identical with other methods; it aims at bringing the will of the people into submission[2]." Critics of Parliamentary democracy would also support the contention that "whereas the qualification for a share of the work in Parliament is the possession of a 'Voice' – a vote – the qualification for a share of the work of government is – a Powerful Interest... should Parliament, by means of its 'Voices' attempt to register decisions antagonistic to the governing interests, it would promptly find itself paralysed... 'The Principles of democracy' affect the nature of government no more than straws in a storm: nor are

---

[1] *The Egoist*, 16 February 1916.
[2] *The Egoist*, 1 September 1915.

they intended to. But they are capable of mollifying the governed people, which is what they are designed to do[1]."

But this analysis of power, based on an uncompromising, amoral, aggressive individualism, clearly and fundamentally differed in its origins from that of Socialism. The socialist belief in class solidarity and "brotherhood" was an anathema to Dora as it negated the individual and its ego. "Oh universal brotherhood, universal love, sameness, monotony, extinction! Mankind pressing onward to Unity, swept forward to the one impulse of the bosom of the Type! Like those swine which it says somewhere, were swept into the Gaderine Sea[2]!" At the heart of her difference with Socialism, of course, was an opposition to collective action and organization along with curtailment of total individual autonomy for the common good. Instead of liberation through class action (which in itself saw oppression as class-based, not due to an *ad hoc* group of powerful and successful individuals), Dora still seemed to regard this as possible through an act of will, through an incredible act of assertion. Even so, her calls to the oppressed to resolve their own oppression could still be appealing and not without their merit. "The poor," she argued, "will cease to be poor when they refuse to be: the downtrodden will disappear when they decide to stand up; the hungry will have bread when they take it[3]."

---

[1] *The Egoist*, 1 September 1915.
[2] *The Egoist*, 15 January 1914.
[3] *The Egoist*, 1 January 1914. Yet - who makes the bread?

Dora's tirade against causes, ideas and rights also continued to argue that to "claim" a right (as with the vote) was to accept the greater power of the person (or state) the claim was made to. It was a plea for protection, the act of a beggar[1]. Indeed, her attack on "causists" and "rightists" could reach vulgar, if somewhat colourful heights. "The notion," Dora argued, "which enables the Saviours of Society to develop in their steamiest heads is that of 'equality' and to take this notion to pieces is a process after the nature of a cold douche which should do much to reduce the humanitarian temperature to the level of common sense[2]."

As with *The Freewoman* and especially *The New Freewoman*, Dora angered her critics who could not stomach her amoral and individualist stance nor her attacks on rights and causes. One correspondent, Henry Meulin, for example, was particularly critical, arguing, not unjustifiably, that "The philosophy of Egoism rests upon unverifiable assumption[3]." Another, in a letter to Dora, wondered "whether you are in earnest or only buffooning[4]." Dora was certainly not "buffooning," though her position continued to isolate her politically, especially from feminism and anarchism. She was on her own, acknowledging her debt to Stirner but refusing even the label 'Stirnerist[5].'" This exasperated others, especially Tucker who was still smarting from their unresolved debate over Proudhon. Tucker eventually wrote

---

[1]   *The Egoist*, 1 July 1914.
[2]   *The Egoist*, 15 July 1914.
[3]   *The Egoist*, 15 January 1914.
[4]   *The Egoist*, 16 February 1914.
[5]   *The Egoist*, 15 January 1914.

in March 1914 that he was going to disassociate himself from the paper[1]. What Dora could not stand about the "clerico-libertarianism" of Proudhon and Tucker was their notion that individual autonomy in a "free" society could be curtailed and justified through appeals to "duty," "Conscience" and "the love of man." What Dora stood for, in her own words, was "a vulgar, simple satisfaction according to taste – a tub for Diogenes; a continent for Napoleon; all that I desire for me, if we can get them[2]."

The only label Dora appeared willing to accept was Tucker's description of her as "egoist and archist." Rejecting what she regarded as his moralism, she wrote that she wanted "living according to personal desire: life according to whim: life without principle: the essentially immoral life... the satisfaction of individual wants is the only 'authority' we 'respect.'" This seemed rather grand for a woman leading such a quiet life in Southport but Tucker, for one, had had enough: "against what is *The Egoist* rebelling?," he asked. "Against rebellion? Or having discovered you are not an anarchist, am I now to discover that you are not even a rebel[3]?" But Tucker suffered, to Marsden, from his moralism substituting the old demands of the Church with the "oughts" and appeals of such empty concepts as "goodness," "humanity" and "justice." In "Illusions of Anarchism," written in the autumn of 1914, she would only accept only the

---

[1] *The Egoist*, 16 March 1914.
[2] *The Egoist*, 2 March 1914 (Diogenes was a Greek cynic philosopher). Reflecting on this surely leads to a fight where only the most powerful win?
[3] *The Egoist*, 16 March 1914.

label "archist" defined by her as "one who seeks to establish, maintain and protect by the strongest weapons at his disposal, the law of his own interests... the world falls to him who can take it[1]."

This was not only an amoral picture but a bleak one as well, a recipe for continual conflict with its glorification and justification of aggression to defend and extend individual wants and interests. Implicit behind Tucker's argument was surely the question of how to escape this nightmare of a continual free for all. Moreover (and this follows on from a central weakness of Stirnerism) was the ego itself totally removed from society and its values? In other words, how far were those "wants" value-free? Marsden, like Stirner, "could not free the ego of its cultural determinants simply by refusing to recognize their substance[2]." Dora's individualism may have justified her own life; it was hardly a blueprint for a free and liberated society.

Both the positive and negative aspects of Marsden's political position, however, could perhaps be better judged when applied to concrete issues, for example, the war.

The possibility of war with Germany and the Austrian-Hungarian Empire had been growing for some time. There were many issues at stake – the breakup of the Hapsburg's Empire, Serb nationalism, Russian expansionism and German power – yet the central conflict (in Africa as well as Europe) was over the struggle for

---

[1]   *The Egoist*, 15 September 1914.
[2]   Goodheart (1968) p. 119.

markets and trade. This was, of course, hidden in the wave of jingoism that certainly swept the country (but not with total success) after the assassination of the Austrian Archduke Franz Ferdinand in June 1914 which finally led to war in August. Reactions to the war were mixed, even within pro- and anti-camps. The former included rabid jingoes as well as reluctant supporters who were aware of the carnage war could, and did, bring. Opponents of the war were even more mixed. They ranged from liberal pacifists who regarded war as unbecoming in civilized nations and those who saw the conflict as an inevitable result of capitalism's struggle for profit. Many expected the war to be short but as it dragged on, opposition grew. Lastly, though its outbreak in 1914 subdued the militant temper of the working class this too resurfaced as the carnage and the inequality of sacrifice between the classes on the Home Front became ever more apparent. As the war continued workers of all belligerent countries became increasingly conscious that there was nothing in it for them – a consciousness which, in part, explains the revolutionary movement that swept across Russia and Europe in 1917 and 1918.

Typically, Dora sided neither with the jingoistic patriotism of the Right nor with the opposition of the Left but seemed initially to regard the war almost as a clash of egos on a national scale. It was not moral or justified on one side or the other but was in fact an expression of "natural" human instinct which it would be folly to ignore or condemn. "The error," Dora wrote:

which give birth to objections which proved no objections arose from a failure to realise the existence of imperative human instincts which only war can fully justify, and have as much force with a pacifist as with any jingo... To remain too long at peace is dulling and disappointing for ability as it would be for a young singer or violinist to practice scales and exercises interminably without the hope of one day putting their powers of strength to receive the verdict of the world[1].

Surprising though this view of the war may be, Dora none the less saw through the hypocrisy of contemporary justifications of it, as "a war to end wars" or "a war for democracy." Simply "We are fighting Germany because the Germans would settle our hash for us shortly if we didn't... As for the Germans," she cynically added, "one must suppose that their motives are very similar to those of the land grabbing highwaymen who made the British Empire for us[2]." Dora too saw through the sham of international "justice" and "law," arguing that what counted, as in society itself, was not law but power. She noted in particular the hypocrisy of British appeals to international law over Belgium and Denmark whose neutrality and independence had been quashed by "illegal" German invasion. Britain was not interested in their independence *per se*, but only as part of a status quo that preserved her interests[3]. "The right of Denmark and Belgium to exist," Dora insisted, "lies in the fact

---

[1] *The Egoist*, 15 August 1914. This almost sounds like Mussolini and his defence of war. This has uncomfortable resonance with the ideas of a lance corporal in the German Army who became Chancellor and Fuhrer in 1933.
[2] *The Egoist*, 1 September 1914.
[3] *The Egoist*, 15 September 1914.

that their existence as buffers is very useful to England[1]."

Dora also stood aloof from the pacifist opposition to the war. She was scathing about pacifist women in particular. Many suffragists had opposed the war, seeing it as an extension of male physical force, and there had been a major split in the National Union of Women's Suffrage Societies over this issue[2]. Women like Margaret Ashton and Helena Swanwick wanted a negotiated peace as early as 1915. They and other suffragists like Catherine Marshall therefore supported the International Women's Suffrage Conference held in The Hague where this and a truce were on the agenda. But to Dora, their attitude and that of others who were calling for an international agreement which would guarantee the neutrality of Belgium, ignored the reality of international relations. She condemned the thinking of:

> suffragist women of America and of such as Mrs. Swanwick, Margaret Ashton, Mrs. Philip Snowden here have: i.e. that conventions, treaties, words and documents are the bases of a community's existence rather than tempers, ambition, will and power. They don't realise that the conventions are only a superstructure erected on a stability which follows upon an apprehension of the relative powers represented by conflicting powers and wills: the apprehension itself being arrived at only after actual conflict has rendered it unmistakable[3].

In fact, Dora could be seen to have been a supporter of the war albeit from a rather specialized and unique

---

[1] *The Egoist*, 2 November 1914.
[2] Garner, pp. 23-5.
[3] Dora Marsden to Harriet Shaw Weaver, 6 January 1916.

viewpoint. She certainly wanted the war pursued fully, arguing, for example, that "the delayers of peace are those who would temper down the ferocity which would wage war only at its deadliest." Further, she became a firm supporter of conscription: "everything which militates against the British Empire becoming a military camp until victory is assured is treason[1]." Yet Marsden's motives were not simple jingoism, for part of her support for conscription was based on the hope that armed individuals would be more able to secure their goals once the war was over. For example, in reply to a *Times* article at the beginning of the war which stated that the old class conflict was "artificial" in comparison to that on the continent, she countered "perhaps we as 'workers' shall emerge at the far side of this crisis capable of waging a conflict to which the term 'artificial' can be less justifiably applied[2]." Moreover, it was clear to her, as sure as "night follows day that men who have prepared themselves to defend their country will find themselves better equipped to defend themselves[3]."

Revolutionary Socialists might have sympathized with this but had a far more rigorous attitude to the war. Like Lenin, they saw the war largely as a battle between German and British capitalism for trade, markets and profit. The only benefit they envisaged was that by increasing economic and social crisis within the warring countries, class consciousness and thus the revolution would be hastened. Arming the workers as soldiers

---

[1]   *The Egoist*, 1 June 1915.
[2]   *The Egoist*, 15 August 1914.
[3]   *The Egoist*, 1 February 1915.

would help to this end. But this position envisaged the arming of a class not a hotch-potch of disparate individuals. It saw the war in economic terms and not merely as a clash of "national interests," a sort of Egoism writ large. Dora's analysis clearly did not fit this position – or indeed any other. She was alienated from the liberal suffragist pacifist view and also from the jingos. Once again, she was on her own.

Before the war began, Dora still felt unable to resist attacking her old adversary, the WSPU. As before, her vitriolic attacks on the Pankhursts often had feminist implications. This was clearly evident in her continued denunciation of Christabel's *The Great Scourge and How to End It*. As discussed above, Christabel had claimed that most men had venereal disease and that the prime reason for opposition to woman's suffrage came from men concerned that enfranchised women would stop their promiscuity. Until women had the vote, she concluded they should be wary of any sexual contact with men. "Votes for Women, Chastity for Men!" was a provocative and memorable rallying cry, and Christabel was certainly correct in attacking the hypocrisy of many men. Ultimately of course *The Great Scourge* was a call for upholding the "ideal" values of chastity, marriage and monogamy.

Given Dora's attitude to contemporary moral values it was hardly surprising that she should oppose Christabel's position. In particular, Dora criticized *The Great Scourge* for its denial of women's sexuality and its failure to examine the issues that lay behind the myth of purity. Apart from that, Dora, among others, believed that

Christabel's statistics on venereal disease were so exaggerated that they made nonsense of her argument. If over 70 per cent of men at one time or another had VD, then "the number of those who are free from it neither means nor matters – we are all tainted and presumably inoculated in fact[1]." Concern over venereal disease was certainly real at the time, if only because of the uncertainty of cures, but Christabel's tirade appalled many feminists. Rebecca West, for example, declared that her remarks on sex were "utterly valueless and were a matter for scalding tears[2]." But to Dora it provided another example of the stupidity and crassness of Mrs. Pankhurst's favourite daughter. It also gave Dora the opportunity to reveal her more humourous, lighter side. She attacked Christabel in rhyme:

[1]   *The Egoist*, 2 February 1914.
[2]   Quoted in Mitchell, p. 228.

These are the doctors

Who Told The Tale

Of the Scrofulous Child

Of the infected wife

Of the lustful man

Who before his marriage

Visited the woman

Who poverty led

To wander the streets

To minister to friends

Who contracted the disease

Which was the scourge

Which distressed the spiritual ideals

Of the Normal Woman who regards the Sex Act as the Final Pledge of her Faith and Love[1].

Dora's reaction to *The Great Scourge* was based on a totally different conception of morality and, of course, on personal animosity towards Christabel. While noting that Christabel never once ventured "the indiscretion of an individual observation but contents herself with the repetition of the tale of social illnesses such as the maiden of 16 on the orange box at the corner has for a long time made us familiar with," Dora concluded: "If Miss Pankhurst desires to exploit human boredom and the ravages of dirt she will require to call in the aid of a

---

[1] *The Egoist*, 2 February 1914.

more subtle intelligence than she herself appears to possess[1]." Later, she added that, in her whole career, Christabel had only expressed two opinions "one watches with interest for the third[2]." Others too joined in the fun. The Canadian feminist R. B. Kerr, for example, argued that "her obvious ignorance of life is a great handicap to Miss Pankhurst[3]," while even Ezra Pound, posing as Bastien von Helmholtz, felt she "has as much intellect as a guinea pig[4]."

Dora's lingering bitterness over her treatment by the WSPU remained with her throughout *The Egoist* period. Her attitude was obviously politically-based but under the surface was guided by the pain of rejection and betrayal. Dora had risked her life for the Union but no doubt felt she was dropped when her independence became too great to be tolerated by the leaders. As we have seen, Dora politically was moving away from the WSPU anyway but the personal aspect of the split must not be ignored. It was fuelled too by a feeling that Christabel and Emmeline Pankhurst only favoured wealthy, titled women, not the plain Janes (or Doras) of this world. This was hinted at in Marsden's review of Lady Constance Lytton's book *Prison and Prisoners* which appeared in *The Egoist* in May 1914. As a suffragette, Constance had entered WSPU folklore by disguising herself as a plain working-class woman, "Jane Warton," and creating a scandal by revealing the vast difference in treatment after "Jane's" arrest in January

---

[1] *The Egoist*, 2 February 1914.
[2] *The Egoist*, 15 June 1914.
[3] *The Egoist*, 16 March, 1914.
[4] *The Egoist*, 1 July 1914.

1910 from that she received as Lady Lytton some months previously when she was quickly released from jail. Dora mischievously wondered what would have happened if Lytton had "done another Jane Warton on the very capable, very astute and very charming persons, Mrs. Pankhurst or Mrs. Pethick-Lawrence. Had she adopted another role, say plain 'Martha Jones' and presented herself at Clement's Inn as a deputant would she have 'rested' in Miss Christabel's boudoir? In faith, love and truth we declare unto her she would not. No, not, not NOT." Contrary to Lytton's view, Dora felt that "one would need to travel far before encountering a trio of women (Pethick-Lawrence, Emmeline and Christabel) as selfish as the former committee of the WSPU[1]."

Dora remained critical of suffragism as a whole and not just that of the WSPU. She viewed the largest and most important suffrage society, the NUWSS, and its growing relationship with the Labour Movement with disdain. Dora felt that suffragists in the National Union "would like to be the 'intellectual' party: unfortunately strict suffrage and intellect will not lie down together." They should stick to simple arguments, perhaps none simpler than the Pankhurstian "Give us the vote, never mind why, or we will burn your house down if you don't." (WSPU arson attacks continued throughout 1914.) To Marsden, when asked where her paper stood in position to women's suffrage, the answer was unequivocally clear: "'Nowhere,' since the suffrage is wholly a matter of indifference[2]."

---

[1] *The Egoist*, 15 May 1914. See also Lytton (1912).
[2] *The Egoist*, 15 June 1914.

However, the debate surrounding Christabel's *Great Scourge* and suffragism in general reflected some interest in feminism even though Dora herself would have certainly rejected the label "feminist" in 1914. R. B. Kerr continued to write to the paper as occasionally did F. W. Stella-Browne who remained a subscriber throughout the paper's life. The latter was particularly vociferous in her defence of the American Margaret Sanger, who was being prosecuted for her attempts to spread information on birth control. Commenting on American suffragists" somewhat guarded defence of Sanger, Stella-Browne argued: "I suppose we should be thankful that they have not hastened to repudiate Mrs. Sanger and all her works, as the English leaders de-nounced *The Freewoman* 3 years ago[1]." Other suffrag-ists and feminists, for example Catherine Tolson, Bessie Heyes, Edith How-Martyn and Rona Robinson, re-mained subscribers too, even though they were a minor-ity. The vast majority of *Freewoman* subscribers did not take a subscription to *The Egoist*: in spite of its ancestry, the paper's prime concern was no longer feminism[2].

None the less, discussions, sometimes extremely frank discussions, on the position of women did surface in the paper if only in 1914 and if only due to further re-actions to suffragism. "H. S. C.," for example, praised Dora's attack on the limits of Christabel's posturing on morality and felt that women's sexuality and drive had to be recognized and be seen as equally "legitimate" to

---

[1] *The Egoist*, 1 July 1914. Rose Witcop was prosecuted in 1922 for publishing a book by Sanger on birth control.
[2] See *The Freewoman*, *The Egoist* subscription lists.

that of men. Sex itself "Is too important to be hidden... the sex act as a normal, regular and completed function is as necessary as eating... God save us from sexual constipation[1]." Beeban and Noel Teulon Porter agreed, and went into some detail on how women could help themselves to be sexually fulfilled[2]. Others struck a more cautious note with one (male) reader making the pertinent point that "it is a significant fact that all these sweeping statements about the sexual 'needs' of women are made by men... we wish to indulge our low pleasures, so we assume in women greater 'needs' in this line and pat ourselves on the back for satisfying them. What high souled martyrs we are[3]!" Dora intervened occasionally in this discussion if only to emphasize her distaste for the concept of "morality" and her belief that the only morality that counted was that conceived by the Ego[4].

Dora herself argued that she had had enough of "the feminist corpse[5]," though she wrote to Harriet Weaver on 16 September 1914 that she was considering writing on "The position of women as revealed by the war." She still occasionally reminisced privately about her suffragette days too[6], but as her interest in philosophy increased and became almost totally time-consuming, her references to women declined. Her importance to feminism was however still occasionally recognized.

[1] *The Egoist*, 16 February 1914.
[2] *The Egoist*, 2, 16 March 1914.
[3] *The Egoist*, 16 March 1914.
[4] *The Egoist*, 2 March 1914.
[5] *The Egoist*, 1 October 1914.
[6] See, for example, Marsden to Weaver, October 1915.

Requesting an interview in 1917, Mabel Potter Dagget, an American journalist and feminist working for the *Pictorial Review*, referred to Dora as "the representative of one branch of the feminist movement in England[1]." Dora was unsure about meeting her although she was attracted to the possibility of free publicity for *The Egoist* in America. She wrote to Harriet, "I am not keen to be identified with the feminist 'stunt' particularly: but if the *P. R.* were a paper of any standing it might be worthwhile trying it on just to keep the Americans alive to the fact that the paper still lives and thrives." In the end, and somewhat sadly for the founding editor of the most radical feminist journal of the early Twentieth Century, Dora concluded: "That anything I say about women isn't worth a journey to Lancashire to listen to[2]."

By the time of Dagget's enquiry Dora was no longer editor of *The Egoist*. Harriet Shaw Weaver, somewhat reluctantly, had taken over the editorial chair in the summer of 1914 and Dora had assumed the role of contributing editor. Ostensibly, this was to allow her to concentrate on her philosophical research and writings. She intended to continue her regular column of "Views and Comments" but she was also going to begin a series on "The Philosophical Basis of Egoism" in July[3]. However, Dora's concern for philosophy was not the only reason for the change. It was also linked to two other persistent and lifelong problems of the paper, its finances and the intermittent struggle for control.

---

[1]   Mabel Potter Dagget to Dora Marsden, 23 February 1917.
[2]   Dora Marsden to Harriet Shaw Weaver, March 1917.
[3]   *The Egoist*, 15 June 1914.

Financially, as with *The Freewoman* and *The New Freewoman*, *The Egoist* was extremely weak which as Catherine Wood noticed, was hardly surprising given the nature of its concerns. It was extremely unlikely to attract advertising revenue while such a journal was even less likely to attract an audience understandably distracted by the war[1]. The potential revenue from sales was in any case limited for the print run (not the number of copies sold) only exceeded one thousand once, in May 1915, and was usually nearer to seven hundred and fifty, reduced to four hundred by 1919[2]. In each year income derived solely from the paper was exceeded by expenditure and this sorry state of affairs was only remedied by anonymous donations, namely gifts from Harriet Shaw Weaver.

The financial problem was linked to and complicated by a struggle for control of the paper itself. This was usually associated with Ezra Pound and his circle. As early as January 1914, Pound was hoping to increase his influence by persuading Amy Lowell, an American patron of the arts, to finance the paper. Both Dora and Harriet, though conscious of the paper's perilous financial position, were apprehensive, and eventually Dora proposed a solution which must have been aired at the beginning of the year. She wrote to Weaver in March that if "*The Egoist* spark of intelligence is not to be extinguished under Miss Lowell's respectable hulk" that Harriet "Become sole editor on and after June 15th[3]."

---

[1] Wartime restriction on newspaper was also a problem.
[2] *The Egoist* account book.
[3] Dora Marsden to Harriet Shaw Weaver, 19 March 1914.

Harriet's reaction to this proposal is unknown, a victim of her unfortunate decision to destroy much of her correspondence with Dora in 1944[1]. None the less, in spite of possible apprehension over Pound, Harriet was determined to maintain a journal for new and creative talent and to continue to provide a platform for Dora's writings. Though she had no experience of editing, she finally agreed to take over the editorial chair. She hoped it would be temporary but Dora acted as if it was a permanent appointment. For Dora it was ideal. An editor-backer of Pound's choosing would be a threat to her position on the paper but with Harriet in charge her independence was guaranteed. Dora even tempered her suspicions of Pound, finding him "Very amiable. I feel sure we are doing the very best for the paper in changing matters as we are doing now[2]."

Dora was relieved by the new arrangement as it gave her more time for her own work but it also further isolated her from the day-to-day running of the paper. The centre of operations was now entirely in London as the printing of the paper moved to the capital in the summer of 1914. Partly as a result of this, and out of loyalty to Dora, Grace Jardine formally resigned her post in June as well. With typical generosity, however, Harriet offered to pay her wages for continuing to be

---

[1]   For a biographer of Harriet's friend, this act was indeed unfortunate. A note with the surviving letters in the Weaver collection reads "I destroyed the bulk of Dora Marsden's letters – and in particular, the more personal ones." She probably did this in an attempt to disguise her financial gifts to Dora and *The Egoist*, but also, I suspect, to hide some of the differences, possibly even rows between them.

[2]   Dora Marsden to Harriet Shaw Weaver, 3 April 1914.

Dora's personal assistant. Grace did remain involved both with the paper and Dora, though eventually she became a traveller for the publishers Hodder and Stoughton. Dora's personal isolation increased as a result of the changes although she remained involved in *The Egoist*'s affairs – if from a distance – until its end in December 1919.

In particular, Dora, in a reversal of roles, was especially helpful and supportive towards Harriet as she grappled with her new task. Commenting on the 15 July issue she wrote: "Dearest Editor... the paper looks extremely well: we were lost in interest over it this morning: breakfast plus *The Egoist* lasted until 11:45... please accept my congratulations." Dora further felt that rather than just editing the paper, Harriet ought to write more material herself, beginning perhaps with a version of the old *Freewoman* "Notes of the Week." "*I am sure*," she continued, "you could do them in just the way we have been wanting them done for so long. And I don't know who else can. Why not have a shot[1]?" Later, when Harriet had written an article under the pseudonym Josephine Wright, she congratulated her fulsomely: "Please do some more: your comments and quotes are far more refreshing than the laboured things. The paper needs lightening: obviously to lighten it is your destiny[2]."

But the relationship between the Southport-based Dora and her editor was, unsurprisingly perhaps, not without its problems. In particular, Dora's insistence on

---

[1] Dora Marsden to Harriet Shaw Weaver, 15 July 1914.
[2] Dora Marsden to Harriet Shaw Weaver, 16 September 1914.

accuracy in her own material led to large printers' bills for corrections. Also her copy was almost always late. The correspondence between the two, though often reflecting both women's wit and humour, constantly referred to the lateness of Dora's articles. Even the normally cool Weaver began to get exasperated. Dora promised to amend her "sinful life ...s'elp me Gawd!" and even claimed to be a "reformed character[1]," but still her articles kept arriving late or at the very last minute. Finally, Harriet let off steam in a marvellous parody of Shakespeare's *Tempest* which for its wit alone is worth quoting in full:

[1]   Dora Marsden to Harriet Shaw Weaver, 17, 19 July 1914.

With apologies to Caliban

You made me edit, and my profit on't

Is, I know how to curse. May headaches never quit you

For learning me to edit! When first thou cam'st

Thou talkedst smooth, and madest light of it; wouldst tell me

No need to worry so. And I believed you.

Cursed be that I did so! All the charms

Of Ainsdale, sands, winds, rabbits, light on you!

For I am all the editors you have

(Until your book is published), which was first

But mine own happy self. And now you stie me

In a vile office, whiles you do keep from me

The whole o' your article. Sometimes am I

So short of copy that I'm driven to make

A leader out of Carter's trash. Shrugs thou, Malice?

If thou neglects or dost unwillingly

What I command, I'll pester thee with postcards,

Fill all thy house with swearing telegrams

Thou'lt blush to meet the postman in the street.

As wicked words, as e're Miss Jardine swore

As stupid printers in her hottest mood.

I'll wire you every day. Your conscience† hears me

And yet I needs must curse.

† Note to the 400th edition: This is an error. Recent researches
   have shown that she never had one[1].

---

[1]   Harriet Shaw Weaver to Dora Marsden, August 1914.

Even this wonderful joke, which clearly reflected Weaver's own hidden talents, did not have the desired effect. The arrival of Dora's copy continued to be erratic and late. Quite clearly, this was due to the complexity of the material and Dora's constant revision in a search for absolute accuracy. Grace tried to mediate between the two, and more than once apologized to Harriet on Dora's behalf. When Dora, for example, was writing on the philosopher Berkeley, Grace felt that the lateness of the finished article was due to the subject which required "Almost endless writing and rewriting to make it understandable... Dora says," adding almost pathetically, "That Berkeley would have taken ten years to publish anything so assertive if that is any consolation to you for the fact that your contributory editor takes a month and then is struck for want of time. We recommend ourselves for mercy[1]." This was a common plea – "I recommend myself for mercy and a light sentence[2]." But in general, Weaver tended to tolerate Dora's behaviour with gentle humour. This reflected the strength of the relationship between them and it reflected too Harriet's faith in Dora. Moreover, there was no jealousy in Dora's attitude to Harriet, but rather admiration and support, even if this was sometimes expressed in a mischievous way. "Now: re H. S. W. *You* are a horror: a villain: a ----!!! It is imperative you should produce an article... *where* are those moral discourses? You burnt them – wretch! So you have got to write on 'modern tendencies of thought' or something like it as a punishment richly

---

[1] Grace Jardine to Harriet Shaw Weaver, 23 February 1915.
[2] Dora Marsden to Harriet Shaw Weaver, September 1916.

deserved[1]."

The paper continued, though, to lurch into financial difficulties and in 1915 it became a monthly. Weaver's confidence as an editor grew, however, and she quickly became the lynchpin of *The Egoist*. In spite of Harriet's central role, though, it is very noticeable how keen she was to consult Dora on developments regarding the paper. This was achieved mainly through the voluminous and almost daily correspondence between the two women but also by Dora's occasional visits to London and Harriet's to Southport. Harriet came north in December 1914 while Dora went to London for official meetings four times in 1916 and once in 1919. In other words, though Dora's personal isolation increased during this period, she did remain involved with the paper, if not with the actual day-to-day organization.

In particular, the two women consulted each other fully over the problems of survival and the struggle for control. As early as 1914, this was already an issue even though the Lowell "bid" never materialized. Yet both women knew that the paper was in serious trouble and Dora was constantly making suggestions for its revitalization. For example, she hoped to woo back Rebecca West[2], and she hoped too to exploit the rumoured death in the summer of 1914 of her old adversary, *The New Age*. Dora even suggested trying to engage *The New Age*'s Bechhofer, who had written the skit on *The Free-*

---

[1] Dora Marsden to Harriet Shaw Weaver, n.d., *c*. September / October 1916. The constant rewriting and subsequent delay became a central feature of Dora's work throughout the rest of her life.

[2] Dora Marsden to Harriet Shaw Weaver, 30 July 1914.

woman and had just published another on the letters page of *The Egoist*. Aldington took this seriously and suggested cutting the correspondence down but Dora admonished him for "becoming jumpy with nerves" about it. "What does the young man imagine the paper is to live on in the way of popular interest? Not on Imagist poetry surely?" She concluded, "If we can get Bechhofer and Rebecca West we could make things go – especially in an empty field[1]."

By the autumn of 1914 Dora was insisting: "We ought to be making the most of the few months we are keeping alive. I am certain everyone expected us to go under[2]," and she even seemed half-hopeful that the Lowell offer would after all be realized. But by the end of the year, Dora clearly had doubts about *The Egoist*'s survival and asked Harriet for circulation details "because it isn't much use bringing out a paper that has no readers, is it[3]?"

By the following autumn, the paper's fortunes had not revived, and even Weaver seemed to have had enough. In her biographer's words, she realized that she had been "priming a pump that was going to need priming for ever[4]." The paper's most interesting serial, Joyce's *A Portrait of the Artist as a Young Man*, had ended and Dora's articles continued to be obtuse as well as late: *The Egoist* was almost dead.

---

[1]   Dora Marsden to Harriet Shaw Weaver, 30 July 1914. In the end neither joined the paper.
[2]   Dora Marsden to Harriet Shaw Weaver, 3 September 1914.
[3]   Dora Marsden to Harriet Shaw Weaver, 30 November 1914.
[4]   Lidderdale and Nicholson, p. 105.

Dora was well aware of the precarious state of the paper's position and in October 1915 wrote to Harriet a long and thoughtful letter on its prospects. *The Egoist*, Dora clearly realized, was "slowly but surely fizzling out... We are rapidly reaching the bottom of the slope." To her, the major problem was that it:

> has no unity; it is not vitalised or dominated by any united purpose which can be made to grow increasingly attractive and intelligible to readers. It is not bright because it has no leaven: what should be the yeast to lighten the heaviness of Egoism is the equally unleavened heaviness of Imagism... The paper is trying to serve two masters, and while one master – one purpose – is absolutely essential: two make a deadening combination.

Dora not only felt Imagism and Egoism were separate entities but together created the central weakness from which the paper suffered. She was aware too that both subjects could be dull. As things stood, "we are not merely risking failure but are actively courting it." She went on to suggest three possible plans of action:

a. Drop the paper entirely before our audience drops us and while we can, give out some plausible excuse such as "The War" and so save our reputation and money.

b. Take the whole question of reviewing our audience in hand and the first essential for this is to give the paper unity. Either Imagism must go: or Egoism must go. If it is Egoism which is to drop out your course is clear. Mr. Aldington will run the Imagist poets and if there is anything in them they are likely to win a modest success given the advantage of a journal and time. Perhaps also money can be influenced if I disappeared: Miss Lovell perhaps would come if I went. Such a course would be sensible from a journalistic point of view: that is it would give the paper at least the *hope* of succeeding. The other way, and of course the one whose desirability it is my business to plead is: –

c. Pulling up sharp while we have a nucleus of circulation left and so draw the attention of our readers to the fact that matters are going to be changed. This course would save money on three issues which saved sum could be used in advertising our reappearance.

Some of Dora's ideas were quite startling but change was needed if *The Egoist* was to survive. Indeed, given the additional problems of "divided purposes, absentee contributors and directors" it was, as Dora wrote, a "miracle that there is a sheet left to tell the tale at all." Dora did not ignore her own responsibility for the paper's position. She realized the problem of being an absentee in Southport but, more unusual for her, she realized too that her own articles were not particularly attractive. "My mind," she complained, "has gone placid; the smallest attempt at articulateness seems to cost more effort than the thing when said is worth. I *could* write metaphysics here: I *can't* vitalise a paper from here; nor from anywhere else until I have dragged myself out of the depths of indifference in which I sink."

What she suggested was that the paper should be suspended for three months, that she should return to London and new writers be recruited in time for its resumption. These were to include Rebecca West – "she *is* somebody now"- and Margaret Storm Jameson. Aldington was to have less control, leaving "us free to rake in some of the poets of a different brand than the Imagists." Evidently, Dora intended coming to London, meeting people and assuming a much more direct role in running the paper. She even suggested becoming *The Egoist*'s drama critic though perhaps "under a name less burdened with 'Philosophy' than 'D. M.[1]'"

This fascinating letter is illuminating in many ways, not least of which is Dora's attitude to Imagism. Far from inter-relating with it, she saw Imagism as a major factor behind the paper's decline and wanted it dropped or reduced. In another letter written in the same month, she told Harriet not to "forget about the November number: tell R. A. on no account must they take up the whole issue[2]." Moreover, the first letter clearly indicates that she wanted to take a more direct and responsible role in the running of the paper. In all, it raises some intriguing questions. Had Dora tired of the isolation of Ainsdale, was she yearning for a more active and social life? Had she grown tired of her philosophical research

---

[1] Dora Marsden to Harriet Shaw Weaver, n.d. *c*. October 1915.
[2] Dora Marsden to Harriet Shaw Weaver, n.d. *c*. October 1915.

for, in this clear-sighted mood, she must have realized that there would be little time for philosophy if she returned to London? Most intriguingly of all, did Dora suggest "lassooing" Rebecca West and Margaret Storm Jameson while demoting Aldington because she resented the male dominance of the paper and wanted more women writers?

Unfortunately, Harriet's response to Dora's suggestions has not come to light[1] although perhaps part of her answer can be guessed through the fact that she decided to soldier on without any major changes. Perhaps she felt the suggestions were not feasible, perhaps too, Weaver felt more warmly towards the Imagists than Dora did. It may well be that her worries were assuaged by a slight (and temporary) increase in circulation. But whatever the reason, and in spite of Zepplin raids in London, Harriet evidently decided to continue publishing the paper with her contributing editor still ensconced on the Lancashire coast. Dora herself does not appear to have pursued her October manifesto, nor did Harriet's failure to act on it seem to bother her. On the contrary, the New Year opened well with Dora claiming the January 1916 issue was "very good, much more varied than usual." She added Harriet's "views and comments read very well indeed: consider yourself established and an institution henceforth[2]."

In many ways, it was a pity that Dora did not follow her own suggestions, particularly the idea of breaking her own self-imposed exile and returning to London.

---

[1] Very likely, Harriet's reply was destroyed by her in 1944.
[2] Dora Marsden to Harriet Shaw Weaver, 6 January 1916.

Why did she decide not to go? Had Harriet put her off, advising her to complete her book on philosophy in the peace and quiet of the Lancashire coast? But surely, Weaver would have welcomed Marsden's help and in any case, could not prevent her from coming? The evidence suggests rather that Dora was scared, frightened of a return to a more active and public life after her three-year retreat. By now, she probably preferred her own small, yet secure world. But the decision had many repercussions. First, it meant that her writings went largely unchallenged by direct debate. She had to work out their complexities on her own and this became a tremendous mental and physical strain. This was increased by another consequence of her decision to stay in Southport for it meant her sense of worth and a public validation of this could only come through her writings: of course, that is why they were so important to her. And finally, it meant that any future attempt to join the world in a more active, social, even political way would be even more difficult to fulfill. The failure to carry out the proposal to return to London was, in my opinion, crucial.

By the New Year, Harriet had clearly decided to carry on. In many ways and beyond her financial support, *The Egoist* was her paper. She was an active editor who began to be more confident about her own writing. Perhaps buoyed up by New Year optimism, she opened 1916 with a proud and defiant defence of the paper. "It has," she declared:

skirted all movements and caught on to none... *The Egoist* is wedded to no belief from which it is willing to be divorced. To probe to the depths of human nature, to keep its curiosity in it fresh and alert, to regard nothing in human nature as foreign to it, but to hold itself ready to bring to the surface what may be found, without any predetermination to fling back all but unwelcome facts – such are the high and uncommon pretensions upon which it bases its claims to provenance[1].

Harriet was not so overconfident or insensitive not to continue to seek Dora's advice on matters affecting the paper, especially when, in the spring, there was yet another attempt by others at a takeover. In February, Dora felt that Pound was again trying to gain control. She complained to Harriet of "the way these individuals, Pound, R. A. or anyone else put on the audacity to ask for the whole paper. It isn't good for us and I hope you won't allow it to be done[2]." Indeed, Pound, backed by the promise of £120 a year from John Quinn, hoped to lease some of the paper from Harriet. This section of the paper would then, of course, be under his control. This may have seemed reasonable to him yet in effect it would have resulted in *The Egoist* subsidizing Pound while putting Richard Aldington, as assistant editor, in an awkward situation. It certainly would have given Pound more clout.

Dora's reaction to his latest proposal was predictable though she did not want to throw away completely the chance of further money. She saw Pound's

---

[1] *The Egoist*, January 1916.
[2] Dora Marsden to Harriet Shaw Weaver, 2 February 1916.

suggestion as part of a continuing friction between him and Aldington, whom, as Dora saw it, he wanted to replace. "It is a question of E. P. and his friends against R. A. and his friends. We rub out R. A.'s name on the editorial staff and put in Pound's (which by the way as they are sworn foes will create a mild scandal). Well, of course, which gang do they prefer? That is the question." Dora herself thought "*very little* of Pound's supposed big sums to be expended on contributors of his own choosing." She noted that he did not propose simply putting the money into the New Freewoman Company Ltd, as this would not give him the same degree of control. Dora concluded that Pound wanted to replace Aldington "all on the strength of some phantom sums which he doesn't even propose we shall ever handle. He reduces *our* editorial power to zero. Fixed items he allows for – he bags the rest. He really is ingenious." On the other hand, Dora realized, *The Egoist* needed Pound's material and influence. Further, perhaps, his money could be used to attract new contributors. Thus, she told Harriet to keep "sweet and gracious" to Pound, and to tell him that they were going to think the offer over. Dora even admitted that "Pound is... more *entertaining* than R. A." but she still had "a genuine mistrust" of the American. Finally, she advised Harriet never to "cede any rights over the space of the paper[1]."

In this case Pound's money was apparently real and perhaps Dora's isolation from London coloured and exaggerated her suspicions of him. Harriet seemed to have warmed to Pound though she appreciated Dora's remark

---

[1] Dora Marsden to Harriet Shaw Weaver, 31 March 1916.

that he liked to play the "little god among his friends[1]."
Pound himself emphatically denied he wanted to replace
Aldington[2], but again, in the end the offer lapsed. Dora
was clearly concerned about the paper but though she
realized the need for new revenue she mistrusted Pound.
Perhaps too, though this is not directly raised in her correspondence, she was concerned that the increase in his
power on the paper would adversely affect her position,
making *The Egoist* even more of a literary review and
her own work look even more out of place than it already did.

Pound was nothing if not persistent and he returned
to the fray the following spring with promises of cash to
pay contributors. Dora was again sceptical – "you know
I think the offer is mythical" – but her scepticism was
overruled by her realistic assessment that Pound was too
important to lose[3]. For this reason Dora, notwithstanding
her worry over her own position on the paper, concurred
with Weaver's suggestion of offering him a contributing
editor's post as long as Harriet retained ultimate control
as editor. To Dora's relief, after he had secured an appointment with *The Little Review* Pound did not take the
post. None the less she was annoyed at what she regarded as his duplicity. She accused him of being "cool
and high handed in the last degree" for continuing to
press for a post on *The Egoist* while negotiating with
The Little Review. Dora was, moreover, concerned that
he was going to use *The Egoist* as a mutual appreciation

---

[1]   Dora Marsden to Harriet Shaw Weaver, 31 March 1916.
[2]   Ezra Pound to Harriet Shaw Weaver, 4 April 1916.
[3]   Dora Marsden to Harriet Shaw Weaver, 1 February 1916.

society for himself and his friends. "Apparently," Dora argued humorously:

> he is going to use *The Egoist* as a sounding board for the assertion of his merit and that of his followers and I suppose now of his 'Master" W. B. Yeats. We must mind we don't become too ridiculous in connection with this sort of thing. The Imagists: by each other, Mr. R. A., E. P. by himself; E. P. also by another. Eliot by E. P., Joyce by E. P., W. B. Yeats (father!) by E. P. alias Eliot... and so on and so on. It only requires (as I've said before) you to do me and me you in order to provoke the very type to "inextinguishable laughter[1].

Ultimately, Pound suggested T. S. Eliot, whom he had met in 1914, as assistant editor and, after checking with Aldington's wife H. D. that this would be acceptable to them, Eliot took up the post in June 1917[2]. Dora liked Eliot's work although "as with all the new poets, *thought* runs a trifle thin." She was moreover still concerned about Pound's intentions for "You see: we and E. P. have totally differing conceptions of what *The Egoist* is to be. He is for *capturing* it: we are for maintaining it... My opinion of Mr. Pound remains what it has been for a long time: that he is too clever by one half. He is such a schemer that he schemes himself into people's mistrust[3]."

Dora's fears that Pound would assume a proprietary position through Eliot fortunately proved groundless although "the hardy annual" of reorganization appeared for the last time in 1918. On this occasion, it was initi-

---

[1]   Dora Marsden to Harriet Shaw Weaver, 6 May 1916.
[2]   Aldington had been called up to the war.
[3]   Dora Marsden to Harriet Shaw Weaver, 16 May 1917.

ated by Captain (later Sir Herbert) Read, the poet and art critic. He suggested a merger of *The Egoist* with other literary journals combined with a shop or gallery. Though Dora felt that Ezra Pound may well have been behind it, she did not dismiss Read's suggestion entirely and saw "their offer as a tribute to our staying power and solidity. Six years of existence commends some little acknowledgement quite on its own account. Let us crow!" Dora felt this offer differed from the others, seeing it as a proposal to amalgamate rather than "a veiled invitation to us to terminate our existence in their interest." Indeed, she was keen about the merger and the shop and suggested their combined strength would even allow them to purchase their own printing press. "I am really extremely keen: the whole thing has enormous possibilities. If the proposal matures and we get on there is no reason why they should not take an interest in the extension of *The Egoist*; perhaps in a dim and distant future modify its form and make it a real force. As for helping the young and struggling: heaven knows we don't want to wallow in profits. All we want is to escape the arms of the official receiver[1]."

Harriet, ever the realist, was less enthusiastic, realizing the difficulties of the scheme, but Dora remained "still undisillusioned" especially given *The Egoist*'s perilous state. There had only been one issue for November-December 1918 and in 1919 the price had risen to 9d. What Dora conceived was the creation of "Egoist Monthly Publications," publishing books, pamphlets and a monthly review containing *The Egoist* and other titles,

---

[1]   Dora Marsden to Harriet Shaw Weaver, 30 October 1918.

each with their own editor and control. This would not only cut costs by sharing them but would be a radical departure from the usual methods of publishing such magazines. Evidently excited, she playfully ended "Therefore, ma'am, NOT in Heraclitean vein, do I again recommend unto you this charming delightful yea lucrative scheme[1]."

It was not only the lighter side of Dora Marsden that was reflected in her reactions to this scheme but also her obvious concern for the paper and her wish that it should continue. Harriet may well have been right to doubt its feasibility but none the less it did seem that it "would create quite an innovation in journalistic publishing[2]." Dora was not sure whether she could work with others but she realized something must be done if *The Egoist* as a paper was not to die. But by this time Harriet was in any cast increasingly concerned with publishing Joyce and the offer eventually collapsed as did *The Egoist* itself in December 1919.

❦

The Egoist has been renowned for many years as the first English journal to publish the work of James Joyce. Joyce was without question one of the most gifted and original writers of the early Twentieth Century. He was, in style and content, one of the most controversial too for he ignored orthodox literary and moral conventions. As a result, his work often fell foul of the law and was difficult to publish. Without the perception of his talent by others and without the personal and fi-

---

[1]   Dora Marsden to Harriet Shaw Weaver, 21 October 1918.
[2]   Dora Marsden to Harriet Shaw Weaver, 21 November 1918.

nancial support of some key figures, it is unlikely that Joyce, a restless and impecunious man who lived most of his life in Europe away from his native Ireland, would ever have become the literary giant he is today[1].

One central character in Joyce's early career was Ezra Pound who, for all his own faults, quickly recognized the Irishman's talents. Pound thus promoted his work in *The Egoist* and later, in his own *Little Review*. Equally important was Harriet Shaw Weaver who personally and financially supported Joyce throughout his troubled life. Still occasionally misrepresented as "a wealthy American[2]," Lidderdale and Nicholson's biography of Weaver finally gave Harriet the credit she deserved. Yet, though much smaller in comparison, the contribution of Dora Marsden has been overlooked. First, Dora had been responsible, in an indirect way, for bringing Joyce and Harriet Weaver together through her papers *The Freewoman*, *The New Freewoman* and *The Egoist*. Second, though far from keen on *Ulysses*, Dora welcomed Joyce's work in *The Egoist* and was willing to risk prison in a fight for its right to be published. Dora also never interfered with Harriet's decision to promote and publish Joyce when Harriet took over the editorship of the paper.

Finally, Dora must take some belated credit too for the decision to publish *A Portrait of the Artist as a Young Man*, in serial form in *The Egoist* in 1914. There remains some dispute over who originally sent the manuscript to Pound who, with reservations about the lan-

---

[1]   Ellman (1966).
[2]   Mitchell (1977), p. 357.

guage, passed it on to Dora yet it was she who decided on publication, announcing in January 1914 that the series was to begin the next month. Harriet, whose astounding generosity was only matched by her integrity, was always ready to acknowledge this. Many years later, for example, she insisted to Stuart Gilbert, who had known Joyce since 1927 and who became the editor of his published letters in 1957, that Dora too must have credit for the publication of *A Portrait*. Writing to Gilbert's publisher she asked: "Under 1914. Please change '(thanks to Miss Weaver)' to '(thanks initially to Miss Dora Marsden)' as it was she to whom Mr. Pound had sent the typescript of the first three chapters of the *Portrait* and who had accepted it for serialising in *The Egoist* – before she handed over the technical side to me[1]." Dora did not read all of *A Portrait* until it was in book form yet she had accepted the first three chapters and, with Grace Jardine, saw they came back from the printers unaltered. What would have happened if Dora had refused the manuscript it is difficult to say, yet it was through the January announcement in *The Egoist* that Weaver first heard of Joyce and it was Marsden's decision that gave the Irishman his first major breakthrough in England.

Once *The Egoist*'s editor and printer were located in London, it would seem inevitable that Dora, in Ainsdale, would become of peripheral importance to Joyce. But though Weaver became the pivotal figure and Dora's role much less direct, she remained influential and supportive to both as the correspondence between

---

[1]   Weaver to Huebsch, 8 June 1955.

the two women shows. When, for example, Truscott's, *The Egoist*'s printers in London, objected to part of a chapter from *A Portrait*, Dora commiserated with her friend. "I am afraid," she wrote on 3 November 1914 "that Truscott's have far too naughty minds for us: only Heaven can guess at the dark imaginings of their 'Directory Board!'"

The difficulty with Truscott's was repeated when a publisher was sought to print it in book form. Eventually, Weaver decided to publish it herself through the New Freewoman Company Ltd., which became The Egoist Ltd. in the autumn of 1916. Harriet would by now have done this independently if Dora, as a member of the Board, had refused but, as usual, out of regard for Dora and procedure, she formally asked her permission. Marsden was indeed somewhat nervous about the new venture, concerned that they both might end up in the bankruptcy court but finally she agreed[1]. Only when she knew Dora did not object did she write to Joyce with a firm offer of publication[2]. It was not until later that Dora realized that Harriet was in any case willing personally to make good any financial loss on the project.

Though more concerned with her own work and the various attempts to take over the paper, Dora none the less was willing to defend Joyce and his publication by *The Egoist*. She suggested to Harriet that she should write a leader defending Joyce. This duly appeared in March 1916. This also announced their forthcoming publication of *A Portrait* although at the last minute the

---

[1]   Dora Marsden to Harriet Shaw Weaver, 12 January 1916.
[2]   Harriet Shaw Weaver to James Joyce, 14 January 1916.

printers, Richard Clay and Sons, withdrew. The unsigned article stated that they wanted to publish the book "not because we desire to saddle ourselves with fresh responsibilities at this difficult time, but in order to save a work of exceedingly high merit from oblivion[1]." Harriet informed Joyce that "it was Miss Marsden's suggestion to talk of your book in the March number... in fact the article should have been signed by her for though it was my foundation, she worked it up[2]."

After a long struggle, which involved having to print the book in the USA, The Egoist Press finally published *A Portrait* in February 1917 – a tribute to Joyce, Weaver and, to some extent, Dora. Certainly, Dora now felt that the book was excellent and was prepared for a fight. On receiving her copy she remarked, "it looks exceedingly well and the novel itself is really tip top... the four sermons and the Parcell passage are unsurpassable. I hope it will have success... The passage about the relative merits of Christ and Tsar will give them plenty of ground to move on, without counting the fruity 'langwidge.' Our rule now is to 'wait and see,' I suppose[3]."

They did not have to wait long. Unsuspecting and respectable libraries returned the novel and there were rumours of a possible prosecution. Dora welcomed the latter, partly to defend Joyce, but also because she saw the immense commercial possibilities of a sensational trial. "Let them send the book and the police by all means and we'll have a *cause célèbre* with H. G. Wells

---

[1]   *The Egoist*, 1 March 1916.
[2]   Harriet Shaw Weaver to James Joyce, 15 April 1916.
[3]   Dora Marsden to Harriet Shaw Weaver, February 1917.

and Clutton Brock [*The Times'* Literary critic] and other pillars of respectability as witnesses. A good solicitor and select witnesses and a blessed police court trial would be worth a £1,000 worth of advertising[1]!" Did she even consider and welcome that she too might become involved?

The book certainly met critical acclaim by, among others, H. G. Wells and Clutton Brock, and Dora was quick to praise Harriet. With some foresight she told her: "You will have established a little niche for yourself in literary history. When the opposition which a famous book had to overcome is recorded there you are as Saviours[2]!" Joyce too was delighted and passed on his congratulations to Harriet and "the firm." When Harriet informed Dora of this, she again complemented her friend for publishing "the book of the season... How nice of J. J. to think that the 'firm' should have feelings and require patting on the head. I think he must be a nice man in spite of his reputation for quarrelling with all the world," adding in a nice touch: "It's wretched he should have this trouble with his eyes[3]" (Joyce suffered from glaucoma, an insidious disease of the eyes).

Harriet wanted a second edition of *A Portrait* published but as with the first met considerable obstacles, again from printers. Dora sympathized with her – "It is wretched about the *Portrait*: you are being given a time with it." She suggested that Harriet should try Johnson's, *The Egoist*'s old printers in Southport. Dora felt it

[1] Dora Marsden to Harriet Shaw Weaver, 2 March 1917.
[2] Dora Marsden to Harriet Shaw Weaver, 2 March 1917.
[3] Dora Marsden to Harriet Shaw Weaver, 9 May 1917.

was worth a try for both she and Grace were on good terms with their manager, Sammy Wilkinson, even though she feared the book was on "The Black List of the Printers Association." Dora added that she would send "Grace over to interview him and let her point out all the difficulties of the situation[1]." The plan was a success and the firm finally agreed to print the book.

The publication of *Ulysses* with its own "fruity langwidge" was, if anything, more difficult than that of *A Portrait*. Harriet again hoped to serialize it in *The Egoist* but only one installment appeared in the January-February 1919 issue, and eventually the idea had to be abandoned. Dora's part in this was minimal though, as before, she was willing to risk prison in Joyce's defence[2]. Compared to Weaver, of course, her whole contribution to the development of Joyce's career was marginal but still, in an indirect way, significant. She certainly had respect for him and it was a feeling that was reciprocated. His letters to Harriet often enquired after Dora or thanked her for her help[3]. Years later, Joyce too seemed to be genuinely concerned about the publication of Dora's own work, sympathizing, as a "fellow sufferer," with her poor health[4]. Joyce and Marsden never met but it is not difficult to understand his gratitude to her or her sympathy with him. Dora's paper had provided an outlet for his work and, through Harriet, a lifelong friend and benefactor. For her part, Dora could

---

[1]   Dora Marsden to Harriet Shaw Weaver, 17 August 1917.
[2]   Dora Marsden to Harriet Shaw Weaver, 7 June 1922.
[3]   For example, see James Joyce to Harriet Shaw Weaver, 1 January 1918; 6 August 1919.
[4]   James Joyce to Harriet Shaw Weaver, 2 December 1928, 19 October 1929.

sympathize, even identifying with another lonely writer and his predicament. Perhaps, too, she was identifying (in her own eyes) with another tortured genius with a message for the world.

By 1918, Dora was totally immersed in her own project on philosophy and though willing to defend Joyce, she was far from keen on *Ulysses*. She wrote to Harriet: "I have just read Episode III of *Ulysses*. My dear editor, go down on your knees and thank your stars for possessing one writer who is CLEAR! That's me!! Joyce is – my word! He is appalling. If the British Public will struggle with this production it is equal to anything Fate could have in store for it[1]."

If the "British Public" struggled with Joyce's prose they had an almost impossible task in unravelling Dora's own philosophical ramblings in *The Egoist*. Of course, this was in part due to the complexity of the subject, yet Dora's quest for definitive statements made the problem worse. Her interest in philosophy, it will be recalled, went back to her university days in Manchester, where she studied under the famous philosopher Professor Samuel Alexander[2]. In 1911, though caught in the birth and running of *The Freewoman*, Grenville (as mentioned above) had given her a contract to write a book on philosophy to include, among others, examinations of the German philosophers, Nietzsche and Wieninger. From 1912 onwards, in spite of lapses, this concern never left her, finally resulting in her decision to resign

---

[1] Dora Marsden to Harriet Shaw Weaver, 10 May 1918.
[2] In her autobiographical notes she claimed that she conceived the idea to write a book on philosophy at school.

as editor of *The Egoist* in order to concentrate on researching the "Philosophical Basis of Egoism[1]."

Dora's Stirnerian-based Egoism was at the heart of the paper until its demise in 1919. As such, it suffered from the same weaknesses of Egoism discussed above. In particular, it tended to be based on unsubstantiated assertion. It lacked realism and was expressed in inexorable prose. Again, this was in part not surprising given her personal and intellectual isolation in Southport but it was further complicated by Marsden's determination for absolute definition of some deeply complex and intangible terms and concepts. Lidderdale and Nicholson point out too that Dora suffered from being a pioneer in the field. The end result was usually articles that were difficult to comprehend and follow. It is interesting to speculate how many of the two hundred to three hundred readers of *The Egoist* actually bothered to read them, perhaps Hughes was right and most did ignore her work[2]. None the less, Dora's philosophical research and writing were now in many ways her life, her *raison d'être*. What value did they have and what, if anything, do they tell us of Dora herself?

Dora's philosophical position in 1914 was still based on Stirner yet it is clear that she had been influenced by other writers too, such as Nietzsche, Wieninger and the French philosopher Bergson. While renouncing the rabid misogyny of the German philosopher Nietzsche, Dora would have appreciated his passionate indi-

---

[1] *The Egoist*, 15 June 1914.
[2] Hughes, G. *Imagism and the Imagists.* London: Stanford University Press 1931.

vidualism and his hatred of democracy of equals. The unabashed elistism of Nietzsche with his supermen creating by will and force a social order with themselves, and other members of their aristocracy at the top of the heap, would also appeal to the implicit elitism of Stirnerism. The superman as super-egoist? Nietzsche of course, had some similarities with Stirner while Wieninger, in his *Sex and Character* had rather more interest for feminists[1]. It is likely too that Dora was influenced by the French philosopher Henri Bergson who enjoyed some popularity among the left in the 1900s. Indeed, Dora published an extract of his work in *The New Freewoman*'s last issue of 15 December 1913 under the title "The Philosophy of Ideas." What probably attracted Dora to him was, in part, his belief in a vital life-force but more especially his view that this was connected to a need for creation and a desire for expression which does not come from intellect but the intuition of man. As one contemporary socialist reviewer of Bergson put it: "Its highest form, its creative aspect is only fully realised in those manifestations of intense passion for life which both produce the works of genius and induce their appreciation in men of lesser gifts. Momentarily – too rarely perhaps – a flash of vivid illumination breaks through the mechanical investiture of our routine, humdrum life, then we apprehend[2]."

Bergson's emphasis on intuition, the reference to genius and his attempt to make sense of the world as a

---

[1] Wieninger, (1906). His views were discussed by Dora in *The Freewoman*, 13 June 1912.

[2] J. R. Milnes, *The Link*, February 1912.

whole appealed to Dora. This became evident as her research progressed. However, Dora insisted that an absolutely clear semantic framework was necessary if a valid understanding of the world was to be achieved. The search for absolute definition of terms was so crucial that her prime concern could be seen to have become "linguistic philosophy." Understandably perhaps, the search for "true" definition of terms and meanings became extremely complicated and obtuse, especially given Dora's own personal social isolation. Moreover, her quest for absolute definition was pursued outside of life and reality, and only inside her own world, her own mind. Recognizing this only made the problem worse and, in the end, as she realized, her philosophy tended to rely more and more on assertion. It also became a great mental strain and as Lidderdale and Nicholson observed, "It became progressively more difficult to write and much more difficult to read[1]."

Dora emphasized the importance of language in her "Truth and Reality" series which began in March 1915. It was retitled "Lingual Psychology" in July 1916. However, though linguistic enquiry became crucial to her, Dora's semantic research was still connected to Egoism and, in some ways her "war with words" followed on from her denunciation of such concepts as "Liberty," "Freedom" and "Justice." "To blast the word," she wrote, "to reduce it to its function of instrument is the enfranchisement of the human kind: the imminent new assertion of its next reach in power[2]."

[1]   Lidderdale and Nicholson, p. 101.
[2]   *The Egoist*, 1 January 1915.

This was clearly what Marsden was attempting to do in the "Truth and Reality" series of March, April and May 1915. However, her Egoism, her belief in a world for and defined by the individual Ego, was continually emphasized. Dora claimed that "A thing has Being when it is felt, and it 'is' only to those who feel it. 'Being' begins and ends in the feeling experience of the Ego of which it forms some specific mode[1]." Things, she admitted, obviously had different uses according to the perceiver or user of them. Thus, a piece of wood on a lake had a different meaning to a carpenter than to a drowning man. But from this hardly original observation she went on to argue that the world itself exists only through the Ego – the wood has no substance in itself. "All things," Dora felt, "are purely individual. The 'nature' which things are supposed to have are the inverted appearances of our own potentialities in regard to them... All things are then feelings related to our purposes and achievements[2]."

This was a logical extension of her Egoism, now applied to the nature of the world itself. When Dora returned to the subject in June 1916, under the grand title "Lingual Psychology – A New Conception of the Function of Philosophical Enquiry," she tried, not always with success, to elaborate her position. With a typical flourish, she began by denouncing other philosophers. They often claimed it was impossible fully to understand reality because of the problematic nature and rela-

---

[1] *The Egoist*, 1 May 1915.
[2] *The Egoist*. Thus a naturalist and a lumberjack would see a tree in a different light according to their 'ego.'

tionship of mind and matter, the impossible circle[1]. Does matter exist independently of the mind that perceives it? Part of their problem, to Dora, was imprecision in their philosophical enquiry in general and their use of words in particular. They had been especially lax with words and now "philosophy has to initiate a closer scrutiny of terms, and particularly of those whose import has been assumed to be self-evident. In the scrutiny and ultimate redefinition of the primary elements of speech... lie the new hopes and prospects of philosophy[2]."

After a somewhat ironic plea for clarity and definition, Dora continued to develop her own Egoistic analysis. In September 1916, after acknowledging some debt to the English philosopher Berkeley, who claimed that matter only existed when perceived by man, she tried to explain herself through the following equation: "A thing is a thing felt or perceived by an individual: a thing is therefore part of the individual's own feelings therefore things are part and parcel of the individual, the Ego." Following on from this, "The precondition of all language is the Ego;" by a careful analysis of words, an understanding of the Ego and the world itself becomes possible[3]. The origins of language and mind were inextricably linked and the inability to realize this was due to misconceiving language as a mere communicative tool. Language was much more than this to Dora who described it as "The very fabric itself of intellect and self-consciousness[4]," crucial to an understanding of reality

---

[1] *The Egoist*, 1 July 1916.
[2] *The Egoist*, 1 August 1916.
[3] *The Egoist*, 1 September 1916.
[4] *The Egoist*, 1 April 1917.

and the world.

Dora attempted to illustrate this by referring to an interesting story concerning Laura Bridgeman, a deaf, blind mute. According to Dora, Bridgeman's case reflected the human need to name all things, in order to understand the world and to develop an intellect. This, of course, was usually achieved through the use of the sensory organs, principally those of sight and sound. These were obviously denied to Bridgman but her drive for understanding led her to intellect via "reading" through the raised letters placed on things put out for her to touch. From this she acquired language, intellect and knowledge, ultimately going on to write her autobiography. Whether Dora's account of Laura Bridgman or the story itself, is true, does not matter here for it is used only to reflect Dora's belief in the crucial importance of language through which the external world becomes intelligible to the individual[1].

To Dora, it was possible to understand the "nature of the world to the human mind[2]," for in fact they were one. "The world *plus* the organism," Dora claimed, "form one: a universe: an Ego[3]." Life itself is "the power to project an external world" the form of that world being dependent on the organism which experiences it. One cannot exist without the other – "there is no organism without its projected or externalised world; and there is no world which is not the expression of the par-

---

[1] I have discovered this story is indeed true. J. W. Trent: "Laura Dewey Bridgman." *Encyclopedia Britannica* 2018.
[2] *The Egoist*, 1 March 1918.
[3] *The Egoist*, 1 August 1918.

ticular organic power of the body which projects it. The external world is thus the expression of the properties of the organism which experiences it[1]."

From April 1918 the series, now under the heading "Philosophy: the Science of Signs," began to become incredibly obtuse and repetitive. However, Dora's interest in Space and Time (which was also examined by Bergson) began here and she developed this further in the 1920s. Dora's "philosophical egoism" still remained central to her analysis and towards the end some of her earlier clarity occasionally returned. To her, Egoism was the only "philosophical theory owning a sound logic... every attempt on the part of the philosopher to deal drastically with the nature of knowledge, leads him to egoism: that is the position that external nature has no existence independent of the organism which owns it." Egoism "denied the absolute and independent existence of the external world[2]" to her, a truism not even denied by death. Time was not linear, Dora argued, but circular and the death of one organism was a sort of fertilization of the universe as a whole. "May not dying," she pondered, "constitute life's innate compulsion to put into employ the sole means capable of enabling it, when it has spent itself beyond a point, to renew its youth and vigour in perpetuity[3]."

Dora's philosophy suffered from several weaknesses caused by her unremitting individualism, which in itself could be traced to her commitment to the ideas

---

[1]   *The Egoist*, 1 March 1918.
[2]   *The Egoist*, 1 July 1919.
[3]   *The Egoist*, 1 September 1919.

of Max Stirner. Basically, Dora refused to acknowledge the social context and influence on both ideas and the pursuit of knowledge itself. Neither the object under review nor the philosopher interpreting it existed in a social vacuum, free from external pressures. Dora's philosophy and political position refused to accept this, even though, ironically, she proved it herself; her individualism reflected (and in some ways compensated for) her political and social isolation and powerlessness. Moreover, as Marx argued, "philosophers have only interpreted the world in various ways, but the real task is to change it." This Dora was singularly failing to do. She had been politically inactive for several years and her views clearly had little relevance during the First World War. In her defence, it could be said that she was working in a field which was, and still is, extremely complex, yet this was an argument for a *more* social life not an isolated one in Southport, with only her mother and Grace. Both were, in their own ways, intelligent women, yet Dora needed to defend and sharpen her views in open discussion with others interested in her line of enquiry. The odd skirmish in the pages of *The Egoist* could be no substitute for this. It was the lack of social and intellectual intercourse and the subsequent lonely mental struggles with "truth," "reality" and so on that, of course, explain her increasingly excruciating and long-winded style. One example, worthy of the *New Age*'s satirist Bechofer, is perhaps worth quoting in full:

Our third guiding principle is one so obvious that its obviousness serves not only to justify the omission of its renumeration, but the omission also of its observance; it might be allowed to pass without saying. In the circumstances it seems advisable to enumerate it[1].

The strain of working in isolation with such complex material was clearly beginning to tell.

Finally, Dora's philosophy had little if anything to do with feminism. This was perhaps made clear during a skirmish in 1917 with the writer William Carlos Williams. He had been attracted to the ideas of Wieninger as had Dora. Marsden would have particularly welcomed those parts of his analysis which could be interpreted as calling on women to make themselves more independent from men by refusing to accept artificial modes of behaviour. Yet she could not agree, as we have already seen, with his notion of separate male and female psychologies. Williams made the mistake of praising Dora in April for creating "a militant female psychology." Dora replied that his criticism "will be more helpful when he makes clearer what the distinction is which he draws between male and female psychology. Is it anything beyond the fact that the one is written by a man, the other by a woman[2]?" Williams did reply, in August, but Dora had lost interest in the discussion.

Dora did however return to one of her feminist friends, Rebecca West, in 1918. Though she complained to Harriet, "I can't make headway with Rebecca. I can't

---

[1] *The Egoist*, 1 May 1918.
[2] *The Egoist*, 1 April 1917.

warm up the subject somehow[1]," she did finally manage to write a review of her work. This at least showed that she could return to a more direct style and it also reflected Dora's critical attitude to West. First, she reminded readers that Rebecca had her first opportunity on "[*The*] *Freewoman*, that journalistic grub form of which *The Egoist* is the winged development." She recalled that the paper's editorial staff had clubbed together to pay the newcomer's wages: "Thus it was that Miss Rebecca West made her entry into literature." Second, Dora was critical of her book under review, *The Return of the Soldier* (which was made into a film in 1982). She claimed that West's debatory style did not suit her for "she is not a debater; she is not a fighter; her spirits do not rise at the prospect of a scrap[2]." Rebecca did not appreciate this criticism, partly, according to Dora, because "she is used to all praise[3]."

Quite clearly there was some conflict between the two women – they had lost touch with each other since 1913. Dora even complained to Harriet how much "in a most peculiar way, these personal things seem to burn up the brain tissues[4]." What lay behind Dora's hostility? Was she envious of Rebecca's subsequent success? Certainly their lives and careers had seemed to move in opposite directions, with West achieving national recognition in spite of her controversial affair with Wells and the condemnation she faced following the birth of their son. Dora did end the review with some praise, but it

---

[1] Dora Marsden to Harriet Shaw Weaver, 6 August 1918.
[2] *The Egoist*, 1 October 1918.
[3] Dora Marsden to Harriet Shaw Weaver, 31 October 1918.
[4] Dora Marsden to Harriet Shaw Weaver, 31 October 1918.

was guarded. "It is certain," she concluded:

> that Rebecca West possesses brilliant gifts: the world has acknowledged them; and we think it probable that she possesses others of an even more solid worth. There exists, therefore, every hope that when she emerges from the groping twilight of the process of finding herself and her true form, she will be able to combine indisputable high gifts with the high, but necessary, moral forces, of courage, independence and unashamed truth[1].

Dora too still possessed "brilliant gifts, courage and independence," yet it was years since they had been recognized: Rebecca, like Dora's other *protégés*, had long since overtaken her.

Dora did consider once more breaking from her philosophical research to comment on the revolutionary situation in Britain at the end of the war. Certainly, the class struggle, fuelled by the disillusionment following peace and inspired by the success of Lenin and the Bolsheviks, returned to pre-war levels. Dora also knew that *The Egoist* was almost dead and realized that more direct and relevant material was needed. "The fact of the matter is," she wrote to Harriet, "I think we are on the verge of social and political and economic events of the first magnitude. Calm as everything seems we are in the throes of world convulsion of which the war itself is only the smallest part." A little ludicrously, perhaps, she wondered how far she could influence or be a part of this forthcoming ferment: "I feel," she continued, "enormous events are immediately abroad and we've got to ask ourselves whether we are a force sufficiently strong

---

[1]   *The Egoist*, 1 October 1918.

to exercise an appreciable influence on these events. Those articles I proposed some time ago on 'instead of economic revolution' seem now to me more urgently necessary than ever in this lull before the storm. In fact we ought to really *talk* these matters forthwith. Do you think it can be managed? And if so how[1]?" Clearly Dora had been thinking of this for some time and at the end of 1918, *The Egoist* announced that while her philosophical series were going to be "remodelled for publication in book form, Miss Marsden will contribute to *The Egoist* a short series of articles aiming at the analysis of the factors in the existing social situation. Later she will begin a new philosophical series 'The Logic of Morals[2].'"

Dora's political commentary did not materialize and at the end of 1919, after six years of precarious life, *The Egoist* finally collapsed and died. Its readership was always small and it had dwindled further at the end. By this time Harriet Weaver wanted anyway to concentrate solely on publishing Joyce, a wish that coincided well with Dora's need for more time to complete her philosophical research without the distraction of the paper. Though its death went largely unnoticed, its importance to modernist literature was immeasurable. It provided an outlet for an astonishing array of radical and innovatory talent from Pound and the Imagists, to James Joyce. Again, Weaver's role in Joyce's career was crucial, though Marsden must take some, belated, credit too.

Some commentators have tried to link Imagism with Dora's Egoistic philosophy and perhaps there were

---

[1]   Dora Marsden to Harriet Shaw Weaver, 4 December 1918.
[2]   *The Egoist*, November / December 1918.

some parallels in their fascination with words and their individualism. Indeed, some would argue that they shared an arrogant elitism too, a belief in their own genius which placed them far above the common throng. Weaver (1971) tries to trace a link between Marsden and Imagism, arguing that it can be traced to *The New Freewoman* period[1]. Certainly, Dora did occasionally comment on art in that paper (for example, 15 August, 1 November 1913) but whether there was an inextricable link between her views and Imagism remains controversial, a debate that must be pursued by others. What is certain is that Dora was constantly apprehensive about Pound's role on *The Egoist* and that she located Imagism as a major weakness of the paper in 1915. By that time too, Dora herself felt there was no link between the new poetry and her own philosophy.

Politically, Dora continued to pursue a line that though often startlingly acute about power, was in all meanings of the word, individual. Indeed, it was almost as if she sought a unique position, unwilling to temper it in response to criticism, ever more unwilling to slot it in with anyone else. Her general attacks on orthodox values and arguments always placed her outside mainstream political debate but they were so peculiar, so fiercely independent that they placed her outside feminist and anarchist positions too. Anarchist interest in *The Egoist* quickly diminished and, in spite of the loyalty of some of the old *Freewomen*, so did that of the feminists. Dora, in part driven by personal animosity, still made trenchant attacks on the Pankhursts but had no

---

[1]   Weaver (1971), p. 27.

time for the suffragist pacifists, or peace women, of 1915, nor indeed for the "feminist corpse" at all. Her individualism and her attitude to power originally came out of her analysis of the powerlessness of women but her "feminist" label had been abandoned years ago; the only label she would accept was "Egoist."

Dora Marsden, though, was a lonely and isolated Egoist who increasingly lived and validated her life through her writings. Her disdain for political movements and collective action, alongside her call for individuals to pursue their own line, fitted in neatly with her own life and withdrawal from politics. Her political comments could be perceptive but the force of her views on power were surely and ironically only matched by her own powerlessness. *The Egoist* was not *The Times*, and was read by a mere few hundred people, many of whom may well have ignored her work, as Hughes suggested. The more obtuse her philosophical articles became, the less well they were received.

The key questions must surely be – why did Dora retire into this personal and political isolation? Why did she invest almost all her energy and life into her work? Obviously, the political background had changed, with the war subduing both the suffrage and the feminist movements. Yet she had already withdrawn from these before 1914 and her isolation had already begun. Dora herself argued that she needed to withdraw in order to concentrate on her book on philosophy in the belief that it could indeed become a seminal work. There may well be some truth in this even though it was guided by an exaggerated view of her own ability; on its own it is surely not enough.

Perhaps the real reason for her isolation and her total absorption in her work was that together they were used to prevent her reflecting on her own life, her own feelings about herself, perhaps even her own sense of failure. After all, her own circle – Rona Robinson, Rebecca West, Grace Jardine – had all moved on and were making their own successful careers in science, literature, and in Grace's case, publishing. Even the retiring Harriet Weaver was something of a success in literary circles. Others, too, like Joyce, H. D., Aldington, Eliot, Pound and the rest were, or were becoming, successful in their field. Dora, approaching forty, was living alone with her mother, with no job, no career and no income. The fiercely independent Egoist was dependent for financial and emotional succour from others. She was gambling all on her work, hoping this eventually would give her recognition and a feeling of self-worth: surely even Egoists cannot do this on their own. Yet this was an extremely risky gamble to take and was a long way from the front page of the *Daily Mirror* or the roof of Southport's Empire Hall. Dora may well have been a brave and beautiful spirit but in 1919, with the exception of a few dwindling friends, she was also a lonely and forgotten one, a *Kami* in the wilderness.

Seldom Seen, 1920 – 1935

Seldom Seen

The really magic thing about the place is the atmosphere which makes everything indescribably seductively lovely. These last two weeks in October and the first ten days of November have been the most beautiful I have ever experienced. I shall never forget it. One has seemed to be living and working through a crystal globe flushed with every kind of soft but penetrating light. Spring was crude compared with it... Will you join? Do think seriously about it. It is quite an addition to one's experience. I have never before experienced anything like it. You are a dear to write to this benighted spot as regularly as if it were Xian land. No one else seems to... The rest of the world is very well able to get along without us... It is very lonely.

Dora Marsden to Harriet Shaw Weaver

Seldom Seen, Ullswater, 12 November 1920

It may be that the wisdom she has obtained is not communicable, but I am sure to some far peak of wisdom she must have attained, and I cannot think it is not good for the race when some of its component atoms reach projection even if they cannot transmit it to their fellows.

Rebecca West

Time and Tide, 16 July 1926

For most of the fifteen years from 1920 to 1935, Seldom Seen, near Glenridding in the Lake District, was Dora and Hannah Marsden's home. Though plagued with ill health, Dora persevered with her research and finally published, through The Egoist Press, two volumes – *The Definition of the Godhead* (1928) and *Mysteries of Christianity* (1930). But these achievements came at the cost of a severe strain in her relationship with Harriet Shaw Weaver and ultimately at the price too of her physical and mental health. In 1930 Dora suffered a nervous breakdown followed, five years later, by another, from which she never fully recovered. She became further isolated, a lonely and pathetic figure, doomed to spend the last twenty-five years of her life in hospital. The years at Seldom Seen ended in tragedy; it is difficult to write about Dora's life in this period without sharing its sadness.

❦

Seldom Seen was indeed a "benighted spot" nestling on the lower slopes of Helvellyn, one of the highest mountains of the Lake District. The nearest village is Glennridding, over two miles and a good walk away. Glencoyne Cottages formed a row of ten originally built for miners working further up and beyond the mouth of the Glencoynedale spring which flows past them. At one time there was a thriving community there with nearly thirty children educated in a schoolhouse just below the row. By the time Dora moved in this was no longer in use, as the miners and their families had left for Glenridding. All the buildings were originally owned by Lady Mabel Howard who gradually sold them off to pay for her son's gambling debts. Edith Allsup, who lived there until the 1950s, bought some of them in 1917; the rest were let. Though ownership of the cottages in the 1920s is complex and unclear, it seems that she bought them all in 1923, later selling some as her funds ran out. Dora and Hannah originally rented a single cottage but, with Harriet's help, moved into numbers 4 and 5 in 1923, with Harriet herself renting number 6 next door[1].

The picturesque and well-appointed dwellings of today make it difficult to imagine the reality of life there in the 1920s. There was no electricity and water had to be drawn from the spring. An earth closet was at the back. Laundry would usually have to be done in the stream. Access was either by a steep path from Glencoyne Farm or a lane through Glencoyne Wood reached, for most visitors, only after a bumpy ride on the solid-tyre daily bus from Penrith. Provisions had to be collected from Glenridding though dairy products were delivered from the farm. In short, life at Seldom Seen was spartan and, in winter, bleak – Harriet Weaver complained it was so cold in 1930, that she had to get dressed in bed, and then had to break the ice in the pipe that was connected to the spring[2].

---

[1] Alice Ryan to Vera Farnell, 1 November 1970; Nancy Bell to Les Garner, July 1984; Eric Allsup to Les Garner, 21 September 1984.
[2] Harriet Shaw Weaver to Sylvia Beach, 25 February 1930.

It is not known how Dora came across Seldom Seen, or even when she and her mother moved there. She had proposed taking a holiday in the Lake District in 1916 and perhaps she saw Glencoyne Cottages for the first time then[1]. Certainly by 1919 she was looking for somewhere to live so that she could get on with her book. Dora even briefly considered returning to Manchester[2], but eventually settled in the Lake District. Though she welcomed the peace and quiet, it was, with hindsight, a fateful choice since, for most of the year it was a truly isolated spot, visited by few. Even Mrs. Chapelhow, the old school teacher, had committed suicide there, partly because the children had gone but also because of the loneliness[3].

When Dora and Hannah, now in her seventies, arrived only Edith Allsup was in permanent residence. A tall, bony woman with enormous teeth, Allsup contrasted sharply with Dora though she had at one stage been a governess[4]. She was eccentric and was particularly keen on animals. She had a large retriever and a donkey, Neddy, which when Edith drove her trap would often elicit the local cry "Watch out here comes lang legs and long lugs!" Edith even kept a monkey for a few weeks too, but as it frequently escaped this pet had to

---

[1] Dora Marsden to Harriet Shaw Weaver, 2 February 1916. She may have visited the Lake District before the war to attend a Fabian Summer School, usually held at Keswick.

[2] Dora Marsden to Harriet Shaw Weaver, 18 September 1919.

[3] Nancy Bell to Les Garner, July 1984.

[4] Relatives tend to prefer this spelling of the family name, though Allsop is sometimes used. Eric Allsup to Les Garner, 21 September 1984.

go[1]. Edith and Dora did not get on together, partly because Edith was staunchly Conservative in her politics but also because Dora wanted to be left alone. As early as 1920, Edith was annoying Marsden by peering through her windows trying to see what her new neighbour was up to. In 1923, she served Dora with a notice to quit which Dora as a sitting tenant ignored.

The only other regular and local contact would be the daily visits from the postwoman and from the nearby farm. Florence Pye, who took milk, eggs and butter to Dora from September 1929 to May 1932, was occasionally invited in for a chat. Like everyone else who met her she noticed what "a very sweet old lady" Hannah Marsden was but, ominously, how Dora herself was "definitely in her own little world[2]." The postwoman, Edna Cox, agreed but felt that being highly strung was not unusual for one so clever[3]. Edna became friendly with Dora and eventually she became her typist, using an old machine Dora had brought with her. Edna not only had to struggle with the volume of mail that was sent to Dora but also her illegible handwriting which she often found difficult to decipher. Dora and Edna's relationship was more professional than personal yet Edna's understandable inability always to decipher Dora's handwriting correctly was to lead to a major and disastrous row between them in the 1930s.

Apart from the frequent and crucial visits of Harriet Shaw Weaver, Dora's life was indeed isolated. Occa-

[1]   Florence Pye to Les Garner, 15 October 1984.
[2]   Florence Pye to Les Garner, 15 October 1984.
[3]   Ronnie Cox to Les Garner, 13 June 1984.

sionally her sister, Eleanor, and her children would come for a brief summer holiday but generally there continued to be little contact with the rest of the family. (Later, Eleanor and her husband, the Reverend James Dyson, were extremely supportive when she became seriously ill.) Dora's other contacts were the unwelcome ones of summer visitors. These on the whole annoyed her and distracted her from her work. Dora frequently complained of "long drawn out summer[s] in this hotel-like 'life in a row[1].'" Many of these temporary residents tried to make her acquaintance, no doubt curious about the writer in their midst. Sometimes they would provide Dora with some amusement and light relief but she generally resisted any social advances. She reported, for example, of two families and their six children that they were all bored. "The two papas are musicians... One of the mamas is *bored stiff* she says she can't stand it" – but she still refused their offer of tea[2].

Dora herself must have intrigued the visitors, shunning company to work all day on her book. To some of them, she became a source of ridicule. According to Weaver, some of the MP Ellen Wilkinson's friends, "professional women," who rented a cottage in the summer of 1926 regarded Dora as a "droll humbug, posing as a hermit and as writing a book which, however, will not get past its first paragraph... while they themselves are most important personages with well-paid jobs, coming up here for well-earned holidays[3]." One visitor,

---

[1] Dora Marsden to Harriet Shaw Weaver, 22 December 1932.
[2] Dora Marsden to Harriet Shaw Weaver, 1 April 1926.
[3] Harriet Shaw Weaver to Margaret Storm Jameson, 20 November 1928.

Alice Ryan, who had bought one of the cottages, was even a little frightened of Dora and was "rather prejudiced against her after I came very near losing my life as I thought through her." Dora and Alice, were chopping down a dilapidated woodshed when she "suddenly realised that Dora was brandishing her axe almost on top of me and when I moved away she followed at once. That went on for some little time until I made an excuse for leaving the work to her... Of course it would have been pure accident had the axe cut part of me but I felt nervous." It is unlikely that Dora intended to hurt her neighbour, more that her mind was on other and loftier things. After all, she told Vivien Hartley and Phyllis Owen, two friends of Ryan's, that she was writing a book "which was to be greater than all the works of Plato, Aristotle and Bergson[1]."

Dora's life at Seldom Seen was in other ways odd yet it occasionally had its lighter side too. It was certainly ironic that this erstwhile writer of 'Space and Time' should have a clock that was permanently fast and could not be re-set. It was odd too that she kept her fire going all year except "for the odd day or two when the temperature runs up to 80 or 90 in the shade[2]?" Yet Dora could find time to amuse her niece and nephew, Elaine and Philip. They remember her as sometimes stern but they recall her taking them walking and swimming too. Ronald Cox, Edna's son, recalls having to suffer the affectionate nickname "Ronald Donald" while Mrs. Marsden made him drinks of hot milk. He also remembers

---

[1]   Alice Ryan to Vera Farnell, 1 November 1960.
[2]   Harriet Shaw Weaver to Sylvia Beach, 22 June 1925.

Dora taking him for a walk in the woods, pointing out nests and red squirrels[1].

Dora lived a spartan life but could become enthusiastic about making her home comfortable to live in. When she and Hannah moved into 4 and 5 in 1922, Dora pestered Harriet to bring up candles, lamp shades, material for blinds and artificial flowers, though "in view of my mild speculation setting up as a housebuilder I am compelled to ask the prices of all commodities nowadays down to that of a pound of cheese[2]." Dora could always appreciate the countryside although "this sunshine makes comments on things that are almost insulting... the strong light in at the little black window says deplorable things about the scullery and staircase[3]." And finally, to the enjoyment of all, including Hannah, came the introduction of a gramophone player which Harriet brought with her in 1926. Harriet, Dora and Hannah would often stay up late listening to James Joyce reading from *Ulysses* or, in a lighter mood, Mr. Mac's "Moon of my Delight[4]." Diversions were completed by the acquisition of a much-loved cat, Sara, around the same time.

None the less, these lighter moments in Dora's life were themselves rare and were increasingly overshadowed by isolation, overwork and poor physical and mental health. Dora was thirty-eight years old when she arrived at Glencoyn and it is not surprising that her

---

[1]   Ronnie Cox to Les Garner, 13 June 1984.
[2]   Dora Marsden to Harriet Shaw Weaver, 9 October 1922.
[3]   Dora Marsden to Harriet Shaw Weaver, 8 March 1932.
[4]   Harriet Shaw Weaver to Sylvia Beach, 14 June, 13 August 1926.

health, already not robust, should suffer in such harsh conditions. Her letters to Harriet nearly always contained a reference to her physical condition. In 1912, for example, she complained to Harriet that "scarcely one day in three is a good working day owing to my head, which I now believe is incurable[1]." One year later, she told Harriet of her strenuous efforts on her research "but lying up about every third day with the headache is the nemesis for working hard[2]." Dora also suffered from insomnia, largely caused through her unremitting concentration and worry over her work. She claimed that this resulted in her brain remaining "most fully awake[3]." Continual sleeplessness is a great physical as well as mental strain which leads to extensive fatigue and tiredness. Dora seemed to suffer from this frequently, complaining in 1925 that "I have been sleeping wretchedly... from 12:30 until 8:30 completely wide awake[4]." This nagging problem was exacerbated by, and no doubt linked to, that of her nerves which by 1926 were "so jagged and tingled and hot." Though cod liver oil seemed to help as it had in 1916 "when things were at their worst... I sleep no better than before[5]." Harriet, who knew that Dora also suffered from lumbago, realized that "Miss Marsden's work is much delayed by her constant attacks of biliousness and sleeplessness. She is badly in need of a thorough rest and change[6]."

[1] Dora Marsden to Harriet Shaw Weaver, 21 March 1921.
[2] Dora Marsden to Harriet Shaw Weaver, 13 March 1922.
[3] Dora Marsden to Harriet Shaw Weaver, 11 July 1924.
[4] Dora Marsden to Harriet Shaw Weaver, 7 October 1925.
[5] Dora Marsden to Harriet Shaw Weaver, 22 March 1926.
[6] Harriet Shaw Weaver to Dora Marsden, 15 December 1925. Concerns over Dora's health were a continuing theme from at least 1912, if not

Fortunately, Dora could occasionally escape by visiting her sister Eleanor Dyson, but she refused to take the complete rest that was so obviously needed. She had chosen Seldom Seen for its solitude, to get the peace and quiet necessary, she felt, to complete her work. Certainly, whether on one of her night walks or on her thinking seats in Glencoyne Wood, there was time and space for tranquil contemplation and thought. The view from her favourite bench that still overlooks Lake Ullswater today must at times have given her inspiration. Yet Seldom Seen clearly had disadvantages too besides the more obvious physical drawbacks of Winter weather and spartan living conditions. Apart from being physically isolated it was socially and intellectually isolated too. There were no libraries, no residents who could discuss and support her work. Indeed, Dora shunned contact with Edith Allsup and only enjoyed a working relationship with Edna Cox. Dora sometimes saw the limitations of Seldom Seen and once or twice considered a return to London. This might have improved her physical health yet after so many years in isolation it is difficult to see how she would have coped with a return to the capital and a more social life. In any case, as Weaver and others learned, she did not take criticism easily or lightly. The virtues of Seldom Seen for Dora Marsden were in some ways paradoxical and contradictory. On the one hand, the peace and seclusion were ideal, allowing her to pursue her work without interference. On the other, they encouraged her withdrawal and social isola-

---

before. Symptoms referred to here align with the neurasthenia she complained of in Southport.

tion. Moreover, bereft now even of the odd skirmish in the correspondence pages of *The Egoist*, life at Seldom Seen meant her work developed without the benefit of debate and positive criticism. In turn, this accentuated her absolute belief in the validity of her opinions and the direction of her work. The danger of this, of course, is clear. What would happen if both were ignored and ridiculed when she finally shared her message with the world outside?

Dora was at first confident that her work on philosophy would soon be completed and it is possible that she regarded Seldom Seen as only a temporary home. Certainly she did not consider living there for the next fifteen years, if only in consideration of her mother. But her health, her drive for perfection and the ever-widening scope of her research resulted in continual extensions of deadlines and delay in publication. Even when her two books were published, Dora regarded them as only part of a five- (later a seven-) volume series.

Harriet, who loyally stuck to Dora throughout, soon became aware of the obstacles preventing the completion of her work. As early as 1919, she had noted yet another new element – mysticism – in Marsden's work and affectionately labelled her "the same old spinner of webs[1]." None the less, even Harriet was dismayed to find on her first visit to Seldom Seen, in 1920, that Dora had only completed two chapters of her book. She had not got much further the following year. Dora herself tried to explain the reasons for delay in a fascinating let-

---

[1] Harriet Shaw Weaver to Dora Marsden, 2, 12 August 1919.

ter to Harriet in the spring. She needed extra time, for other writers in the field were "thinking their way out as they go along. They seem to publish at a stage which I should regard as the snowed-under-stage. They never seem to emerge. I do, owing to my hunger and thirst for mental clearness." Dora felt motivated by her "great need to state problems more clearly even if this results in stating their difficulties clearly. I need to know what the real question at issue is and I'd rather be impaled on the difficulty than find an easy way round it." Though sounding arrogant, Dora argued that she was not bragging but could not work in any other way, even though the result was constant revision and rewriting. It also meant that the scope of her research was forever increasing. This letter, for example, concluded with a request for a book on "Germination and its electrical aspects[1]."

By 1922, though, Dora was optimistic about finishing her work and even asked Harriet "how long it takes to get a book set up after a delivery of a manuscript." She hoped to get one volume (on philosophy) finished by June or July, the second, "on the nature of life and sensation," by October[2]. This was hopelessly optimistic although to some extent Dora was delayed by her concern over the publication of James Joyce's *Ulysses*. This, like *A Portrait of the Artist as a Young Man* was proving to be extraordinarily difficult. Eventually, it was published by Sylvia Beach in Paris and Harriet took and distributed some copies in England in the spring. (Harriet got to know Beach, an American who owned the

[1]   Dora Marsden to Harriet Shaw Weaver, 21 March 1921.
[2]   Dora Marsden to Harriet Shaw Weaver, 13 March 1922.

Shakespeare and Co. bookshop in Paris, through Joyce. They worked together on publishing the first edition of *Ulysses* and subsequently became life-long friends.) After some initial reviews, which ranged from complimentary to hostile, there seemed to be a lull. This prompted Dora to ask: "What has happened to *Ulysses*? Has the storm burst or is the author to be destroyed by silence[1]?"

At this stage, Dora admitted to Harriet that she had not read the book completely (Harriet had bought her a copy) and her query over Joyce reflected probably only a passing interest, more a concern for Harriet than anything else. This situation changed once the really hostile reviews began and the prospect of a controversial public fight seemed likely. Harriet wanted to bring out her own Egoist edition even though this risked almost inevitable prosecution for publishing pornographic and obscene material. *The Sunday Express'* editor, James Douglas, for example, had damned *Ulysses* as "the most infamously obscene book in ancient or modern literature. The obscenity of Rabelais is innocent compared with its leprous and scabrous horrors[2]." Given this sort of hysterical reaction, Harriet felt that a private edition would be less prone to prosecution as distribution could be more closely supervised and sent to those less likely to take the publishers to court. Dora, spoiling for a fight to defend a principle rather than the book itself, disagreed. She condemned "the unpleasant minded ladies who do the reviewing on the respectable journals" and argued that the Egoist Press should publish an ordinary edition

---

[1]   Dora Marsden to Harriet Shaw Weaver, 13 March 1922.
[2]   *Sunday Express*, 28 May 1922.

as soon as possible. "If these people have decided, as seems certain, to take a firm line in the case of *Ulysses*, we shall have to take one still firmer and force them to make us into martyrs." Writing in the summer, she concluded, "I presently simply crave for a quiet time for the next few months to finish my opus but as I told you, prison, first class, will suit me perhaps better than Glencoyne. Fewer visitors and fewer distractions[1]."

Harriet was nervous about publishing an ordinary edition but Dora was adamant: "we cannot countenance the undertaking of a private edition by ourselves. As far as we are concerned it is, in my opinion, all or nothing ... [*Ulysses* was] the kind of a book which not only ought to be written but ought to be pressed upon the public for perusal. That is what the difference between a public and a private edition amounts to." If there was to be another private edition, Dora added, Sylvia Beach ought to do it. Harriet, heartened by Dora's support, passed on her ideas to Beach in Paris. She admitted her own "nervousness / or cowardice" over an ordinary edition but felt she could face prosecution if Dora came to London to help. "It would," she conceded, "be a very great relief to me to know she was free to support the case for *Ulysses*; if, as is only too likely, a prosecution should follow publication in this country, and the chances of a favourable verdict would be very much increased[2]." Harriet still had faith in Dora's fighting spirit and (for the only time in the Seldom Seen period) welcomed the possibility of her return

---

[1] Dora Marsden to Harriet Shaw Weaver, 7 June 1922.
[2] Harriet Shaw Weaver to Dora Marsden, 22 July 1922.

to London. In the end, however, a private edition, printed in Paris, was published by The Egoist Press in the autumn and Dora was left to concentrate on her work.

Harriet and Dora's discussion over *Ulysses* is fascinating on many levels especially considering Dora's apparent dislike of the book. The debate reflected Dora's courage, willing at forty to risk prison again and, possibly, a desire to leave Glencoyne too. Whether the latter was due to a wish to avoid the troublesome summer hordes or was rooted in a deeper desire to escape the year-long isolation of Seldom Seen is not clear. However, it was also a genuine attempt to help her friend, courageous in her own way but also terrified of facing open and public controversy on her own. Certainly, both felt (rightly or wrongly) that Dora would have been more capable of defending the book in open court than Harriet. Weaver clearly respected Dora's courage and felt her reputation and fighting skills would help to defeat a prosecution of The Egoist Press[1].

In the end, a trial was not necessary, Dora did not go to London but remained in Seldom Seen. Indeed, this was the only time that Harriet seriously considered the possibility of having Dora live near her. Harriet understandably refused to let her loyalty and love for Dora overwhelm all her other intellectual and personal interests. Dora on several occasions asked her to live permanently in Seldom Seen and though she did rent a cottage for her visits, Harriet could not do this, realizing that ul-

---

[1] I now wonder if Dora wished to be in the limelight again - to be on the front page of the *Daily Mirror* again.

timately she would merely become Dora's dogsbody. Harriet did all she could to help, seeking out and forwarding obscure books to Glencoyne, even helping her to move into the double cottage. But to live with Dora in Glencoyne or London, would have been too great a burden for even Harriet Shaw Weaver to bear.

Dora's work, as ever, continued to expand. By October 1922 even she realized that she was getting bogged down but felt she could "hasten publication if I omitted the volume on *Mind* and issued the two on *The Nature of the Philosophical Enquiry* and *The Nature of Life*." Yet Dora was reluctant to do this for "the three make a whole. The fourth on Time and Space can be neglected to the dim and distant future!" Each of these concerns were highly complex, deserving single-minded attention yet Dora seemed incapable of organizing and working on them separately. The result, of course, was more delay, compounded by constant revision. "I have begun," she wrote, "to revise from the beginning. I thought it was just a matter of reading through but I have now mauled the whole thing about so that I don't know how long it will take me to put it back into clean shape[1]." The problem was exacerbated by the ever-expanding boundaries of research which by 1923 and 1924 included atomic structure, astronomy and theology. Not surprisingly, the strain continued to take its toll and in November 1923, Harriet reported to Sylvia Beach that Dora was ill again[2].

---

[1]   Dora Marsden to Harriet Shaw Weaver, 9 October 1922.
[2]   Harriet Shaw Weaver to Sylvia Beach, 28 November 1923.

In 1924, however, Dora's research took a further twist but this time even Harriet felt that Dora was on the verge of an exciting new discovery. To back up part of her metaphysical research, which eventually went into *The Definition of the Godhead*, Dora wanted to prove that magnetism and gravity were in fact the same thing but with different names. To show this, she began to see whether it was related to the "pull" of the planets around the sun. She asked Harriet, who began to share Dora's interest, for a whole range of books, including an almanac of astronomy which covered the last 200 years[1]. Dora further asked her to go and play with a model of planetary orbits at the Royal Astronomical Society to see if sun spot activity was indeed connected to the position of the planets[2].

Throughout the summer both women immersed themselves in research even though Harriet was also involved in winding up The Egoist Press. They were both excited by their discoveries and Dora even became convinced that her sun-spots could be used to prove Einstein wrong. Einstein through his theory of relativity, believed that as time and space were relative and not fixed terms, it was impossible to predict what would occur in a physical system – for example, the universe. Dora believed otherwise and wrote to Harriet that "this shifting of the magnetic poles in the course of the ages corresponds to the absolute movements of the solar system among the stars. Hence ocular proof of the *absolute* no-

---

[1]   Dora Marsden to Harriet Shaw Weaver, 3 June 1924.
[2]   Dora Marsden to Harriet Shaw Weaver, 10 July 1924.

tion of heavenly bodies. Whence: *Exit Einstein*[1]." Dora's theory on sun-spot activity was not entirely novel but could be traced back to the Nineteenth Century. Interest in sun spots was high in the USA in the 1920s and there have been more recent attempts to prove the correlation between these and the planets. The most recent exploration of the theory however, by Gribbin and Plagemann, even the authors accept is not infallible[2].

The drawback of the summer excitement was a further reorganization of Dora's work. She now wanted to include another volume, *Space, Time and Gravitation*, with an appendix by Weaver. T. S. Eliot encouraged Harriet and even showed an interest in the book. Dora however was, surprisingly, difficult about this, demanding high royalties of thirty-three and one-third per cent and demanding anonymity for herself and Harriet. Dora said she was not concerned about criticism of an impersonal theory but felt it could distract her from her other work. "And, as I shall still have to plough through Book IV, before I publish Books I and II it is indispensible that my peace of mind should be provided for and this can only be done by withdrawing my name entirely[3]."

Thus by the end of 1924 Dora was working on four volumes: *The Nature of Philosophical Enquiry* (her first venture); *Mind; The Nature of Life*; and *Space, Time and Gravitation*. Dora seemed incapable of concentrating on one, even the first, begun so many years ago, and

[1]   Dora Marsden to Harriet Shaw Weaver, 11 July 1924.
[2]   Gribbin and Plagemann (1983). For information on the history of the theory, thanks are due to Prof. J. Meadows, Leicester University. See Meadows to L. Garner, 30 April 1984.
[3]   Dora Marsden to Harriet Shaw Weaver, 10 (?) July 1924.

none was ready for publication. Indeed, as her interests were ever-widening, the requests for further material continued to flow thick and fast. In the summer she wanted a book that "gives the bare bones of the relationship of Nineteenth-Century physics and mathematics in Germany to Humanism[1]," and by the end of the year she was asking Sylvia Beach in Paris to track down Duheim's *"La Théorie Physique"* and *"Le Système du Monde[2]."* She also wanted an obscure article by the French scientist and philosopher, Duheim *"Les Idées d'Auguste Comte sur la Mathématique"* which was written in 1898 or 1899. Dora was particularly keen on having the whole of Duheim's work (five volumes) but by the end of 1925 a distinctly religious interest was also evident. Perhaps the width of Dora's interests can be best judged by the following shopping list sent, via Harriet, to Sylvia Beach:

1. *Le Théorie mathématique des sciences*. E. Halévy

2. *La pensée antique*. J. Fabre

3. *Histoire de la philosophie atomique*. Mabilleau

4. *Pour l'histoire de la science héllène*. Paul Tanning

5. *Histoire du dogma de la divinité de Jesus Christ*. Reville

6. *Le Mysterie de Platen*. Prat

7. *Les Origines et la Nature du Zohan*. Karppe

8. *Problème de la classification des sciences d'Augustine St Thomas*. Martineau[3]

---

[1] Dora Marsden to Harriet Shaw Weaver, 10 (?) July 1924.
[2] Harriet Shaw Weaver to Sylvia Beach, 19 December 1924.
[3] Harriet Shaw Weaver to Sylvia Beach, 15 December 1925.

Though Sylvia Beach's secretary translated some of the material for her, Dora often read in the original French, a language she had learned many years ago in Manchester. This obviously would increase the strain on her, further delaying the completion of her work. Yet she remained optimistic in the Autumn of 1925. In September, for example, Harriet reported that she was "making a great effort to finish the first two volumes of her series and to have them ready for a publisher in January – and hopes to have a further two ready by the end of 1926 – till then she will take no holiday[1]." The Weaver-Beach book service was, coincidentally, crucial to Dora's research. Sylvia was perhaps motivated here by her friendship with Harriet, yet she became interested in Dora too. Dora still managed, even at a distance, to get others to work on her behalf.

None the less, by 1926 the situation was getting hopeless, worsened further by Dora's health and lack of sleep. Eventually, she realized the need to concentrate on just one aspect of her work, as Harriet had suggested at the beginning of the year. Harriet's advice finally caused her to:

> look very seriously at the situation in which I find myself apropos of which I have had a good many projects in my head. Finally at last I have however decided exactly what I am going to do... the one and only cause of my condition is worry over my work and that its only cure is to get some part at least finished and off my mind... accordingly I have decided to narrow down my present work.

---

[1] Harriet Shaw Weaver to Sylvia Beach, 22 September 1925.

Sensibly, Dora felt that by postponing some historical research and concentrating on two volumes she would "feel relieved in not having to keep my thoughts playing over so wide a field and probably shall make quicker progress[1]." She hoped this new strategy would help her nerves and relieve her sleeplessness.

For some time Dora's plan seemed to work and she was pleased to report to Harriet that the effects were "very good indeed. The whole thing is falling into shape, my mind is lightened to the extent of having shaken off the consideration of what was nothing less than the whole history of civilisation and, once more, I can see the end of my labour. I cannot tell you what relief I have felt." Harriet would also be pleased for herself for the revision of Dora's timetable meant there was less pressure on her to complete her symposium on the changing definitions and interpretations of Time and Space. (Dora had asked her to do this, hoping it could be included in one of her volumes.) In fact, Dora felt Harriet should consider publishing this work separately and even encouraged her with offers of help. "I think that you would make a very valuable and interesting collection. My advice is: Do it!"

Harriet eventually abandoned the idea of publishing the symposium although her manuscript, *A Symposium on Time* which is at Oxford, makes clear and interesting reading[2]. In this Harriet makes a gracious reference to Dora's help even though her own misgivings about Marsden in the mid-1920s had begun. In particular, as

---

[1]   Dora Marsden to Harriet Shaw Weaver, 22 March 1926.
[2]   This is at Oxford Philosophy Library, Merton Street.

an atheist, Weaver objected to Marsden's developing interest in religion. Moreover, she neither understood nor accepted Dora's belief, as espoused in *The Definition of the Godhead*, that Time and Space were, respectively, male and female. Neither could Harriet accept Dora's notion that God was a woman. Years later, Harriet revealed that the "Holy Ghost was a female deity to whom [Dora] used to pray and who, she believed, intervened on her behalf[3]." Harriet, though remaining loyal throughout, also became increasingly frustrated by Dora's inability to accept criticism and her unwillingness to discuss her work at all. Dora was quick to fly off the handle, following this with a period of sulking. This happened once over the apparently trivial question of the angles of an isosceles triangle. Harriet and Dora had a row over this at Seldom Seen; for once, Dora's niece recalls, Marsden was right.

On the whole, having faced a similar problem with her other genius, James Joyce, Harriet subdued her criticism of Dora however difficult and tricky this became. Dora wanted Harriet to give her unqualified support, on her own terms without questioning her work. The unwillingness to discuss her writing, of course, completed Dora's intellectual isolation and was, undoubtedly, a further factor in her mental strain and the disaster of the 1930s. What is surprising is that it reflected a lack of trust in Harriet, her devoted lifelong friend and benefactor.

---

[3]   Harriet Shaw Weaver to Bjorn Rasmussen, 28 March 1961.

The deterioration in Harriet and Dora's relationship finally came to the surface in the autumn of 1928, just before Dora, at last, was ready to publish *The Definition of the Godhead*. Dora argued that Harriet was not committed to her work while Harriet retorted that Dora was ruthless. Harriet hurtfully, though accurately, added that Joyce's work was at least as good as hers. While Weaver confided in Joyce, arguing that the row had been brewing for years, Dora turned to Margaret Storm Jameson. Jameson had met Dora before the war and like so many others had been greatly impressed by her "pure intellect." She had offered reviews for *The Egoist* in 1914[1]. Subsequently, of course, she became a renowned and popular novelist. Margaret never seemed to lose her faith in Dora and clearly took her side in the row. "Miss Weaver," she argued, "is rather in the position of listening to God arguing about the creation when she listens to you about your work. She hasn't the equipment to deal with it in conversation... I can't, I simply can't think that anyone for one moment could suppose that the work of James Joyce is comparable in value to yours. It is too absurd. She can't, possibly, Dora[2]."

This was the type of praise Dora wanted to hear and eventually Harriet withdrew her criticism and began to appear to share Dora's determination to publish. In fact, nothing, not even expert advice from her old professor, the philosopher Samuel Alexander would prevent her. Dora, very sensibly, had asked Alexander to comment on the manuscript for *Definition of the Godhead* in

[1]   Margaret Storm Jameson to Dora Marsden, 1 January 1914.
[2]   Margaret Storm Jameson to Dora Marsden, 26 September 1928.

the spring of 1928. The professor, though kindness itself in not wishing to upset his former pupil, admitted he had "mixed feelings about the book." He added that he appreciated Dora's originality "and am astonished by the mass of knowledge you have required... yet I do not think you should try to publish it in its present form." Alexander felt that *Definition* was in reality two books "a statement of philosophy and a critical history of philosophy and opinion" and as such, not suitable for publication. He particularly disliked what he regarded as Dora's uninformed criticism of other disciplines than her own but he did concede that her "treatment of philosophical doctrines, for example the 'proof of God's existence' I found very interesting indeed." Sensitive to the last he ended "I do much dislike throwing cold water over your enthusiasm and your quite splendid devotion. But I do say consider it again. I think too you have made the book unnecessarily partake of a character of a personal confession[1]."

Dora's former professor was ideally suited to criticize her work. He was an acknowledged expert in his field and his concerns had mirrored and influenced those of Dora. In 1920, for example, he had published *Space, Time and the Deity*. Yet Dora refused even to listen to his kindly advice, preferring to accept Jameson's view that "Alexander is a fool, a blasphemous fool[2]." Dora's reaction was not to sit back and ponder his considered view – her egoism could not allow that, even from him –

---

[1] Samuel Alexander to Dora Marsden, 13 May 1928.
[2] Margaret Storm Jameson to Dora Marsden, 3 January 1928 (*sic.*) (actual year was 1929).

but to work even more furiously to get the book published. To this end, she enlisted the help of Storm Jameson, who was so clearly still impressed by what she regarded as Dora's genius. Thus, in spite of recently resigning from the publishers Knopf, and a serious operation, Margaret began to work tirelessly on Dora's behalf.

Whether Jameson was convinced of the merits of Dora's book or was still influenced by her first impression of her, it is difficult to judge, yet her generous compliments would have been warmly welcome. She wrote to Dora that she was "staggered by the immensity of your achievement... it is incredible and magnificent[1]." Her role at this stage was to hawk the manuscript of *Definition of the Godhead* around various publishers in the hope that one would take it. Though convinced herself of its value she warned Dora that not many would be interested, particularly given the suggested price of a guinea. Someone surely would accept her "great work of sensational merit and revolutionary in effect[2]," but she did not have much success. To comfort Dora, eleven days later she added the truism that "all publishers are slow as well as stupid[3]."

No publisher was interested and once again Harriet stepped in to rescue Dora's work from oblivion. The Egoist Press was resurrected to publish *Definition* and was, as Harriet probably realized, the only publisher that would do so. In reality, of course, it meant that Harriet herself would, at her own cost, be publishing the book.

---

[1] Margaret Storm Jameson to Dora Marsden, 1 September 1928.
[2] Margaret Storm Jameson to Dora Marsden, 1 September 1928.
[3] Margaret Storm Jameson to Dora Marsden, 12 September 1928.

As such, this decision was a testimony to her devotion and love for her wayward and troublesome friend. Harriet, though disliking much of the book and though not consulted over decisions affecting it (for example, the choice of printers, Charles Burchall of Liverpool), threw herself into the fray. Not surprisingly, cordial relations between her and Dora were re-established: "we are quite happy now," she wrote to Sylvia Beach[1], though the differences between them remained.

Harriet typed letters, ran to the post box to deliver them and generally did all she could to promote what she loyally called Dora's "wonderful book[2]." Margaret Storm Jameson continued to work zealously on Dora's behalf too. Her task now was to solicit favourable reviews from appropriate sources, for example, the *Journal of the Institute of Philosophical Studies*[3]. She also wanted to enlist the support of women who knew Dora before the war. Though Harriet had tactfully advised Margaret not to write to Ellen Wilkinson because of her friend's attitude to Dora[4], she did attempt to contact both Emmeline Pethick-Lawrence and Rebecca West.

The old network of suffragists and feminists was now much weaker than before the war but at least Pethick-Lawrence remembered Dora well. According to Storm Jameson, Emmeline said, "I always had a very special feeling and affection for Dora Marsden and admiration for her brain and courage, therefore I shall ap-

---

[1] Harriet Shaw Weaver to Sylvia Beach, 18 October 1928.
[2] Harriet Shaw Weaver to Sylvia Beach, 18 October 1928.
[3] Margaret Storm Jameson to Dora Marsden, 15 October 1928.
[4] Harriet Shaw Weaver to Margaret Storm Jameson, 15 November 1928.

proach the book with warm anticipation[1]." Margaret also hoped to contact Mrs. Leisenring and H. G. Wells. "I hesitate to say this," she mischievously wrote to Weaver about getting Wells to comment on the book, "but Rebecca West could do a lot in this way." Margaret hoped too that she might interest the Woolfs ("such nice people")[2]. Even Joyce, though suffering from poor sight, was roped in. "I am looking forward," he wrote to Harriet about the book, "to thieveries on an unheard scale as soon as I can find an accomplice as rascally minded as myself to read it to me[3]."

Finally, "after a very great push[4]," *The Definition of the Godhead* was published on 1 December 1928. It was dedicated to:

THE GREAT NAME

HUSHED AMONG US FOR SO LONG

of

HER HEAVEN,

THE MIGHTY MOTHER

of

ALL

A curious dedication which reflected Dora's conversion to the concept of a divine force. This certainly did not fit into her old amoral Egoism which excluded God. It certainly did not fit into her wartime philosophy

---

[1]   Margaret Storm Jameson to Harriet Shaw Weaver, 28 March 1928.
[2]   Margaret Storm Jameson to Harriet Shaw Weaver, 5 November 1928.
[3]   James Joyce to Harriet Shaw Weaver, 2 December 1928.
[4]   Harriet Shaw Weaver to Sylvia Beach, 4 December 1928.

either. In 1917, for example, she was aghast at the news that Alexander was trying to fit God into his work. "*Horrible piece of news,*" she had written to Harriet, "Professor Alexander's first Gifford lecture in Glasgow was ... on Time, Space *and the Deity*! ... I told you he would never have 'Lingual Philosophy[1].'" Gradually, however, through her examination of Space and Time, the "first principles" of the Universe, and through her study of Alexander's *Space, Time and the Deity* Dora was drawn to the notion of a divine force; her mission now was to prove objectively God's existence through a vast and interlocking examination of science, philosophy and religion.

This was no small task as she admitted on the dustjacket. "This work," Dora wrote:

> is the first volume of a philosophy which claims to affect the intellectual rehabilitation of the dogmas of Christian theology in terms of the characters of the first principles of physics, i.e. Space and Time... But to solve the riddle of the first principles solutions are required to those age-old problems of philosophy and theology which impart into human culture its heavily tangled undergrowth. This opening work, therefore, presents these solutions, unifying by means of them the whole body of human knowledge and re-interpreting all the great issues of mankind's cultural history.

Dora was all set to explain God and the Universe: the old arrogance and supreme self-confidence remained.

---

[1] Dora Marsden to Harriet Shaw Weaver, 1 February 1917.

She began in Book One, "Concerning the Method to be Adopted in this Inquiry," with a declaration that all philosophers wished to "unravel the scheme of the universe." To do this, they have to establish "first principles." Her "central argument," she continued, "is that the universe is grounded in radical substances which may, very well, be called first principles; that out of these substances the world of nature is generated; and that, for this reason, they are to be accounted divine[1]." The role of the philosopher was to define what these first principles were. To Dora, most philosophers had singularly failed to do this. They never adequately defined their terms, particularly "absolute," "being," "nature," "space," "time," "motion," even the term "definition" itself. Though Dora accepted this was difficult, she contended it was possible and thus, in the end, no longer necessary to subscribe to "the dogma of the inherent unknowability of the universe[2]."

At the heart of her argument was the notion that the first principles "the universe's inherently irreducible, indecomposable, incorruptible substances... its eternal foundations[3]" were space, the world mother and time, the world father. Space and time were the raw materials of the universe, they were eternal, not born of anything and therefore immortal. They were supernatural and divine, crucial to the definition of the godhead. If this could be defined authoritatively, its importance to the world would be immeasurable. "If men's idea of God

---

[1]   Marsden (1928), p. 19.
[2]   Marsden (1928), p. 30.
[3]   Marsden (1928), p. 76.

be, as we believe, the governing factor of their lives a right idea of God must perforce be human life's basic good, and it as such that the 'deepest want of our age' has been sensed as being a new definition of the God-head[1]." This was Dora's mission, the driving force behind the years of exhausting work, divinely ordained to help the world.

Dora argued that mankind always possessed a sub-mental sense of the importance and relation between Time, Space and the Godhead. Though discussed more fully in *Mysteries of Christianity*, Dora continued that this could be seen in all religions and indeed, in every act of worship. She felt, for example, that sacrifice and resurrection rituals, alongside a belief in the soul, were common to all religions and were, in effect, used to reflect and glorify the immortality of the universe. Thus:

> Christian theology, art and ritual have meaning no less certainly than the hieroglyphics of the Rosetta stone; and just as the latter were made to yield up their significance in terms of their demotic and Greek equivalents, so can the former be made to yield up theirs in terms of the findings of the science of the first principles read in the light of the findings of the comparative studies of religions and mythology[2].

All this, of course, seemed a long way from Dora's earlier concerns, especially those of 1910 to 1914. In particular, it seemed to have little to do with feminism or a Stirnerian-based individualism. But perhaps there were some links, her reference to God as a woman, for

---

[1]   Marsden (1928), p. 108.
[2]   Marsden (1928), dust-jacket.

example. It would, though, be stretching the point beyond credulity to argue that *Definition of the Godhead* was overtly feminist, and based on feminist concerns. It was, though, an extremely individual approach, based, as with Egoism, on assertion. It reflected too, Dora's undying belief in her own qualities and her role as a writer with a message not just for women, but the world itself. What greater task could there be in trying to explain the universe and God? On the other hand, it could be argued that in trying to unravel the mysteries of the Universe, resorting to God was an easy option.

Dora hoped the book would create a sensation and accordingly review copies were sent to the leading national and regional papers. Presentation copies were also sent to such luminaries as G. B. Shaw, Bertrand Russell and a host of university professors and clerics. Russell, probably like many others, decided that he could not help the book and the hoped-for sensation did not occur. Not everyone shared Margaret Storm Jameson's view of the book that "this is the superb beginning of an achievement that must dwarf everything done in philosophy since the era begun by Newton. I hope to heaven it moves[1]." But nothing did move, nothing happened, the book was received with a deafening silence. The slavishly loyal tried to reassure Dora by putting the lack of reaction down, as Jameson put it, to a "fear of an unknown greatness[2]." However, unbeknown to both women, two reviews had appeared by this time, in Dora's old adversary, *The New Age* and the *Times Liter-*

---

[1]   Margaret Storm Jameson to Dora Marsden, 8 December 1928.
[2]   Margaret Storm Jameson to Dora Marsden, 15 February 1929.

ary Supplement. Understandably, perhaps, the first was kept from Dora by Harriet for it ridiculed both the author and her book, "Alas! only the first of a series to be published, very appropriately by The Egoist Press." "N. M." began the review by stating: "Miss Marsden has written a weighty volume to prove that there really are such things as Time and Space, and that they are not the same thing, matters which most of us are quite ready to take for granted." From this, "N. M." continued, Dora tried to define God. "I had begun to hope that she might establish the exact length, breadth, and height of the Deity, perhaps with a view to painting Him (or Her), but I was doomed to disappointment. I therefore consoled myself with the reflection that a person whose taste in human prose is so execrable as Miss Marsden's would certainly have made a mess of the Divine wall papers." "N. M." concluded that "behind Miss Marsden's 'spatial extension' nonsense there lies... a philosophy old as the hills and fresh as the morning. And when she approaches this, Miss Marsden achieves one or two phrases which almost make the book worth reading[1]."

The *TLS* took Dora's work more seriously. She would have been comforted by its concluding remarks that "her knowledge of philosophy is thoroughly adequate and her critical powers considerable." Yet the reviewer felt that her work "Depends on a belief in the vision of immediate truth bestowed on the primitive 'mythopoeic' mind which many may hesitate to accept[2]." In other words, many of Dora's conclusions, as

---

[1] *The New Age*, 27 December 1928.
[2] *The Times Literary Supplement*, 7 February 1929.

before, relied on assertion. Finally, the only other review that has come to light was in the obscure *Congregational Quarterly* of April 1929. This was sent to her by her brother-in-law, the Reverend James Dyson. He felt the reviewer, A. T. S. James, had probably never read the book but was probably saying this more out of kindness than the knowledge that it was true. James felt the labour that had gone into the book was "immense and Miss Marsden is courageous almost to a fault," but though he did not want to be discouraging "the obvious fact is that Miss Marsden greatly overstrains her abilities. If she would be content to try something of a more moderate compass, she would do much better work."

Though Margaret Storm Jameson was "futilely raging over the neglect of your work" and felt, like George Fox "That I'd like to run through London saying 'Woe, woe, to this bloody town' (for) they must acknowledge you before long[1]," the acknowledgement of Dora's genius was not forthcoming. None the less, after a short break with her sister Eleanor in Preston, Dora returned to Seldom Seen in a surprisingly confident mood. Though she had probably only seen James' review (clearly no one had told her about the *New Age*'s) and though she herself could not explain her optimism, she wrote that she had "this feeling that the book will quite speedily make itself felt." She hoped that Rebecca West would publish something on it soon[2]. In fact, the book was not so much selling badly, it was hardly selling at

[1]   Margaret Storm Jameson to Dora Marsden, 15 February 1929.
[2]   Dora Marsden to Harriet Shaw Weaver, 9 March 1929. West never received the book.

all. Her greatest success, in fact her only success, was at Grace Jardine's shop in Manchester. Grace had sold four copies, one to Rona Robinson. Harriet's account book shows receipts for six books sold, giving an income of £4 9s. against total expenditure of £549 18s. Hardly a commercial success, let alone a personal one.

None the less, Dora appeared to work well throughout 1929 and in her excitement felt that another two volumes would be ready in November. *The Definition of the Godhead* had promised, besides Weaver's work on Space and Time, three more volumes by Dora – *The Mystery of Time*, *The Immemorial Cross* and *The Constitution of Mind and Knowledge*. In the end only one volume, *The Mysteries of Christianity*, was published, in 1930. Again the book was dedicated to a woman and one who thoroughly deserved it, given her lifetime love and devotion to Dora.

ACKNOWLEDGEMENT.

WITH GLAD THANKFULNESS FOR

THE PRIVILEGE, THE AUTHOR HERE

ACKNOWLEDGES HOW MUCH THIS ENTIRE LABOUR,

HAS MEANT THE GREAT PERSONAL DEVOTION

OF HER DEAREST FRIEND AND

LIFELONG COMPANION

HER MOTHER

(Harriet received no mention in either book.)

The Mysteries of Christianity in many ways followed on from *The Definition of the Godhead*. In particular, Dora wanted to show that all religions, even those that were not Christian or pre-dated Christianity, had rites and symbols which were linked by their common recognition of the Universe, Time and Space. "Mysteries," she explained on the dust-jacket, was a term used in this context for "theoretical dogmas" which in reality were not mysterious at all. Ultimately, "they resolve into a claim that the universe hangs together after a certain manner that the dogmas themselves definitely indicate. The mysteries have, therefore, every right to the respect ordinarily afforded to scientific postulates, being, as they are, essentially scientific, what through their character has been obscured through their supremely comprehensive bearing." Dora added that, therefore, the "Mysteries of Christianity can be accepted as containing the substance of the religious mysteries everywhere" and gave an example of the cross. (This belief explains the presence on the borders of both books' jackets of the hooked cross, the swastika, plagiarized by the Nazis). Not only the cross but the notion of the immaculate conception, the virgin birth, atonement, epiphany and resurrection were, to Dora, common in all religions and often pre-dated Christianity. Thus the mysteries of Christianity were not novel but found everywhere, "setting forth as they do, universally accepted findings as to the characters of the dual elements or Godhead identified in our earlier volume with Time the World Father and Space the World Mother[1]."

Dora argued there were four grades of theological knowledge – knowledge of the divine (covered in *Defi-*

---

[1]   Marsden (1930), p. 14.

nition), knowledge of religious symbolism and ritual (for the next volume) and what she wanted to explore in *Mysteries*, knowledge of salvation and of the kingdom of heaven. This was fairly straightforward, as was her exposition on the similarities between Christian stories and festivals and those of the pagans. However, Dora became increasingly obtuse as she tried to elucidate her views on Father Time and Mother Space, the "divine parents" of the world, and their connection with the cross. "Time," for example, "is the breadth of the universe. The logos is therefore the world lung as well as the world ovary. It is the labyrinthe world – bagpipes that speak when the world breathes through them[1]."

Though by page ninety-two Dora claimed "so far, all plain sailing," nothing could have been further from the truth for the author's prose was long-winded and obscure. However, Dora's genderizing of the "first principles" did lead to a clear demarcation of what she referred to as "masculinist monotheism." In other words, Dora felt that men, particularly male priests, had devalued female images in most religions and replaced them with those of men. She was, for example, virulent in her criticism of the Christian Trinity of the "Father, Son and Holy Ghost." In fact the ancient Trinity, to her, was of three women, though evidently "no dogma has suffered greater distortion under the influence of masculinist monotheism." The Greek trinity of Zeus, Hades and Poseidon was a fabrication too, created by Homer to belittle that of the three women, Hera, Aphrodite and Pallas. In fact, Dora saw evidence and clues to a female trinity

---
[1]   Marsden (1930), p. 46.

almost everywhere, in Britannia's tripod, in the Prince of Wales' feathers, even in the pawnbroker's golden balls. Though somewhat exaggerated, these views marked a link with some of her pre-war concerns and would no doubt be regarded by some as constituting a spiritual or mystical form of feminism.

Dora's views on evolution also reflected her continuing elitism and again constituted a justification of her own isolated life. She claimed, in Chapter 12, "The Kingdom of Heaven, Darwinism, and Christianity," that there was a cosmic law guiding evolution. This involved, unlike Darwin, not a natural but a supernatural selection process. There were five stages of evolution, A to E, with E marking the highest stage, the kingdom of heaven. Eventually evolution will lead to supermen (a term Dora used for both sexes) who would try to lead the rest to E. In many ways this reflected the work of the Greek philosopher Plato who similarly classified people according to their understanding of "true" knowledge. Dora would also have concurred with his argument that this knowledge could only be attained after years of isolated study. Dora's supermen could only have achieved it too if they led a pure, abstemious and chaste life, for to gain true knowledge the body has to "maintain its integrity... the rupturing of men's sexual integrity causes his brain to become a leaking vessel so far as this grade of knowledge is concerned[1]."

---

[1] Marsden (1930), p. 188. It should be pointed out that Marsden's 'supermen' had nothing in common with Nietzsche's crazed and brutal warriors.

"Nothing in the universe," Dora conceded, "can obliterate sex[1]" but for genuine truth-seekers it had to be abandoned. Indeed – and this obviously mirrors the rationale behind the lives of nuns and priests – chastity for the supermen was essential for it "is the world's bulwark against the tide of world-waste represented by the seminal incontinence that is carrying mankind away from the saving lives of the logos[2]." For true holiness to be realized there was a need for "an utter dissociation from the parts that are involved in the processes of physical generation[3]."

Of course, Dora's views on sex and the need for abstinence for those seeking the truth of the universe were, yet again, a thinly disguised justification of her own life since at least 1921. Not surprisingly, given the different contexts of 1911, 1921 and 1931, they differed markedly from those expressed during the halcyon days of *The Freewoman*. Then Dora was politically active, debating and exchanging ideas with others, her paper acting as a forum for debate. But her developing interest in individualism and her removal from social and political interaction took this stimulus away, increasingly leaving her mentally as well as politically isolated. Curiously though – and Dora would have refuted this – there is a link between her analysis of 1911, 1921 and 1931: they showed again that ideas do not come from heaven but are, in part, due to the interaction with the social, political and personal environment. Thus her isolation and

---

[1] Marsden (1930), p. 193.
[2] Marsden (1930), p. 201.
[3] Marsden (1930), p. 264.

poverty could be explained away by her determination to be a superman, one who eschewed earthly pleasures in an attempt to gain true holiness and knowledge. Working in a damp, draughty cottage and living on a subsistence level was a duty for "the acquiring of knowledge shall, with missionary fervour, be insisted on, as the prime Christian duty of every individual[1]."

Finally, though her anti-materialism could perhaps be traced back to before the war, Dora's position in the 1920s and early 1930s led to a fierce denunciation of "modern" woman. This was not altogether unusual for prewar feminists though Dora herself was obviously influenced by the ridicule, if not hostility, of some of the young women who visited Seldom Seen. She condemned them and what she saw as women's obsession with the rule of the "purse," "refinement" and children:

> And their time, thought and energy being thus given over to activities having to do solely with feeding, clothing and interests connected with the reproduction of the species, women foster a state of society that is essentially sub-human by diverting the world's work into the unworthy channels where it merely vastly multiplies the means of gratifying the characteristically sub-human instincts. Hence... the intense vulgarity of existing society[2].

Harriet Shaw Weaver would have disapproved of this and indeed of much else in the book, but as usual, she kept quiet and loyally supported her friend. However, the publication of *Mysteries* was preceded by yet another illuminatory row between the two women. It be-

---

[1]   Marsden (1930), p. 289.
[2]   Marsden (1930), p. 283.

gan over conflicting requests from Dora and Harriet to the printer Captain Birchall who had shown remarkable patience in dealing with the author and her innumerable corrections and changes. Dora had initially asked Harriet to supervise the printing but began to send Birchall new instructions on her own. She felt that Weaver was countermanding her orders and complained that Birchall would only accept them if they went through her first. "*That*, I suppose, because you are the firm's bank reference... no businessman," she continued "in the five continents would hold so intolerable position... as managing director of The Egoist Press I absolutely refuse any longer to condone the villainous vulgarity of the situation. Well, that's that[1]." Dora wanted to send a fierce letter of complaint to Birchall but Harriet, in a remarkably restrained reply, advised against this but the "poor woman" agreed to leave it to Dora to decide. Harriet could have added that she too was a director of The Egoist Press and, of course, it was only through her money that Dora was being published at all. She complained that Dora wanted to make all the decisions while she had to do most of the work needed to get the book published. However, with remarkable loyalty she still ended her letter "With much love, Josephine[2]" (a pet name she only used with close friends).

Instead of accepting this gentle rebuke, Dora exploded in a way which reflected the mental strain of the

---

[1]   Dora Marsden to Harriet Shaw Weaver, 20 December 1929.
[2]   Harriet Shaw Weaver to Dora Marsden, 21 December 1929. The nickname came from her maternal grandfather's father, Joseph Wright. She had first used it in his memory as a pen name to her first article in *The Egoist*.

last few years. She accused Weaver of being unsympathetic, self-righteous and cruel. Her actions to Dora, were especially hurtful given that she had made a special case for Harriet, allowing her into her private world at Seldom Seen. Revealingly, Dora wrote: "All the persons known to history who have had to announce to the world the message I am announcing have had to go into solitude, the reason being... they are picking up the 'voices' from which they have to draw the substance of their gospel." At first, Dora continued, she did not know why she was drawn to Seldom Seen, she just knew that she had to:

> get away from the noisy voices of the world and listen to something that was already speaking itself in my brain, but very confusedly... I felt I wanted to be shut up in a box: sealed in. And bit by bit, by one means and another, I nearly managed to bring about what I needed, i.e. my entry into solitude to bring this work to the birth and hide my great spiritual miseries in so doing from the eyes of the world.

But, she added, regretfully "In your case, I made an exception. I let you come inside and see all the straining of my mind. I thought I could rely on you. I thought you, though silent, were sympathetic." Dora condemned Harriet for telling others about the row of 1928 and again accused her of insensitivity. "I am not upbraiding you, I am merely pointing out that, standing by as you have been doing, during these last ten years, at a very strange phenomenon, you have completely failed to realise *what* you were standing by... now, even if you wanted to discuss my books with me, I don't think I can do it. It is too late." In spite of the incredible arrogance of this letter and its baseless charges, Dora at least had the grace still to wish Harriet a good Christmas and thanked her for "putting up 'good money' for books which for the prospects seem so dark[1]."

Harriet returned the seasonal greetings but could no longer restrain her anger at Dora's accusations. At last, all Harriet's pent-up feelings about Dora came to the surface. "On account of the recurring crises in our personal relations," she began to explain her point of view. Though admiring "the great power and enormous fertility of your mind and am quite sympathetic (though you don't think so) on the score of your vast and most exhausting mental labours, it is the direction they are applied that sometimes seems to me not so fortunate."

It was not only the direction of Dora's work that she objected to but her overwhelming dogmatism which finds "evidence so dazzlingly overwhelming as to blind you to contrary views." Moreover, Dora's theses were based on "voices" whose authenticity was in doubt. Harriet argued that they were not spiritual but "spring from the deepest routes of the personality." Ever the rationalist, Harriet added "Your 'message' and 'gospel' I therefore believe to be your own... I cannot help distrusting 'inspiration' 'revelation' unless they seek and submit themselves to *reason*, by which I mean to searching scientific physical tests." And as Dora sought "absolute submission to your own views and became antagonised

---

[1] Dora Marsden to Harriet Shaw Weaver, 22 or 23 December 1929. Reflecting on this letter in 2019, I think it illustrates both the arrogance and illness of Marsden at this time.

unless it was yielded to you," Harriet now felt it was pointless trying to discuss her work with her.

Finally, Harriet came to specific criticisms of *Mysteries*. First, she felt it was "a pity to make so much of sex. My view, for what it is worth, is the best way to treat sex is to forget it as far as possible." Second, she did not approve of the elitism inherent in Dora's superman idea – "give humanity a fair chance and trust it I say." Lastly, Harriet felt that "the first half reads (to me) like a wonderful fairy story." In spite of all this she concluded "I am (and expect to continue to be) perfectly willing to do any service for you that I can[1]."

Dora replied to these attacks by writing that she did not want to continue the argument and then promptly did so. This was not surprising given Harriet's frank denunciation of Dora's work and methods. After all, her labour had not only been painstaking but, to her if to no one else, had a crucial message to deliver. She did not want to give Harriet the impression that "the Holy Spirit communicated with mankind after the manner of a ventriloquist!!" but conceded, "at least we are entirely agreed on one point i.e. that we do not speak the same language." She felt Harriet was particularly cruel to upset her just at the moment when her book was due to be published. "I think," Dora wrote, "of a swimmer swimming the Channel in a rough sea forced into a heated argument just when he is gasping to reach the shore." Though not "bitter and hostile" to her, Dora felt Harriet's attitude was a poor reward for the way in which

---

[1]   Harriet Shaw Weaver to Dora Marsden, 31 December 1929.

she rescued Weaver from her shyness twenty years ago. Harriet then was "a gently shy being who needed all the helpful speeches by which one draws out shy children." Finally she argued that she was not "anxious to pressurise you to believe in any philosophy. I gave that up years ago[1]."

For the second time in two years the differences between the two women had erupted into the open. Harriet clearly disliked Dora's methods, and, worse, was severely critical of her work. As Weaver realized, much of *Definition* and *Mysteries* relied on intuition and assertion and the latter was especially elitist. For a rationalist and atheist they were too much to bear. For her part, Dora obviously felt betrayed by her friend and benefactor, a poor reward for bringing Harriet out of her shell so many years ago. Dora had even let Harriet into her privately ordained world yet she did little to try to understand it, criticizing her just as the results of over ten years' efforts were published. Dora's outburst though was risky – after all it was only Harriet's cash that allowed publication – but perhaps she knew, as did James Joyce, that she could rely on her unswerving loyalty. Indeed, though Harriet admitted to having "a combative desire to make a long series of replies" to Dora's accusations she had "a much deeper desire for peace[2]." Dora too calmed down and accepted the olive branch. She even said she was sorry that our correspondence has been of such an uneasy nature and conceded that "your

---

[1] Dora Marsden to Harriet Shaw Weaver, 3 January 1930.
[2] Harriet Shaw Weaver to Dora Marsden, 8 January 1930.

share in it has been so conciliatory[1]."

Dora kept copies of these letters and Harriet's replies so they survived Harriet's destruction of their more personal correspondence. As such they provide a valuable insight into the friction that existed in their relationship. They also show the enduring affection and love they still had for each other. After all Dora's furious outbursts, Harriet ended by sending "much love to the big side of you, which is still liked and loved by what I hope you will recognise as the better side of your well-wisher Josephine[2]."

The argument at the end of 1929 again illuminated the mental strain, if not illness, from which Dora had been suffering for some time. In 1930, she was in a terrible state. Her lifeline, her books, was rapidly disappearing as she began to realize their failure to take the world by storm; sales were virtually non-existent. Indeed, in Harriet's meticulous records there is no evidence that anyone actually bought a copy of *Mysteries*. In fact, Harriet, kind but also shrewd, had only printed 500 copies and of these, only 100 were bound[3]. Most of these were sent out for review but only one appeared, in *The Times Literary Supplement* in May. This stated:

[1]   Dora Marsden to Harriet Shaw Weaver, 25 January 1930.
[2]   Harriet Shaw Weaver to Dora Marsden, 8 January 1930.
[3]   Receipt Book, Egoist Press, Directors' Meeting, 27 November 1931.

Miss Marsden has ranged the whole world of folklore and myth to prove the familiar "mysteries" of the Christian faith are natural growths in the process of human evaluation. Her conclusions are at variance with most students of religion and anthropology, and very often she appears to accommodate her facts to her theories but those who are interested in myth and legend should find something to interest them if they are not bewildered too much by the constant use of curiously hyphenated words and phrases[1].

This would neither help sales nor Dora's state of mind. She was already worried about being in debt to Mrs. Cox who, at the beginning of the year, had not been paid for over two months. Moreover, she was beginning to feel guilty about her mother, ill in bed in a damp room. "I am highly conscience-stricken about her," Dora reported to Harriet. "She has had a second attack[2]." Things were so bad that Dora, now nearly fifty, even considered returning to teaching. Once again, however, Harriet came to her rescue with financial help and succour which was to last until Dora's death in 1960.

Dora still continued to work on her opus which the *Mysteries* had announced consisted of *Time and The Homo-Centric Universe*, *The Immemorial Cross* and *The Constitution of Knowledge* but the future looked bleak. As sales were so poor, the type for *Definition* and *Mysteries*, as Harriet recorded, was "broken up[3]."

---

[1] *The Times Literary Supplement*, 8 May 1930.
[2] Dora Marsden to Harriet Shaw Weaver, 25 January 1930.
[3] Receipt Book.

Dora's breakdown in early 1930 occurred over what at first sight seems to be a trivial affair, a misunderstanding by bookshops over the conditions of sale for *Mysteries of Christianity*. Some of them appeared to think that after a sale or return condition had been cancelled, the book was now available for free distribution. After the effort of the last ten years or so, the reaction of the author can be easily imagined and for some time afterwards only Hannah Marsden could comfort her daughter as she retreated into further personal isolation. The strains and stresses, the work and commitment, the sacrifice of the 1920s could surely have only been bearable to Dora if she had received the acclaim she at least felt she deserved. If her life had been less one-dimensional, if she had not purposely identified herself solely with her work then the failure of her books might not have been so personally disastrous. Yet, with hindsight, her elitism, her individualism, perhaps even her arrogance, all of which could be traced back to before the war, combined, alongside her desire for isolation, to create this dangerous situation. It was a sad, but perhaps inevitable result of her life at Seldom Seen.

However, by the autumn of 1931 Dora had recovered sufficiently to want to put the record straight over the sales of *Mysteries*. Consequently a directors' meeting of The Egoist Press was called. (The only directors were Dora and Harriet.) Who Dora believed would want to read this it is difficult to judge but Harriet went along with the idea, to humour her sick friend. The minutes faithfully recorded that it was "entirely contrary to the facts that any book was given by D. M. except in common consultation with the other member of the board for the purpose stated above of serving in lieu of advertisements." The minutes also made clear that "neither was there any withdrawing of the book from sale, still less on the grounds that the author preferred to give than to sell." Curiously, they also refer to a "deliberate misrepresentation to the booksellers," but this was now "a matter that need not be entered here[1]." Was this a veiled accusation directed at Harriet? Had she given bookshops the impression that Dora's books could be given away? There is no firm proof of this but, and without any maliciousness, it might well have been the case.

On her visit to Seldom Seen in November, Harriet noticed how thin her friend was and for the remainder of her time at Glencoyne, Dora's physical and mental health was poor. Her moods fluctuated between delusive optimism about further volumes and a rational acceptance that her work was over. Sometimes Dora wondered again about a return to teaching, and occasionally she was quite cheerful. In the spring of 1932 for example, her spirits were enlivened by the spring sun and the beauty of the countryside. She thanked Harriet for her fiftieth birthday wishes of "health, happiness and a good capacity for work," and told her she was going to continue and complete her research, now needing a total of six volumes, before finding a job[2]. Harriet, who had abandoned any plans to back and publish Dora again, knew her friend's hopes were delusory, though she still continued to send books up to Glencoyne. Dora had

---

[1]   Egoist Press Directors' Meeting minutes, 27 November 1931.
[2]   Dora Marsden to Harriet Shaw Weaver, 8 March 1932.

hoped she would finish three volumes by Christmas 1932 and the last, the sixth in the series, by spring 1933. Of course these did not materialize even though at the end of 1932 she told Harriet she was determined "to the exclusion of everything... to make this coming year, 1933, see the end of this long literary pilgrimage of six volumes... The task will be very heavy but I still have to be convinced that it is an impossible one[3]."

There seemed little chance of Dora being successfully shaken from this tragic self-delusion, especially since Harriet's visits to Seldom Seen became fewer. Dora was sustained only by her mother and perhaps too by Sara her cat. But Sara died in September 1932. The loss of a loved pet is always sad, yet to Dora, Sara's death had an even more profound effect on her. She had known for some time that the cat was ill but she could not afford to take it to the vet. "Sara just had to push along as poor persons usually have." In spite of being "devotedly attended to" by her niece, Elaine, who was staying at Seldom Seen at the time, Sara died. She was found, after a long damp search, by Dora on the neighbouring hillside. "I had promised myself," Dora wrote in a five-and-a-half page letter to Harriet, "that when my work was finished and began to be profitable Sara would have her comforts and be cared for, but I had been so long that any faith we had had been broken up! Round that thought a hundred others surfaced themselves in my mind and hung heavily over it until my mind extricated itself by vowing to devote itself simply to getting on with the series and finishing it. Not to for-

---

[3] Dora Marsden to Harriet Shaw Weaver, 22 December 1932.

get Sara but to push on with this book 'in memory of Sara' was how it disentangled itself." This long letter was clearly painful to write and is equally painful to read over fifty years later. Its self-delusion and paranoia (Dora felt the neighbours might have poisoned the cat) were matched only by the touching if melancholy description of the cat's funeral from which Dora and her mother finally "hastened away, us two only, before we had been three. So passed Sara from amongst us[1]."

Sara's death, and the importance Dora attached to it, along with the continuing problems of finance, disruptive summer tourists, a sick mother and few personal visits must have made life at Seldom Seen almost unbearable. Dora did at least have a visit from Harriet in May 1934 but this was curtailed by the news of a fire at her flat and she had to return to London. Whether this sparked off the serious withdrawal Dora suffered in the Summer it is hard to tell. Yet from that point on she stopped eating, cut herself off from others, and drew all the curtains in the cottage. In the following year she claimed 1934 was in fact "a very good year and I trust this coming one will be a good and momentous one[2]." It was certainly momentous, but not in the way she intended for Dora was still referring to the completion of her work, now stretched to a total of seven volumes. The seventh (and the number seven had special, mystical meaning to Dora) volume was "all very new matter – philosophical – and could easily take about a year with every relevant book at my disposal." Though again de-

---

[1]   Dora Marsden to Harriet Shaw Weaver, 22 December 1932.
[2]   Dora Marsden to Harriet Shaw Weaver, 4 January 1935.

luding herself, she cheerily added that she looked forward to finishing it and then "I shall seek the thrice blessed joy of companionship and fellowship!"

However, Dora suffered another shock in March when her sixth volume came back from Mrs. Cox "in a condition which made me see stars[1]." After a blazing row, her loyal and long-suffering typist finally left Seldom Seen never to return again. Dora and her mother went to stay with Eleanor and James Dyson at Liverpool, where she even went for an interview to see if she could return to teaching[2]. But there were, perhaps not surprisingly, no posts available for a 53-year-old woman who had last worked as a teacher in 1909.

With no job prospects, no permanent home of her own and her work ridiculed, forgotten or ignored, the future looked bleak. She had written at the beginning of the year in reference to her work that "I can see my way to the end now[3]." But the end she sought in March did not refer to the completion of her work. Dora suffered from an accident from which she never intended to recover. Though breaking her pelvis and leg, she did not die, even after contracting pneumonia. Mentally, however, she never recovered and in many ways her life was over[4].

---

[1]   Dora Marsden to Harriet Shaw Weaver, 6 March 1935.
[2]   Elaine Bate to Les Garner.
[3]   Dora Marsden to Harriet Shaw Weaver, 1 January 1935.
[4]   In fact Dora had tried to commit suicide. I had to treat this delicately in the 1990 original at the request of Elaine Bate.

The fact that Dora could withstand the deprivation and hardship of life at Seldom Seen for over fifteen years was due to her unshakeable self-confidence and her faith in her work and indeed (though misplaced) her enduring courage. It was also due of course to the remarkable support of her mother, and the almost saintly Harriet. Though Dora had long since rejected the label feminist, she still lived a very woman-centred life. Moreover in Weaver and especially Jameson, it was remarkable how she still inspired women to work on her behalf. Even Sylvia Beach, who lived in Paris and who never met Dora, was enrolled into the club. Pre-war feminist networks had been strained (but not destroyed) by the changed circumstances of the 1920s, a strain compounded in Dora's case by her withdrawal to Glencoyne. However, her old circle of friends, with the exception of Mary Gawthorpe now resident in the USA, also remained intact, if somewhat frayed at the edges. Grace occasionally (too occasionally for Dora) went to Seldom Seen in the early 1920s and was the most, in fact only, successful seller of Dora's books. Rebecca West, in *Time and Tide*, remembered her fondly[1], as did Emmeline Pethick-Lawrence, though neither woman had kept in touch with her.

It could be argued that Dora's writings occasionally had feminist implications, for example in her condemnation of "masculine monotheism" or perhaps even in her belief of a female God. But this was a long way from the

---

[1]   *Time and Tide*, 16 July 1926.

glorious radicalism of *The Freewoman*, a long way too from the realities of women's lives in the 1920s and 1930s.

Did Dora's work have any other value? The sunspot theory has been taken up again, though somewhat discredited, while her attempts to link the "mysteries" of different religions had, and still holds, some interest. But, yet again, Dora's life was now solely devoted to interpreting the world, not changing it. The ultimate tragedy of Seldom Seen was that after years of physical and mental struggle neither goal was achieved. Eventually, Dora realized this and not surprisingly, the brave and beautiful spirit of 1911 was broken to a point she herself wanted to extinguish it.

Dumfries

CRICHTON ROYAL INSTITUTION, DUMFRIES.

This little lady sits quietly in her chair all day, most of the time absorbed in her own thoughts. She never mixes with the others. Reads the paper then does some sewing. She still retains the highest opinion of her own work – the last her magnum opus, two volumes of which have been published and five volumes in transcript... The patient regards them as her soul and very precious.

Dumfries Records

1 May 1948

Somehow the inner "ego" of us seems to remain ageless.

Dora Marsden to Harriet Shaw Weaver

14 September 1946

Dora Marsden never recovered from the tragic events of 1935 even though she lived until the end of 1960. Consequently, though this chapter covers twenty-five years of her life, it is very short, its length in itself a sad statement and reflection on Dora's unfulfilled potential in these final years. Dora in the 1930s had realized at times that her work was not going to achieve the acclaim she felt it deserved; 1935 marked the end of her aspirations. Harriet, who had held doubts about her friend's ability and mental state since the 1920s, knew that Dora's struggle was over after visiting her in Liverpool Infirmary. It was clear to Harriet that Dora, her tiny frame dwarfed by the hospital bed, was not only unlikely to return to work and Seldom Seen but, in a real sense, to the world itself. Mentally she was no longer well and the feelings of guilt she had expressed to Weaver over the adverse effect of Winters in the cottage on her elderly mother were compounded by remorse over what she saw as the trouble she had caused by her hospitalization. Physically, however, Dora did recover from the pneumonia and her fractured pelvis but it would not be possible for her again to cope on her own, let alone for her mother, who died the following year. Moreover, her sister, Eleanor, and her kindly husband, the Reverend James Dyson, feared for Dora's personal safety if she was left to fend for herself. They knew that she needed specialist help and attention. Thus in the Autumn of 1935 Dora became a patient at the Crichton Royal Hospital, Dumfries.

The hospital still stands in beautiful grounds just

outside the town and by the time of Dora's arrival had already established a fine reputation for the treatment of mental illness[1]. It was originally founded by a bequest from Dr. James Crichton in the early Nineteenth Century and the building of the hospital was organized by his wife, Elizabeth. Her original idea was to develop a university for Dumfries but she could not get government approval. Instead she decided on the then radical proposal to build a hospital for people with mental illness. Along with its first director W. A. F. Browne, Elizabeth Crichton worked hard to establish the Royal and by 1839 its first patient, Mary Candlish, was admitted. By the end of the century Crichton enjoyed a national if not international reputation for the treatment of its patients. Sadly by the time she became a resident, Dora would be unaware of the pioneering work of Mrs. Crichton and indeed, of her kinswoman, Susan Carnegie, who was responsible for the foundation of the Royal Asylum in Montrose in 1781[2].

Dora entered Crichton on 26 November 1935 in a distressed state. She was not able to communicate rationally, was severely depressed and was diagnosed as suffering from deep melancholia. As part of hospital procedure, a brief personal history was recorded and this makes fascinating reading. In particular, it gives another interpretation of her father's departure. It records his gambling and dissipation of the family wealth but states that it was Hannah who decided to leave him when Dora

[1] In fact the hospital is now closed and forms a business park as well as Dumfries and Galloway College. The last mental health wards were closed in 2013 and marked the final end of the site's use as a hospital.
[2] Easterbrook, C., 1940.

was around eight to ten years old (sometime between 1890 and 1892). Obviously searching for clues to her illness, the records confirmed that at school Dora was clever but did not mix with the other pupils while later on that she was "wrapped up in her work – Head of a Training Centre – and has written three books of a philosophical and theological nature." It briefly mentioned her suffragette days and editorship of an "advanced women's paper" and concluded that:

> For the last twelve years she has lived the life of a recluse alone with her books and her studies. She felt she has found something of great importance in the world of thought – a criticism of philosophy from the earliest days onwards – this work did not create the impression she wanted and she became depressed. In summer 1934 the patient denied herself sufficient food, cut herself off from others and pulled down her blinds to prevent anyone seeing her... Since the end of June [1935] she has become more and more depressed ...[1]

The report stressed both Dora's intelligence and her isolation. It located the failure of her books as central to the cause of her illness, defined by the current psychiatrist at Dumfries, Dr. George S. Stirling, as severe psychotic depression. Though Dora never really fully recovered from this she did occasionally enjoy better periods of health. In 1937, for example, she felt well enough to enjoy a short holiday with her sister Eleanor and she began to take an interest in her surroundings.

Dora remained a reserved figure at the hospital, spending her days in her favourite chair, aloof from the

---

[1] Dumfries, 26 November 1935.

other patients and only speaking when spoken to. In an ironic parody of her father's shoddy business and her mother's skill as a seamstress, she began to sew a little and repair clothes. Indeed, the quality of her work was frequently commented on by the staff. However, Dora was still depressed and felt particularly guilty over her poor financial position, even though the hospital fees were paid for her.

By the beginning of the 1940s there was a little improvement and she even began to attend "arts and crafts" sessions at the hospital. In 1941 she felt ready to go on holiday again. This time, though, she was keen to return to Dumfries, and she went back there one day earlier than planned. Back at Crichton, Dora settled into her usual routine of sewing, reading and silence. Electrical treatment was tried, but without success. Occasionally, though, Dora would take a short walk in the grounds. In fact, there was little real change in the 1940s but she did return to some sort of work at the end of the decade. This often consisted of translating Latin, in her own words (as recorded by the hospital) "not for any practical purpose, but for exercise[1]." She appeared, at this stage, to read nothing but her own two books, still dreaming that one day she would be able to complete the seven-volume series. Dora did talk to the staff a little more about her past, but she must have realized that her dream was highly unlikely to materialize.

Dora also started to cooperate with the staff more in the 1950s, helping them in keeping the ward tidy. But

---

[1] Dumfries, 10 January 1947.

she would become very upset if her own routine was in any way altered. She also began to develop some obsessional features – cutting up her food into seven portions, giving the nurses seven sweets a day, because seven remained a magic number to her, ever since Dora was twenty-nine (i.e. 1911, when *The Freewoman* began), or so she claimed. In the late 1950s, she also began to write, in her own words, "a work of great magnitude," her *magnum opus*. Indeed, throughout 1958 and the first half of 1959 she was writing quite furiously, one nurse commenting in this period that she appeared to do little else. "Writes all day," the nurse reported, "and has bundles of 'manuscript' all around her. Eats well but only sleeps a few hours, her writings dominate her[1]." By the summer of 1959 this burst of activity ended and she returned to sitting quietly, doing little. In her last year she discovered and enjoyed television.

Throughout her seventies Dora's physical health, in spite of her frailty (she weighed only five and one-half stone) remained fairly good. In the 1950s she began to walk with the aid of a chair placed in front of her but in the end it was old age that resulted in her death. On 13 December 1960 Dora had a sudden collapse, losing consciousness at 8:30 p.m. She came to for a brief moment but this brave and beautiful spirit was finally extinguished just after nine.

The twenty-five years Dora spent at Dumfries amounted to a tragic waste of the abilities of a woman who, most clearly before 1914, had shown astounding

---

[1]   Dumfries, 16 April 1959.

physical courage and remarkable intellectual capacities. They were also lonely years although Dora was never entirely deserted, receiving visits and letters from her family, mainly Eleanor, James, Philip and Elaine Dyson, and from Harriet Shaw Weaver, "dear Josephine." Harriet, who in the 1930s had become a Communist, was deeply saddened by Dora's plight, for she had known what talent Dora had possessed. Moreover, Dora's friendship had been crucial to her own development. She paid Dora's fees at Dumfries and continued to write, particularly on anniversaries. Dora, though haphazard in replying, did so occasionally, hoping, for example, that Harriet, though seventy, would always feel young. "Somehow," Dora wrote to her, "the inner 'ego' of us seems to remain ageless[1]."

Dora also, in the 1940s, encouraged Harriet to complete her *Symposium on Time*. She was particularly pleased to hear that her own five chapters on *Time and the Homo-Centric Universe*, were to be included. Eventually though, Harriet abandoned the project again in favour of more urgent "burning political questions[2]." She returned to it in the early 1950s, cutting out the work on *Space* which sadly ended in the wastepaper basket. The manuscript was finally deposited in the Oxford Philosophy Library where, as Harriet feared, it has largely remained unread. This is unfortunate, for Harriet's work is a clear and well-written summary of leading philosophers' attitude to Time. With typical generosity she thanked Dora for her suggestions and advice, re-

---

[1]   Dora Marsden to Harriet Shaw Weaver, 14 September 1946.
[2]   Harriet Shaw Weaver to Sylvia Beach, 25 May 1947.

gretting that Dora was, as originally intended, unable to write an analytic introduction due to ill health[1].

As part of Harriet's pruning of her work, Dora's five chapters were omitted but, loyal as ever, she was determined to find a way to publish them. Ironically, when she succeeded, this became Dora's most successful book. Harriet had originally tried to get the editor of the *Philosophical Quarterly* interested though he felt Dora's chapters were unsuitable for publication. "As I could not consult you," Harriet wrote, "since you do not write letters nowadays, and seeing that no ordinary publisher would accept an unfinished book" she decided to publish it herself. As with *Definition of the Godhead* and *The Mysteries of Christianity*, Harriet's love for Dora overrode commercial considerations and *The Philosophy of Time*, published by The Hollywell Press in 1955, remains a lasting testimony to Harriet's affection. As Dora's brother-in-law, James Dyson wrote to her on 2 September 1955, it was clear that "nobody has had a better or more considerate friend and colleague than you have proved to be[2]."

The Philosophy of Time began well with Dora claiming again that the problem of understanding the concept was due more to the inadequacies of philosophers as much as anything else. In particular, philosophers refused to realize that an understanding of Time can only be made when it is related to the whole scheme of the universe. Even St. Augustine complained that "all

---

[1] Harriet Shaw Weaver, *Symposium on Time*, Oxford Philosophy Library, Merton Street.
[2] *The Philosophy of Time* was reprinted by the Union of Egoists in 2016.

men know what is meant by Time" yet cannot explain it. This, Dora continued, is not "a state of mind limited to a thinker here and there. It is the frankly confessed feeling of thinkers ranging over a period of more than two thousand years, every age and every school of the historic period hardly having sounded the dirge of the incomprehensibility of Time." Dora of course, ever the Egoist, had succeeded where all the others had failed. Time was measured motion but not just ordinary motion but "motion conceived as the mobile principle in its entirety; that is as the father or creative element of the material cosmos[1]."

In spite of her more obscure comments, the pamphlet, with its bold black title on a yellow cover (chosen by Harriet to signify night and day), was attractive and well printed. Indeed, it enjoyed a modest success, easily outselling Dora's other philosophical works. In all, nearly one hundred copies were sold, some sent as far away as Australia, Russia, Italy and India. Foreign interest was raised by an even-handed review, in a circular published by the *International Institute of Philosophy*. This stated that "This volume is made up of what was originally intended to be the introduction of a larger volume prevented from completion by the illness of the authoress. The definition of time as motion measured is defended with frequent reference to the thinkers of the past. At the close, time is also viewed as mobile extension."

As before, many copies were sent out for review

---

[1]   Dumfries, 10 January 1947.

but this time some were actually sold. Foyles and Harrods, for example, even requested extra copies as, ironically, did W. H. Smith's who had tried to censor *The Freewoman* so long ago. None the less, it was not a financial triumph as Harriet only received £17 in sales as against £57 expenditure, but compared to *Definition of the Godhead* and *The Mysteries of Christianity* it was indeed a relative success. "Everyone who has seen the little book," Harriet wrote, "seems to have liked it[1]."

How far Dora was aware of her success it is hard to tell, for surviving letters from the Dumfries period are few. She was certainly aware of Harriet's work and had received a copy herself. Further, it seems likely that the reaction to the pamphlet (and seeing her name in print again) was the major impetus behind the new and final burst of writing that began in 1958. In a Christmas letter to Harriet she wrote that she felt moved to write one last cosmo-historical book... It constitutes the promised *Book of Truth* which is Heaven's Covenant with Creation[2]." This was to be Dora's *magnum opus* and had two autobiographical chapters appended to it, to prove her "pedigree."

Dora hoped that, yet again, Harriet though now aged eighty-three, would help her but she refused, suggesting instead that Dora get her brother, Ewart, to find a typist. Unwisely, Harriet hinted that she might just do it herself if this proposal was not a success[3]. In a flash, just like the old days, Dora seized on the "offer." "Now

---

[1]   Harriet Shaw Weaver to Holywell Press, 20 July 1956.
[2]   Dora Marsden to Harriet Shaw Weaver, 20 December 1958.
[3]   Harriet Shaw Weaver to Dora Marsden, 8 July 1959.

Deity has enabled you," she replied, "to help me with such spectacular help and in so many ways during an almost *full half century* that it seems probable that she will help you to complete the full fifty years... You were not on your own. *You were* a dedicated being[1]." Apart from the pathos of a seventy-seven year old bullying an eighty-three year old, the letter reflected not only Dora's belief in a female god but her continuing view that her work was divinely inspired.

For once Harriet, indeed her friend and benefactor for almost fifty years, refused and, for good measure, reasserted her own atheism. She rejected the idea that her help had been divinely ordained – "if it was your deity who arranged my dedication before birth" she logically argued "I will have to shoulder a not too enviable operation: the encompassing of the death at the age of 14 of my uncle Edward Henry Wright, a healthy and merry boy, in order that his father, my grandfather, should not leave the bulk of his fortune to him[2]."

Perhaps it was this reply that led to the cessation of Dora's writing in the summer of 1959. Perhaps too, she felt let down by her friend, and it appears Dora never wrote to "dear Josephine" again. Harriet was saddened by Dora's death in 1960 and, in spite of her own poor health, did, as a departing gift to her dear friend, type out both the fourteen chapters of the magnum opus and the two of autobiography. Neither is accessible as Dora's descendants feel they contain too many inaccuracies

---

[1]   Dora Marsden to Harriet Shaw Weaver, 19 July 1959.
[2]   Harriet Shaw Weaver to Dora Marsden, 29 July 1959.

and, sadly, too many signs of her mental illness[1].

Dora was buried in Dumfries cemetery in December 1960 with only the Rev. James Dyson in attendance. At the time of writing, her grave is difficult to find, the simple headstone missing. What a sad and anonymous end for such a remarkable woman – suffragette, Freewoman, Egoist and philosopher. Poor Dora.

---

[1]   Sadly, I do not know where these autobiographical notes are or even if they still exist.

Conclusion

I hope you don't have to wait till you are dead to be seen and known.

Margaret Storm Jameson to Dora Marsden

8 December 1928

Dora Marsden left us a heritage in the unembarrassed beauty of our times.

Rebecca West

Time and Tide, 16 July 1926

What, then, can we learn from this study of Dora Marsden's life? What can we say about the life itself? Certainly, as Rebecca West argued in *Time and Tide*, Dora was indeed "one of the most marvellous personalities the nation has produced," even if most of the evidence to substantiate this claim must come from before 1914. Clearly, too, Dora was a brave and beautiful spirit but a wayward spirit, a genius flawed, a talent wasted. This central tragedy of her life started with her withdrawal in 1913 but is linked also to the complex nature of her personality and psyche. It would seem appropriate now, with the outline of Dora's life before us, to make some tentative conclusions on these. But before this is considered in detail it would perhaps be useful first to assess the broader historical importance of her life and work.

To begin with, Dora's early life surely reflects the importance of education in the 1890s and 1900s as an escape route for women. There was already a tradition of women in teaching and the 1870 Education Act only served to increase the demand. For women this provided a unique opportunity, unique because it allowed them to gain independence through a secure, relatively well-paid job without having to struggle against their sharply defined "natural" roles. Some men still objected to women teachers, but overall teaching was an acceptable career for women where engineering, science and medicine, for example, were not.

It was within this context that Dora Marsden got her first job as a pupil teacher at 13. It was a crucial choice for through the scholarship system, where a tiny minority of working-class and lower-middle-class children were "creamed off," it ultimately opened the gates for Dora into higher education, in her case, Manchester University. This process was certainly an improvement in opportunities for women but it was limited. There were still very few women in medicine and science (Rona Robinson being a notable exception), and most women, like Dora, were following "suitable" humanities courses leading to an equally suitable career in teaching. Even on Dora's course there were some differences in the curriculum for men and women. None the less Dora's education at Manchester allowed and encouraged her to think and be independent. It also encouraged her confidence and her feeling of self-worth.

As such, the growth of women teachers created a potential pool of support for feminism and the women's suffrage movement. Indeed, it could be argued that the demand for women teachers created a point of contradiction within Victorian and Edwardian society which was so eager to maintain the "natural" roles of the sexes. For once, it was a contradiction that worked in women's favour. On the one hand, the fact of women working in schools could be rationalized as an extension of their maternal and domestic role but, on the other, their experience as teachers could lead to a questioning of that very role and everything associated with it. After all, how could women be stupid, fit only for a life of domesticity and dependence on a man when, as a teacher, their life and training proved otherwise? Why should women be deprived of a vote purely because of their sex?

Not surprisingly then, many teachers were attracted to the women's suffrage movement. It is surely no coincidence that among other activists, Mary Gawthorpe, Theresa Billington, Rona Robinson and of course Dora herself had all worked in schools. It is no coincidence either that these women, like the Pankhursts, first became active in the suffrage movement in Manchester. The town, as we have seen, already had strong suffragist traditions before the birth of the WSPU in 1903 and it went on to provide many prominent fighters for the cause.

Dora Marsden's part in this battle clearly gives a vivid picture of the vitality, the strength and the weaknesses of the movement, particularly the role played by the WSPU. Dora, Rona and Mary all forfeited secure jobs to work full time for the cause, all risked prison and their health. Mary was an invalid by 1911 and Dora's own health, never robust, did not fully recover after 1910. They were all ostensibly fighting for the vote on the same terms as men which, as adult suffragists constantly pointed out, would have only enfranchised around one million women due to the property qualification outlined above. Yet Dora and the rest did not struggle for hours outside Parliament, face the hostile ridicule of Lord Morley's distinguished audience or risk death from their lofty perch on the Empire Hall for the vote alone. Dora, like so many other suffragettes, saw women's disenfranchisement as symbolic of women's wider oppression, as well as a personal and degrading insult. Others in the Labour and Socialist Movement were questioning the value of the vote itself but, as Victor Grayson, the revolutionary Socialist MP for the Colne Valley put it in his 1909 pamphlet *The Problem of Parliament – A Criticism and a Remedy*, "the right of women to the vote must be discussed on another basis than the value of the franchise. Their claim is to be recognized as intelligent human beings."

Dora's career in the WSPU also shows the weakness of the organization and its strategy. Militancy itself was individualistic and eschewed mass action and its prime aim, pressure on the Liberal government through publicity, meant that each act had to be more eye-catching, or newsworthy, than the last. This built-in escalation could be seen in Dora's own record which culminated in her spectacular heckling of Churchill in Southport. Yet as militancy increased, the risks increased too, with the ultimate price being paid by those women who died after the Black Friday demonstration of 1911 and, of course, by Dora's friend, Emily Wilding Davison. Militancy though showed the limitless ingenuity and courage of women and broke some of the taboos that constricted them. As Winifred Holtby in her *Women in a Changing Civilisation* wrote, "The very recklessness and extremism of militancy had shaken old certainties[1]." In this alone, the campaign helped to change attitudes and contributed to whatever limited progress there was in the inter-war period.

---

[1] Holtby (1934), p. 53.

The militant strategy of the WSPU also had its own contradictions which Dora's departure in 1910 showed so well. Militancy necessitated secrecy and encouraged the autocracy of the leaders. The Pankhursts justified this with a reference to war – generals give orders, the soldiers carry them out. But from 1907, led by Charlotte Despard and Theresa Billington-Greig, the rank and file began to mutiny and continued to do so until the Union folded in 1917. How could they be fighting for independence when it was denied them in their own organization? How could they fight for a democratic reform in such an autocracy? Certainly as "an educated, talented and thoughtful woman" who had "kept watch in the interests of the Union... as few people had the strength, or the brains, or the love to do[1]," Dora greatly resented being told what to do and how to do it. In fact, in her case it was more a case of what *not* to do. This was made clear by the leadership's constraint of her activities in 1910 and particularly over the Bazaar. It was the Union's own point of contradiction; it attracted women of thought, independence and originality but then expected them to leave those qualities behind when they joined the army, to sit tight and await orders from Clement's Inn. Some could accept this; Dora could not.

Growing numbers of women, like Dora's "S.O.S." group in Manchester, also became frustrated with both the political and the feminist limitations of suffragism. Theresa Billington-Greig was one of the first to express this publicly in *The New Age* and then in, *Emancipation*

---

[1] Dora Marsden to Emmeline Pethick-Lawrence, 9 January 1911.

in a Hurry. As Theresa put it, many activists began to realize that the "vote cannot secure of itself any single woman's emancipation... [suffragists] fail to see that large areas in which emancipation is needed lie entirely outside the scope of the vote... a slave woman with a vote will essentially be a slave[1]." Out of this came cries for a greater vision of emancipation and a wider exploration of the oppression of women in all its forms, a discussion and exploration that went beyond the vote. Out of all this too came *The Freewoman.*

The Freewoman was surely Dora Marsden's greatest achievement, an everlasting tribute to her ability and determination. It could not have succeeded without the help of others, most notably Mary Gawthorpe, Grace Jardine and Charles Grenville, but Dora's role was crucial. *The Freewoman* could not have succeeded either without the demand for a wider debate of women's issues outlined above. No doubt suffragists discussed sexuality, contraception and morality in private but to do so publicly within their own papers would hardly be politic. Besides, it would usually clash with the conservative philosophy of suffragist leaders, most of whom accepted contemporary moral values and institutions and wished men would live up to them. But Dora and other "Freewomen" wanted to analyse these same values and institutions and their relationship to women's oppression. She had the courage not only to allow such a discussion but to encourage it too[2].

---

[1]   Billington-Greig (1911), p. 173. As reported by Amy Houghton to Dora Marsden, *c.* 1911.

[2]   As Marsden wrote on 14 March 1912: "We make bold to say that never before the advent of *The Freewoman* has the opportunity [to study sex],

The Freewoman had no "line," no programme, but was the forum for an explosion of radical and controversial ideas. Perhaps, as one newsagent put it, the paper represented the new woman who "doesn't understand herself nor quite knows what she wants. *The Freewoman* seems to be trying to find out[1]." As such *The Freewoman* illustrated the vitality and strength of the English feminist tradition that until recently has been ignored or confined to the struggle for the vote. It also showed the potential of suffragism to raise feminism consciousness beyond its own political and ideological limitations; Mrs. Humphrey Ward was quite right, *The Freewoman* did indeed represent "the dark and dangerous side of the 'Woman Movement.'" It was a threat. It would have been a greater threat still if it had been more closely tied to the militant class struggle of 1911 and 1912. Though sympathetic to certain elements of anarchism and Syndicalism (and *The Freewoman* is a testimony to these traditions too), Marsden's individualism eschewed Socialism, class action and the collective organization of society as a whole. It was to lead her into the political wilderness.

None the less, as Harriet Shaw Weaver put it, *The Freewoman* "must have been edited on a mountain top it breathed so heavily of freedom[2]," even if the mist on Dora's peak prevented her from analysing how to achieve that freedom. But what *The Freewoman* did say

---

either for men or women, in England or elsewhere, been at hand. That is why *The Freewoman*'s advent is so phenomenal."

[1] Quoted in *The New Freewoman* publicity circular announcing the paper's resurrection in 1913.

[2] *Time and Tide*, 16 July 1926.

without any reservation was that women in all areas of their lives, sexually, at home, work, as parents, should have a choice, unrestricted by custom or convention. "The Freewoman wants no ready sphere," Caroline Board wrote in the 14 December 1911 issue, "The Freewoman wants the whole round earth to choose from." How far it contributed to a permanent change in attitude is debatable, though one of its earliest contributors, Rebecca West, thought so. She claimed in the *Time and Tide* article that the paper:

by its candour did an immense service to the world by shattering, as nothing else would, as not the mere cries of intention towards independence had ever done, the romantic conception of women. It pointed out that there were lots of women who were unmated and childless who resented their condition. It pointed out that there were lots of women who were mated and who had children who found elements of dissatisfaction in their position. It even mentioned the existence of abnormalities of instinct. In fact it smashed the romantic pretence that woman had as a birth-right the gift of perfect adaptation, that they were in a bland state of desireless contentment which, when they were beautiful, reminded the onlooker of goddesses and when they were plain were more apt to remind them of a cabbage. If this romantic conception had been true, there would have been no reason for the emancipation of women, since if they could be happy anywhere and anyhow, there was no need to alter their environment. It had to be admitted that women were vexed human beings who suffered intensely from male adaptation to life, and that they were tortured and dangerous if they were not allowed to adapt themselves to life. That admission is the keystone of the modern Feminist movement[1].

The end of *The Freewoman* was deeply felt both in Britain and the USA where Dora's reputation among advanced circles was high. Yet with the help of supporters on both sides of the Atlantic, and in particular through West and Weaver, the paper was reborn as *The New Freewoman* in August 1913. Its feminist supporters and readers however became disenchanted with Dora's Stirnerian-based individualism and her philosophical discourses in general. Dora still made acute comments

---

[1]   Strachey (ed.) (1936), p. 239.

on the WSPU and the powerlessness of women but she had already jettisoned the label "feminist" in May 1913. Along with her growing concern with philosophy, her political development (or lack of it) not only troubled her old supporters but anarchists like Tucker too. Eventually they were, understandably, to desert her, leaving the new literary group around Pound to dominate the paper. Gawthorpe and West had always wanted *The Freewoman* to explore and review modern literature and to help it develop. They did not, however, wish to see it swamp and overcome its feminist concerns. But with Dora away in the North, concentrating on her own work and the relatively inexperienced Weaver and West left in London, this is exactly what happened. It is thus not surprising that the importance of *The New Freewoman* is usually seen in terms of its contribution to modern literature in general, and Imagism in particular.

Ezra Pound certainly wanted to use the paper for himself and his *protégés* but it would be mistaken to locate the "blame" for the decline of feminism in the paper with him and his group. His high-handed manner did contribute to the resignation of West but the principal reason for the change in *The Freewoman*'s successor lay with Dora Marsden and her growing physical, political and intellectual isolation. Her work could still make acute observations about women and power but it was no longer constructed from a feminist perspective. Ideologically, it was Dora's own individualism that eventually subsumed and overwhelmed the overt feminism in the paper. There was still a demand for a radical feminist journal (witness *The Link*, a paper for socialist women for example) but as Dora admitted in the last issue of 15 December 1913, she was no longer willing to satisfy it. If some feminist readers did not approve of the change in direction that was unfortunate but "Primarily the paper is not written for them it is written to please ourselves"; Dora's suggestion for a new title, *The Egoist*, was singularly apposite.

The primary importance of *The Egoist* was, of course, the opportunity it gave to James Joyce. Joycean scholars will always want to claim the paper for themselves, perhaps ignoring other literary contributors, certainly underrating women's role in his early career. Without Weaver, in West's words (again from *Time and Tide*) "the St. Bernard in human form who kept on and on rescuing James Joyce from the continuous alpine storm which raged around him," the Irishman's career would have been radically different; without Marsden its introduction to English readers would have been delayed. It was Dora's persistence and Harriet's money that kept the paper alive and it was Dora who accepted and was so willing to defend *A Portrait*. Weaver and Marsden were *The Egoist* and they performed a miraculous job in keeping the paper alive and open to the "outrageous" work of Joyce. If either woman had dropped out (in 1914 and 1915 at least) the paper would have surely collapsed.

Dora's own political writings in 1914 to 1916 continued to make some acute comments about power and the war, and were particularly scathing in their attacks on liberal ideology. But they became so individualistic that even her anarchist supporters deserted her. 'The

Philosophical Basis of Egoism" was extremely obtuse, though it too could make some telling points. Whether this, and her "Lingual Psychology" made a lasting contribution to philosophical analysis is however extremely debatable. In Dora's defence, as Lidderdale and Nicholson noted, it was "an unlucky accident of history that she came to semantic studies at the early stage, when many of the important books were not yet written[1]," unfortunate too, to be pursuing this research during the war when other issues were understandably more pressing.

Yet Dora had chosen to work in isolation and through this the quality and the relevance of her academic work, however original, was bound to suffer. This clearly applied to her efforts at Seldom Seen although they are not without interest, particularly to students of astronomy and religion. The sun-spot theory has been periodically pursued since while her attempts to link religious mysteries and symbols (also not new) were illuminating. Dora's knowledge of philosophy was vast though not necessarily original. Alexander's advice not to publish was sound but, given Dora's life commitment to her work, always unlikely to be heeded.

Ironically, it was Dora's "asides" that tended to be the most revealing, particularly those on the "modern woman," based, no doubt, on the superior and noisy women that occasionally stayed at Glencoyne. Dora may well have envied their gay and carefree life but would have resented their opinion of her as an old, staid "humbug." After all, Dora could reason that it was her

---

[1] *The Freewoman*, 21 March 1912.

work and her sacrifice that had enabled these women to be free; she deserved their gratitude not their mockery. This feeling was shared by many, but not all women who had been active in the feminist movement before 1914. As Mary Hamilton, who became a Labour MP, put it in *Our Freedom and Its Results*, "Those who fought for the emancipation of their sex and won it, look at the girl of today with a disappointment in which there is more than a hint of bitterness[1]." Dora would not have put it that way but it was no doubt a sentiment she would have shared.

Dora would not even have called herself a feminist in the 1920s but the central, unchanging feature of her life was that from birth until death it was completely woman centred. Indeed, some commentators would argue that the major historical importance of Dora Marsden's life was that it not only reflected the vitality of women's support systems and networks but their value too. They were clearly crucial throughout Dora's unusual life as teacher, suffragette, journalist, individualist, philosopher and writer for she was operating in an hostile world, an independent woman who defiantly flouted conventional sexual stereotyping and expectations. They were perhaps typical of the relationships among independent women in the 1900s, close, intense, even passionate but not necessarily sexual. Quite clearly, without the loving support of her mother and, at varying times, Gawthorpe, Jardine, Robinson, West and Weaver, Dora could not have survived let alone pursue her unusual path. Without the remarkable and enduring love and af-

---

[1] Strachey (ed.) (1936), p. 239.

fection (not to mention money) of "dear Josephine," little would have been possible at all after 1913.

Dora Marsden did not deserve the anonymity that surrounded her death in 1960 yet in many ways it was a fitting end to her life. She was a complex character, brave, courageous, intelligent, gifted certainly, but wayward, dogmatic, elitist and arrogant too. These negative aspects of her personality were evident throughout her life yet they increased dramatically after 1913. They were surely linked to her tendency to withdraw from others, to draw away (especially after the collapse of *The Freewoman*) from an active political and social life. Is it not this that provides the key to her personality and the changes in the quality of her life and writing? If so, what drove Dora into isolation, what were the origins of this destructive and ultimately tragic force?

These awkward questions cannot elicit definitive answers, but one tentative suggestion is that Dora, with one or two exceptions, principally her mother, did not trust anyone but herself. This in part would explain both her need for devotees and the furious rows, with Mary and Harriet for example, when the devotion was tainted by criticism. It would perhaps also explain the severe "loyalty tests" she gave Gawthorpe and Weaver: both failed her, Mary in 1911 and Harriet in 1929.

The only person Dora trusted was her mother Hannah, a central figure throughout her life. It was Hannah, of course, who gave Dora her first and most intimate impression of the potential strength of women, particularly after her father's departure to the USA. Conversely,

Fred, and to some extent her elder brother John, were hardly ideal models of integrity and reliability. Both loved to drink and gamble and Fred preferred to leave rather than stay with his family. It is difficult to be precise about the effect of her father's departure but it could hardly have left her untouched or unscathed; or have fostered a trust in men.

Dora's family experience, alongside that at school and university which proved her own ability, again tended to imply that the only person she could really rely on was herself. Even the trust she had enjoyed with others in the WSPU was tarnished by the end of 1910. The Union's leaders certainly did not trust Dora's judgement, admonishment, it seemed to her, being the only reward for her efforts. No wonder Dora's subsequent attacks on the Pankhursts were so vitriolic and bitter.

Dora's unwillingness to trust others and the belief she could only rely on herself dovetailed neatly into her growing individualism and conversion to Egoism. Stirnerism is surely based, if nothing else, on a lack of trust, with individuals being the only safe and reliable guardian of their own interests.

What is interesting here is the similarity of Dora's life with that of Stirner, in particular the same sharp contrast of their own personal lives and their grand enunciations of the power of the individual. In the 1920s Dora explained her own poverty by referring to her new divinely ordained role as a prophet with a crucial message to deliver to the world: Dora now placed her trust in God. Yet as Harriet and other realized, the Deity and the mission she gave to Dora were both self-constructed, an illusion certainly but one that further justified her withdrawal and indeed her life and work.

The effects of Dora's growing isolation were many and varied. First, it led to a decline in the quality and relevance of her writing. Though elements of individualism could be traced to *The Freewoman* period, it was tempered by her own recent political experience and by the debate in the correspondence columns and the wonderfully innovative Discussion Circles. Though criticism continued in the letters page of *The New Freewoman* and *The Egoist*, Dora had already removed herself to Southport, an increasingly isolated observer who was no longer politically active. The relevance of political ideas must surely come from active struggle but though she continued to make acute observations about power, the quality of Dora's analysis declined as it became the work of an increasingly isolated mind. At the same time, her writing, perhaps not surprisingly, became more and more concerned with self-justification.

The worst personal effect of Dora's retreat was that ultimately she was forced to gamble everything on her work. In some ways, this explains both her inexhaustible search for absolute definition and her continual delay in publication, first of her *Egoist* articles, then of her books. Dora subconsciously at least, knew that she had to get her work absolutely "right"; the world would justify her life and labours by the reception it gave her upon publication. Yet the world's response was poor and, to Dora, severely lacking in gratitude. The hurt she felt in the 1930s manifested itself in even greater withdrawal accompanied by feelings of guilt and unworthiness. She felt guilty about neglecting her aged mother and felt she herself had failed. All the rest of her group from Weaver to Jardine, Robinson to West had all been successful and had done something constructive with their lives. All Dora had, in the 1930s, were two unsaleable books only published in the end because of Harriet's generosity. The result was break-downs, the accident that failed in 1935 and the subsequent twenty-five-year hospitalization in Dumfries.

However, the tragedy of Dora's later years should not be allowed to obscure her historical importance, nor indeed the more positive aspects of her personality. Dora Marsden was a brave and beautiful spirit and a rare one. She could inspire great affection and loyalty, and her writing, especially before the First World War, could be outstanding. Her life also reveals much of the early suffrage and feminist movements and, to a lesser extent perhaps, that of modern literature, certainly that surrounding Pound and of course James Joyce. It was a hard, independent, sometimes brilliant life, perhaps emancipated too yet, personally and politically, it was flawed by her individualism and withdrawal, by her inability to accept and embrace a more social existence and political analysis. The quality and relevance of her political consciousness and writing decreased as her political involvement declined. For a brief and rich period before the First World War, Dora became a crucial part of a political and intellectual ferment which in spite of differences emphasized the crucial relationship between capitalism, power and oppression and the subsequent need for class-consciousness and action. An integral part of this was a socialist feminist position whose origins stretched back to the early Nineteenth Century. In the 1900s this rejected the political limitations of suffragism and the simplistic arguments of the WSPU. It stressed in Isabel Leatham's words in *The Freewoman* that though it may "be possible to have socialism with only a shadow of freedom for women... the complete emancipation of women would be impossible without it[1]." In other words, the radical currents of the period 1910-14, as Dora herself accepted in her interview with the *Evening Standard* in 1911, noted that emancipation from sexual and class oppression required more than an act of will or tinkering with reform – it required revolutionary social and political change. The contributors to *The Freewoman* – surely Dora Marsden's greatest achievement – and Dora herself, brilliantly debated what this would involve. Unfortunately, her own drive to personal and political isolation, aided by her attraction to the elitist and anti-social individualism of Stirner, meant that she would take no part in this activity.

Dora could perhaps reply that she remained a "Freewoman" throughout her life and that her isolation from 1913 onwards was the hard yet worthwhile and almost inevitable cost of her independence. Yet a single emancipated woman – if Dora can be described as such – coming from an individual rather than as part of a mass revolt, is easily consumed and safely dismissed as an intriguing oddity. Many will want to claim Dora Marsden but in spite of her later development and in-

---

[1]   *The Freewoman*, 21 March 1912.

deed, her own loud denials, it is surely clear to which tradition she belongs. In one last lucid moment towards the end of her life Dora may have realized this too. As she said goodbye for what turned out be the last time to her niece, Dora give her one final piece of advice. "Remember, Elaine, always be a feminist." It is as a feminist that this certainly brave, often beautiful and ultimately tragic spirit should be remembered and seen.

Bibliography

This is divided into two major sections of primary and secondary sources.

Primary Sources

The primary sources are organized as follows:

1. Collections of Papers.
2. Other Documentary Records.
3. Newspapers and Periodicals.
4. Miscellaneous Including Interviews and Published Material.

1. Collections of Papers

The Dyson Papers: By far the most important collection of documents used in the compilation of this book. Now in the possession of Princeton University, the collection comprises largely of correspondence connected to Dora's activities during her time with the WSPU, the gestation period for *The Freewoman* and her time as editor of *The Freewoman* and *New Freewoman*. The fascinating exchange between Gawthorpe and Marsden between 1911 and 1912 is contained here, also letters with Rebecca West, H. G. Wells, Guy Aldred, Ezra Pound and others. There is also some material connected to the *Definition of the Godhead*, *Mysteries of Christianity* and *The Philosophy of Time*. It is a crucial collection for students of suffragism, *The*

Freewoman and *The Egoist* – indeed for students of English cultural and political history – and I hope Princeton will allow copies of it to be made available here.

Harriet Shaw Weaver Papers: Held by the British Library, MSS. 57345-57365. This collection holds much crucial correspondence of Harriet Shaw Weaver and many of her literary and business papers. It is particularly important for the letters between her and Dora, Sylvia Beach, James Joyce and others, and for its collection of minutes, accounts, etc. of The New Freewoman Co. and *The Egoist*. It also has some material relating to *The Definition of the Godhead*. Further papers of Weaver's are located in the manuscript and rare books room in the D.M.S. Watson Building, University College Library, Gower St.

Jane Lidderdale Papers: Held in D. M. S. Watson Building, University College Library, Gower St. These consist of material collected by Lidderdale for her biography of H. S. Weaver. It includes letters by the author to Ezra Pound, James Joyce, Sylvia Beach and others.

2. Other Documentary Records

Birth certificates of Fred Marsden, Dora's father, (b. 25 July 1851), Hannah Garside, Dora's mother (b. 15 May 1852), Dora Marsden (b. 5 March 1882).

Marriage certificates of John Marsden and Sara Woodhead, Dora's grandparents on her father's side, 27 January 1851; Fred Marsden and Hannah Garside, 12 April 1875.

Marsden Town School Reports 1890-99 (held at Huddersfield Public Library).

Huddersfield Technical College Annual reports and Prospectus 1895-1900 (also Huddersfield Public Library).

Papers held by John Rylands Library, Manchester University, particularly class registers 1900-3 and on Owen College and its societies.

Kepler Senior School Log Book 1903, held by West Yorkshire Archive Service, Leeds.

Colchester and Harwich Pupil Teachers Centre Log Book and Staff Records, held by Essex Public Record Office.

Minutes of Cheshire County Council Education Committee Vols II-VII 1904 to 1910. Chester PRO.

3. Newspapers and Periodicals These are all held at the British Library, Colindale unless indicated.

Up to suffragette period: *Manchester Guardian*; *Owen's Magazine* (John Ryland's Library, Manchester).

As a suffragette: *Votes for Women* and *The Suffragette* (WSPU); *The Vote* (WFL); *Common Cause* (NUWSS);

The Daily Mail; *The Daily Mirror*; *The Times*; *Manchester Guardian*; *Southport Visitor*; *Anti-Suffrage Review*; *Huddersfield Daily Chronicle*; *Huddersfield Daily Examiner*.

1911 to 1920: Suffrage papers listed above; *The Freewoman*; *The New Freewoman*; *The New Age*; *The Herald of Revolt*; *The Syndicalist*; *The Daily Herald*; *The Link*; *Freedom*; *Evening Standard and St. James Gazette*; *The Morning Post*; *The Times*; *La Vie*.

Post-1920: *Time and Tide*; *Sunday Express*; *The New Age*; *Times Literary Supplement*.

4. Miscellaneous Including Interviews and Published Material

Records: Held at Crichton Royal Hospital, Dumfries (to be consulted only with the permission of family).

Interviews: I doubt whether these should be included as primary sources but none the less include discussions with Rebecca West (30 August 1977, T); Jane Lidderdale (5 September 1983); Mary Nicholson (7 October 1983); Kay Davison (26 July 1984, T); Mary Armitage (28 July 1984); Margaret Gloss (29 October 1984, T); Fiona Billington-Greig (1 April 1985, T); George Holroyd 29 May 1985). The lengthy discussions with Elaine Bate, mainly in the period 1982 to 1985, were crucial too. (The letter 'T' denotes interviews which were recorded.)

Other published material

Aldred, G.: *No Traitors Gait* (Glasgow: Strickland Press, 1956).

Billington-Greig, T.: *The Militant Suffrage Movement / Emancipation in a Hurry* (London: F. Palmer, London, 1911).

Carpenter, E.: *Sex Love and its Place in a Free Society* (Manchester: Labour Press, 1886).

_____ *Loves Coming of Age* (Manchester: Labour Press, 1886).

_____ *The Intermediate Sex / a Study of Some Transitional Types of Men and Women* (Manchester: S. Clarke, 1908).

Carter, H. (ed.): *Women's Suffrage and Militancy* (London: F. Palmer, 1911).

Dell, F.: *Women as World Builders* (Chicago: Forbes, 1913).

Gawthorpe, M.: *Up the Hill to Holloway* (Maine: Traversity Press, 1962).

Goldman, E.: *Anarchism and Other Essays* (New York: Mother Earth, 1910).

Grayson: *The Problem of Parliament / A Criticism and a Remedy* (London: 1909).

Hamilton, C.: *Marriage as a Trade* (London: Chapman & Hall, 1909).

Kenney, A.: *Memories of a Militant* (London: Edward Arnold, 1924).

Lewis, Arthur D.: *Syndicalism and the General Strike / An Explanation* (London: Fisher Unwin, 1912).

Lytton, C.: *Prison and Prisoners* (London: Heinemann's, 1912).

Marsden, D.: *Bondwomen* (New York: National American Women's Suffrage Association, 1912).

_____ *The Definition of The Godhead* (London: Egoist Press, 1928).

_____ *The Mysteries of Christianity* (London: Egoist Press, 1930).

_____ *The Philosophy of Time* (Holywell Press, 1955).

Pankhurst, C.: *The Great Scourge and How to End It* (London: WSPU, 1913).

Pankhurst, E.S.: *The Suffragette / The History of the Women's Militant Suffrage Movement* (New York: Sturgis and Walton, 1911).

Sadler, M.: *Report on Secondary and Higher Education in Essex* (London: Essex Education Committee, 1906).

Stirner, M.: *The Ego and His Own* (London: A. C. Fifield, 1912).

Wilkinson, L.G.: *Revolutionary Socialism and the Women's Movement* (Glasgow: Socialist Labour Party, 1910).

Women's Freedom (London: Freedom Press, 1914).

Symposium on Time: Unpublished MS. by Harriet Shaw Weaver, held at Oxford University Philosophy Library.

Secondary sources

Some readers may have preferred a thematic subdivision of this section but as so many issues with which Dora was concerned with overlap (eg. suffragism and feminism) it was considered unsuitable. All works that are cited in the text are listed alongside others that may prove useful to those who wish to delve further into the subjects, movements and people Dora was involved with.

Adam, R.: *A Woman's Place 1910-1975* (London: Chatto and Windus, 1975).

Adelmann, P.: *The Rise of the Labour Party* (London: Longman's, 1972).

Alpers, A.: *The Life of Katharine Mansfield* (Oxford: OUP, 1982).

Blewitt, N.: *The Peers, The Parties and The People / The General Elections of 1910* (London: Macmillan, London, 1972).

Chew, D.: *The Life and Writings of Ada Neild Chew* (London: Virago, 1982).

Clark, D.: *Radicalism to Socialism: The Portrait of a Northern Constituency in the Formative Years of the Labour Party* (London: Longman, 1981).

_____ *Victor Grayson, Labour's Lost Leader* (London: Quartet, 1985).

Clarke, B.: "Dora Marsden's Egoism and Modern Letters: West, Weaver, Joyce, Pound, Eliot" in *Work and Days*, Vol. 2. No. 2., 1985, pp. 26-47.

Cole, G. D. H. and Postgate, R. S.: *The Common People 1746-1938* (London: Methuen, 1938).

Coote, A. and Campbell, B.: *Sweet Freedom: The Struggle For Women's Liberation* (London: Picador, 1982).

Dangerfield, G.: *The Strange Death of Liberal England* (London:

Paladin, 1970).

Davin, A.: "Imperialism and Motherhood" in *History Workshop Journal*, V, Spring 1978, History Workshop, Oxford.

Dematteis, P. B.: *Individualism and the Social Organism* (New York: Revisionist Press, 1976).

Easterbrook, C.: *The Chronicle of Crichton Royal 1833-1936* (Dumfries: Courier Press, 1940).

Ellman, R. (ed.): *Letters of James Joyce* (London: Faber, 1966)

_____ *James Joyce* (London: OUP 1966).

Ensor, R. C. K.: *England 1817 to 1914* (Oxford: Clarendon Press, 1936).

Faderman, L.: *Surpassing the Love of Men: Romantic Friendship and Love Between Women from the Renaissance to the Present* (London: Women's Press, 1985).

Fiddes, E.: *Chapters in the History of Owen's College and Manchester University 1851-1914* (Manchester: Manchester University, 1937).

Fryer, P.: *The Birth Controllers* (London: Secker and Warburg, 1965).

Fulford, R.: *Votes for Women* (London: Faber and Faber, 1957).

Garner, L.: *Stepping Stones to Women's Liberty: Feminist Ideas in the Women's Suffrage Movement 1900 to 1918* (Aldershot: Gower Press, 1984) (originally Heinemann).

Glendinning, V.: *Rebecca West: A Life* (London: Weidenfeld and Nicolson, 1987).

Goodheart, E.: *The Cult of the Ego: The Self in Modern Literature* (London: Chicago University Press, 1968).

Gribbin, J. and Plagemann, S.: *Beyond the Jupiter Effect* (London: Macdonald, 1983).

Grosskurth, P.: *Havelock Ellis: A Biography* (London: Quartet, 1981).

Groves, R.: *The Strange Case of Victor Grayson* (London: Pluto Press, 1975).

Halévy, E.: *A History of the English People in the Nineteenth Century (2nd edition) Volume V, Imperialism and the Rise of Labour* (London: Benn, 1952).

_____ *A History of the English People in the Nineteenth Century (2nd edition) Volume VI, The Rule of Democracy* (London: Benn, 1952).

Hamilton, R.: *The Liberation of Women: A Study of Patriarchy and Capitalism* (London: Allen and Unwin, 1978).

Harrison, B.: *Separate Spheres: The Opposition to Women's Suffrage* (London: Croom Helm, 1978).

Hesketh, P.: *My Aunt Edith* (London: P. Davies, 1966).

Holtby, W.: *Women in a Changing Civilisation* (London: John Lane, 1934).

Hughes, G.: *Imagism and the Imagists* (London: 1931).

Jameson, M. S.: *Journey from The North: An Autobiography of Margaret Storm Jameson* (London: Collins, 1970).

Jeffreys, S.: *The Spinster and Her Enemies Feminism and Sexuality 1880-1930* (London: Pandora, 1986).

Kamm, J.: *Rapiers and Battleaxes: The Women's Movement and its Aftermath* (London: Allen and Unwin, 1966).

Kendall, W.: *The Revolutionary Movement in Britain 1900-21 / The Origins of British Communism* (London: Weidenfeld and Nicolson, 1969).

Kenner, H.: *The Pound Era* (London: Faber, 1975).

Kraditor, A: *The Ideas of the Women's Suffrage Movement 1890-1920* (New York: Columbia University Press, 1965).

Leach, C. E.: *The Feminist Movement in Manchester, 1903-1914* (Manchester University, M.A. thesis, 1971).

Lidderdale, J. H. and Nicholson, M.: *Dear Miss Weaver / Harriet Shaw Weaver 1876-1961* (London: Faber and Faber, 1970).

Liddington, J. and Norris, J.: *One Hand Tied Behind Us: The Rise of the Women's Suffrage Movement* (London: Virago, 1978).

Liddington, J.: *The Life and Times of a Respectable Rebel: Selina Cooper 1864-1946* (London: Virago, 1984).

Linklater, E.: *An Unhusbanded Life – Charlotte Despard: Suffragette, Socialist and Sinn Feiner* (London: Hutchinson, 1980).

Lockwood, E.: *Colne Valley Folk: The Romance and Enterprise of a Textile Stronghold Heath* (London: Cranton, 1936).

Lockwood, F. E.: *An Ordinary Life: Mrs. J. Lockwood* (London, 1937).

Marcus, J. (ed.) The Young Rebecca: Selected Writings of Rebecca West, Macmillan, London, 1982.

McKenzie, N. and J.: *The Time Traveller: The Life of H. G. Wells* (London: Weidenfeld and Nicolson, 1973)

_____ *The First Fabians* (London: Weidenfeld and Nicolson, 1977).

Mitchell, D.: *The Fighting Pankhursts: A Study in Tenacity* (London: Cape, 1967).

_____ *Queen Christabel: A Biography of Christabel Pankhurst* (London: Macdonald and Jane, 1977).

Morgan, D.: *Suffragists and Liberals: The Politics of Women's Suffrage in Britain* (Oxford: Blackwell, 1975).

Neale, R. S.: "Working Class Women and Women's Suffrage" in *Class and Ideology* (London: Routledge and Kegan Paul, 1972).

Oakley, A.: "The Failure of the Movement for Women's Equality" in *New Statesman*, Vol. 49, No. 881, August, 1979.

Pankhurst, C.: *Unshackled: Or How We Won the Vote* (London: Hutchinson, 1959).

Pankhurst, E. S.: *The Suffragette Movement: An Intimate Account of Persons and Ideals* (London: Longman, 1931).

Parker, S. E. (ed.): *Ego* (privately published magazine on Stirner).

Pearsall, R.: *The Worm in the Bud: The World of Victorian Sexuality* (Harmondsworth: Penguin, 1971).

Pearson, I.: *Marsden Throughout the Ages* (Leeds, 1982).

Pethick-Lawrence, E.: *My Part in a Changing World* (London: Gollancz, 1938).

Raeburn, A.: *The Militant Suffragettes* (London: Michael Joseph, 1973).

Ramelson, M.: *Petticoat Rebellion: A Century of Struggle for Women's Rights* (London: Lawrence and Wishart, 1967).

Ray, G. N.: *H. G. Wells and Rebecca West* (London: Macmillan, 1974).

Richardson, M. R.: *Laugh a Defiance* (London: Weidenfeld and Nicolson, 1953).

Robinson, J. B.: *Memorials of the 1st Marsden Town School* (Huddersfield, 1878).

_____ *Marsden Memorials* (Huddersfield, 1885).

Rosen, A.: *Rise Up Women!: The Militant Campaign of the Women's Social and Political Union 1903-1914* (London: Routledge and Kegan Paul, 1974).

Rover, C.: *Love, Morals and the Feminists* (London: Routledge and Kegan Paul, 1970).

Rowbotham, S.: *Hidden from History: 300 Years of Women's Oppression and the Fight Against It* (London: Pluto Press, 1970).

_____ *A New World for Women: Stella Browne, Socialist and Feminist* (London: Pluto Press, 1977).

_____ (with Weeks, J.): *Socialism and the New Life: The Personal and Sexual Politics of Edward Carpenter and Havelock Ellis* (London: Pluto Press, 1977).

Saywell, R. T.: *The Development of the Feminist Idea in England 1789-1853* (London: London University, MA thesis).

Semmel, B.: *Imperialism and Social Reform: English Social Imperial Thought 1895-1914* (London: Macmillan, 1960).

Showalter, E.: *A Literature of Their Own: British Women Novelists from Brontë to Lessing* (London: Virago, 1978).

Stocks, M.: *Fifty Years in Every Street* (Manchester: Manchester University Press, 1945).

Strachey, R.: *Millicent Garrett Fawcett* (London: Murray, 1931).

_____ (ed.) *Our Freedom and its Results* (London: Woolf, 1936).

Sykes, D. P. E.: *The History of the Colne Valley* (Slaithwaite, 1906).

Thompson, P.: *The Edwardians: The Remaking of British Society* (London: Weidenfeld and Nicolson, 1975).

Trombley, S.: "Personal History" in *History Today*, Vol. XXXV, May, 1985.

Weaver, M.: *William Carlos Williams: The American Background* (London: Cambridge University Press, 1971).

Wieninger, O.: *Sex and Character* (London: Heinemann, 1906).

Wells, H. G.: *Ann Veronica* (London: Dent, 1909).

Whitehead, L. B.: *Bygone Marsden* (Manchester, 1942).

Wilicocks, M. P.: *Towards New Horizons* (London: Bodley Head, 1918).

Woodcock, G.: *Anarchism: A History of Libertarian Ideas and Movements* (Harmondsworth: Penguin, 1962).

Zaretsky, E.: *The Family and Personal Life* (London: Pluto Press, 1976).

Index

Index by Trevor Blake

❦

Marsden, Dora: Career Summary of Life

Marsden, Dora: Character

❦

Marsden, Dora: Family

❦

Marsden, Dora: Health

accident..24, 29
breakdown..24, 29
deterioration.....................19, 24, 29, 106, 110, 356, 433
Insomnia...356, 367p., 407
mental..
.....8, 19, 24, 29, 212, 225p., 282, 339, 349, 355, 357, 389, 395,
398, 403pp., 410, 413
physical..
...29p., 51, 64, 68, 100, 106, 110, 114, 152, 185, 189, 212, 221,
225, 236, 329, 349, 353, 355pp., 363, 367, 394p., 398, 403,
407, 419

❦

Marsden, Dora: Writings (published)

See also: *The Freewoman, The New Freewoman, The Egoist.*

❦

Marsden, Dora: Writings (unpublished)

About the Author

Dr. Les Garner (b. 1952, Oldham) has worked in England for many years in Further and Higher Education, mainly at the University of Greenwich teaching History, Politics and Teacher training. As a Historian, he first came across Dora Marsden in the early 1970s as part of his research at Liverpool University for his PhD on the ideology of the Women's Suffrage movement.

This led to the first of several publications on Suffragism - *Stepping Stones to Women's Liberty: The Ideas of the Women's Suffrage Movement 1900-1918* (Gower Press 1994). Others include "Suffragism and Socialism: Sylvia Pankhust 1903-1914" in *Sylvia Pankhurst: From Artist to Anti-Fascist* (Bullock and Pankhurst, Macmillan 1992). He has published a wide range of articles on access to education, vocationalism and teacher training in England and the former Soviet bloc. He also worked on a range of European funded projects, and has taught in Finland, Estonia and Leningrad.

A committed socialist, longstanding trade unionist and organiser and, since 2015, activist in the Labour Party. He concurs with Isabel Leatham who in 1912 wrote in Dora Marsden's remarkable *Freewoman* that "though it may be possible to have Socialism with only a shadow of freedom for women... the complete emancipation would be impossible without it."

Select Titles from Union of Egoists

Trevor Blake and Kevin I. Slaughter, publishers

The philosophy of egoism as published between 1845 and 1945.
New works of criticism and research, rare works reprinted.
Der Geist / the Journal of Egoism 1845-1945 by Trevor Blake (ed.).

Anarchism and Individualism by Émile Armand.

Dora Marsden Bibliography by Trevor Blake.

The Eagle & the Serpent Index of Names by Trevor Blake.

Max Stirner Bibliography by Trevor Blake.

Anathema / Litanies of Negation by Benjamin DeCasseres.

Fantasia Impromptu / Finis by Benjamin DeCasseres.

New York is Hell by Benjamin DeCasseres.

As I See Nietzsche by Stephanus Fabijanović.

Satanic Lumberjacks and Southron Rebels by Covington Hall.

A Critique of Anarchist Communism by Ken Knudson.

Protagoras. Nietzsche. Stirner by Benedict Lachmann.

The Philosophy of Time by Dora Marsden.

Might is Right: The Authoritative Edition by Ragnar Redbeard.

Egoism by Georgia and Henry Replogle.

The Gospel According to Malfew Seklew by Malfew Seklew.

"I" by C. L. Swartz.

The Right to Ignore the State by Benjamin R. Tucker.

UnionOfEgoists.com